Mastering Financial Management

FT Prentice Hall
FINANCIAL TIMES

In an increasingly competitive world, we believe it's quality of thinking that gives you the edge – an idea that opens new doors, a technique that solves a problem, or an insight that simply makes sense of it all. The more you know, the smarter and faster you can go.

That's why we work with the best minds in business and finance to bring cutting-edge thinking and best learning practice to a global market.

Under a range of leading imprints, including *Financial Times Prentice Hall*, we create world-class print publications and electronic products bringing our readers knowledge, skills and understanding, which can be applied whether studying or at work.

To find out more about Pearson Education publications, or tell us about the books you'd like to find, you can visit us at **www.pearsoned.co.uk**

PEARSON

Mastering
Financial Management

A step-by-step guide to strategies, applications and skills

CLIVE MARSH

**Financial Times
Prentice Hall
is an imprint of**

PEARSON

Harlow, England • London • New York • Boston • San Francisco • Toronto • Sydney • Singapore • Hong Kong
Tokyo • Seoul • Taipei • New Delhi • Cape Town • Madrid • Mexico City • Amsterdam • Munich • Paris • Milan

PEARSON EDUCATION LIMITED

Edinburgh Gate
Harlow CM20 2JE
Tel: +44 (0)1279 623623
Fax: +44 (0)1279 431059
Website: www.pearsoned.co.uk

First published in Great Britain in 2009

ISBN: 978-0-273-72454-4

British Library Cataloguing-in-Publication Data
A catalogue record for this book is available from the British Library

Library of Congress Cataloging-in-Publication Data
A catalog record for this book is available from the Library of Congress

10 9 8 7 6 5 4 3 2 1
13 12 11 10 09

Typeset in 11.5pt Garamond by 3
Printed by Ashford Colour Press Ltd., Gosport

The publisher's policy is to use paper manufactured from sustainable forests.

Contents

Foreword

Money is the life blood of a business. It is the common denominator with which we measure and compare all business activities. Without their full financial evaluation business strategies and plans mean very little. Financial management and its incorporation into every stage of business strategy is a fundamental skill that all executives need in order to identify the financial strategies available and be capable of maximising an organisation's net value through the creation of value and through the financial support of an organisation's business strategy.

Sound financial management creates value and organisational agility through the allocation of scarce capital resources amongst competing business opportunities. It is an aid to the implementation and monitoring of business strategy and helps achieve business objectives. It integrates financial management into business strategy and operations.

This work is based upon my experience as a CFO for large multinational and small companies, working with executive teams to help guide them into areas of value creation by using the financial management techniques described. It is, therefore, a real and practical guide and I have attempted to keep things simple and relevant to the real world. Some topics do border on the academic and at this point I have kept to the professional working aspect of the subject.

Because a wide range of professionals from different disciplines becomes involved in financial management it is not just a subject for accounting and finance executives. However, it is the latter group which has some advantage in learning this subject and for this reason I have started the work with basic accounting and finance principles which are foundation stones for many aspects of financial management. I would like to think that a principal differentiator of this work is its simultaneous breadth and simplification of the subject.

Sustainability, ethics and the 'new world order' following the collapse of financial institutions around the world in 2008/2009 may change priorities, financial markets and corporate financial strategy. In recent years there has been an increasing awareness of sustainability and matching current value creation with longer-term sustainable goals. Forms of sustainable development reporting (SDR) around the world are becoming a common part of corporate reporting and in some countries are required by law. This book includes a chapter on world-class SDR and shows how sustainability can be incorporated in business strategy and supported by sound financial management. Ethics and professionalism in so far as these relate to financial management are covered in a pragmatic way that will help the finance professional avoid 'getting things wrong' and keep out of trouble.

Many professional institutions include financial management in their examination syllabi. Their content varies enormously. I have included a table that shows examination syllabuses and how this works refers to them. I have done this for the Chartered Institute of Bankers in Scotland, the Institute of Chartered Accountants in England and Wales and the Association of Chartered Certified Accountants.

This book is useful as a guide and reference point for the practising professional and also for professional and university students of financial management.

Publisher's acknowledgements

We are grateful to the following for permission to reproduce copyright material:

Sanford Limited in New Zealand for permission to reproduce extracts from the annual report in Chapter 24. Sanford Limited holds no responsibility for this reproduction.

Throughout the book the government for public information on the UK government department web site by the granting of PSI licence number C2008002379.

J Sainsbury plc for an extract report and accounts for the year ended 2007 in Chapter 1.

HMRC for extracts from its public web site used in Chapter 3.

The UK government Statistics Office for information regarding inflation used in Chapter 4.

The International Capital Markets Association for details of updates on international capital markets, details of courses and membership the ICMA web site (www.icmagroup.org).

Sanford Seafood New Zealand for extracts throughout the text on SDR.

The Chartered Banker journal for extracts on professionalism and ethics.

The Competition Commission for extracts from its web site.

The publisher acknowledges the following work used in this book:

The CAPM model mentioned in Chapter 12 and throughout this book was introduced by Jack Treynor, William Sharpe, Jon Lintner and Jan Mossin. It built on the earlier work of Harry Markowitz on diversification and modern portfolio theory. Certain capital structures mentioned in Chapter 13 were the work of Modigliani and Miller. The publisher has been unable to trace the owners of this material or the owners of certain other material that has been used in this text and we would appreciate any information that would enable us to do so.

Reference has been made to web sites throughout this text. In all cases the download date was November 2008. Web information is constantly changing and when making reference to a web site in relation to this text we would recommend that you access the principal web address only and search for the information required using the search tool available on the site.

About the author

Clive Marsh started his business career as a trainee accountant with Mobil in London. At Mobil, Clive held several financial positions including Controls Accountant responsible for financial analysis and controls for UK marine companies reporting to Middle East transportation controllers in New York. Following a period as Works Accountant for a manufacturing subsidiary of the Portals Group, Clive joined Shell UK Exploration and Production as the Project Accountant for the Brent 'C' oil platform construction project. On completion of the project Clive initially worked for Shell Expro in London as Shell UK Budget Accountant. His career with Shell continued with Shell Oil New Zealand as Financial Accountant and then with the Shell New Zealand Holding Company as Group Taxation and Statutory Accountant.

In 1983 Clive joined DataBank Systems, a financial technology company owned by the Bank of New Zealand, Westpac, ANZ and NBNZ. Positions Clive held at DataBank included Manager of Management Accounting, Head of MIS and Finance and Acting Divisional Manager of Corporate Services responsible for HR, training, finance, office services and planning/budgeting integration. As Head of MIS and Finance Clive had responsibility for the financial restructure of DataBank through the swaps market.

Following DataBank, Clive spent time in merchant and corporate banking with Lombank NZ (owned by NatWest), NatWest UK and A&L, where he had responsibility for corporate banking as Area Manager for the South East of England.

In 1996 Clive joined IBM UK Banking, Finance and Securities, managing a number of banking and finance-sector relationships including Lloyds TSB Corporate and Commercial, Lloyds Private Banking, IFL, ALF, LBR and BACS. Then in 2001 Clive joined the consulting industry and spent time with Cap Gemini Ernst & Young, Link ICA, Catalise and Group Partners. Positions he held during this time included Director of Business Development. This was followed by a period back in commercial finance with a subsidiary of Credit Agricole.

During his time in banking and consultancy Clive's clients have been both small and large organisations and in all business sectors, for example Brakes, Lloyds TSB, BACS, The Bank of England, Brands Hatch, Lazards,

IFL, BP (NZ), local authorities, Dawsons, the police, Stena Line, Trafalgar Group and SMEs in all sectors. This experience has given Clive a consummate understanding of business and finance.

Clive's recent publications include 'Professionalism and Ethics' (*The Chartered Banker*, *Scottish Banker*, September 2008), 'Invoice Finance Obstacles' (*National Accountant Australia*, January 2008), 'Banks and Shared Services, an efficient business architecture' (*Journal of Banking and Financial Services of Australasia*, November 2004), 'Human Capital Knowledge Management' (Group Partners, London).

Clive has a master's degree in strategic financial management from Kingston University London, Business School, is a fellow of the Chartered Institute of Bankers in Scotland, a Chartered Banker, a fellow of the Chartered Management Institute and a member/associate chartered accountant of the Institute of Chartered Accountants of New Zealand.

Overview of financial management and its relationship with corporate strategy and the markets

An overview of the purpose of financial management and its relationship with corporate strategy, shareholders, other stakeholders and organisational objectives. The role of financial markets.

■ ■ ■

A DEFINITION OF FINANCIAL MANAGEMENT

Corporate financial management is concerned with the strategic management of an organisation's finances to ensure that its financial objectives are achieved. It is concerned with providing a financial environment to support business strategy and with financial efficiency. Since money is the common denominator for the measurement and control of most aspects of a business, financial management is at the heart of all decision making. One basic assumption of profit-making organisations is the maximisation of shareholders' wealth. Sound financial management plays a major role in this. It is a very wide subject requiring knowledge of aspects of accounting, taxation, management, planning, finance, capital management, investment appraisal, risk management, pricing, dividend policy, financial mathematics, financial markets, economics and strategy. Whilst this single text cannot provide expert knowledge in all of these subjects, it will help professionals and students of professional examinations in finance and banking subjects to master financial management. It provides a step-by-step guide from the basic elements of financial management through to advanced strategic financial management.

Students of accountancy may find that financial management as a subject has been quite specifically, perhaps narrowly, defined by their professional body and does not always include associated subjects such as financial and management accounting. This is because these subjects are covered separately in their syllabi. However, this text will cover the basic elements of these and other associated subjects for the benefit of those financial management students who are not from an accounting background.

A financial manager will prepare a financial plan as an essential element of the corporate plan in order to ensure that both short- and long-term funds are available to meet an organisation's goals and objectives. In doing this the financial manager will need to plan finance to support corporate strategy and consider how financial efficiency might contribute to the maximisation of wealth. Financial management is, then, concerned with both risk management and wealth maximisation through investment and working capital management. It is a multi-discipline subject with an emphasis on bringing together managerial accounting and corporate finance techniques that is concerned with both internal and external market measures.

In summary, the main purposes of financial management are:

Planning	To ensure short- and long-term funds are available to meet an organisation's strategy and objectives.
Decision making	To help make decisions concerning investment, the provision and management of working capital, dividend/distribution/retention policy, risks, project prioritisation, research, resources, mergers, joint ventures, disinvestments, asset disposal and all issues concerning the development and growth of an organisation.
Controlling	To ensure that adequate controls are in place to protect and manage financial resources.
Efficiency	To ensure that assets are used efficiently and provide the returns expected by shareholders.

Strategic financial management (SFM) is the identification of financial strategies available and capable of maximising an organisation's net value through both the creation of value and the financial support of an organisation's business strategy. SFM creates both value and organisational agility through the allocation of scarce capital resources among competing business opportunities. It is an aid to the implementation and monitoring of business strategy and helps achieve business objectives. SFM integrates financial management into business strategy and operations. It is concerned with managing shareholder value and risk and integrating the financial management function with business strategy and the operations of an organisation and is also concerned with the optimal allocation of resources to achieve organisational objectives.

FINANCIAL MANAGEMENT AND CORPORATE STRATEGY

An organisation will set objectives and define a strategy necessary to achieve these objectives. Strategic financial management will help identify which of the possible strategies will maximise the organisation's value by establishing the optimal use of scarce resources.

Corporate objectives

All objectives, whether personal or corporate, should be measurable, time bound, achievable and challenging. Personal and corporate objectives should be closely linked. More about this aspect later.

Corporate objectives are usually high-level statements of intent followed by specific measurable key indicators such as:

■ return on shareholders' funds

- sales and growth
- margins
- market share
- financial position
- customer retention.

A good example of an objective statement with measurable targets is given below in the published J Sainsbury plc report and accounts for the year ended 2007:

> Two and a half years ago we outlined our plan to Make Sainsbury's Great Again ('MSGA').
>
> Our vision is simple: we are here to serve customers well with a choice of great food at fair prices and, by so doing, to provide shareholders with strong, sustainable financial returns. This has driven everything we have done since we outlined our recovery plan in October 2004.
>
> The plan spans three years to March 2008 and as well as fixing a range of basics – such as product availability, supply chain, IT, and price – we committed to make hundreds of small changes every day to improve our customers' shopping experience. To enable us to measure our progress we set some key three-year targets:
>
> The targets we set
>
> - To grow sales (inc VAT ex fuel) by £2.5 billion, with grocery contributing sales of £1.4 billion, non-food products sales of £700 million and convenience stores sales of £400 million
> - To invest at least £400 million in improving product quality and our price position relative to competitors and to find annual buying synergies of 100–150 basis points to be reinvested in the customer offer
> - To deliver operating cost efficiencies of at least £400 million
> - To generate neutral underlying cash flow in 2005/06 and positive cash flow thereafter.
>
> These were demanding targets and the business has had to challenge itself in every area in response.

These corporate objectives clearly define key performance indicators and are followed by an operational review and financial review.

Strategy

Strategy is concerned with the determination of specific actions that will need to be undertaken to achieve objectives. For example, if an organisation operating in the South East of England has an objective of increasing its market share in that territory it might, as a strategy, decide that it needs to increase its sales force. Of course, an organisation operating in a competitive environment will normally not publish its detailed strategy externally. Internally it will normally express strategy in both short- and long-term actions and these may be offensive or defensive strategies.

Examples of strategies, which may be in the short or long term, are given below.

Offensive strategies:

- expansion
- market penetration
- new market development
- takeover and leader strategies
- challenger and innovation strategies.

Defensive strategies:

- market follower
- market niches
- cost reduction.

Financial targets

Specific financial targets may be outlined in an organisation's published corporate report or plan as in the J Sainsbury plc example above, or they may be kept internally, providing the underlying support to the higher-level published corporate objectives. Either way they are likely to include:

- company valuation
- sales
- market share
- profits and margins
- earnings
- dividends payable
- financial stability and health ratios such as liquidity, gearing and stock turnover (Chapters 10 and 11)
- retained earnings.

The calculation of key accounting ratios will be discussed in subsequent chapters. For now it is enough to know the broad category of ratios that forms a part of an organisation's financial targets.

Shareholders will view their wealth derived from a company as coming from the dividends they receive and from the market value of the shares they hold. A company may control the amount of dividends it pays out and the growth in retained earnings and organisational value. However, whilst it does not have much influence over the markets it can report its performance against market trends in its business sector. Certainly the directors of a company should set targets for the things they can influence, such as sales and profits, and have targets for key measures that are meaningful to shareholders. These will include:

- earnings per share (EPS)
- return on capital employed (ROCE)
- yield on investment
- market share.

A company can be valued according to its balance sheet valuation of net assets and liabilities on a going-concern basis. It can also be valued according to the market valuation of its shares being traded and finally on the basis of liquidation or the break-up value of its net assets. The financial targets set by directors will aim to increase overall shareholder value.

A key financial target in most companies is sales value. Most organisations will have targets for sales volumes, selling prices and product mix. Another key sales target is market share. A growth in sales but a reduction in market share may cause concern for the future. Also, whilst an overall growth in sales might show good short-term results, a weak product mix and overdependence on a narrow product range might not bode too well for future years.

Profits (before and after taxation) and gross margin achievements are basic financial targets in most companies. Gross margin percentages are particularly useful when comparing individual product/service contributions towards the overall fixed costs and profits of a company.

A finance manager must ensure that a company's liquidity is adequate to meet its trading terms. A company that 'overtrades' and cannot pay its creditors as they fall due will fail even if it can demonstrate growth and profits. Liquidity and other measures of working capital management (debtors' days, stock turnover, creditors) may not be reported as high-level financial targets or as part of the organisation's strategy but are equally important financial measures. Gearing, the ratio of equity to non-equity debt, is a financial target that is perhaps more obvious to shareholders. A highly geared company, one that has a high level of external debt compared with shareholders' funds, might be more vulnerable in times of rising interest rates. However, a highly geared company that is making high profits will have more earnings to distribute to fewer shareholders than a low-geared company. A financial manager needs to find the optimal but safe level of gearing.

Which financial targets a company decides to make important and key will depend upon what is needed to support the company's overall organisational objectives and strategy. It is important not to make important simply those things that can be easily measured.

The three main types of decisions facing finance managers are generally:

- investment decisions
- financing decisions
- dividend decisions.

Investment decisions concern internal investment projects, external opportunities and disinvestment decisions.

Financing decisions cover the process of selecting appropriate short- and long-term finance. Short-term finance is for working capital and longer-term finance is for long-term assets such as buildings, plant and equipment. Here the finance manager must choose the appropriate, most cost-effective and least risky source of funds and will require a knowledge of the financial markets.

Dividend decisions are notoriously complex. Not only are they related to financing decisions but there may also be international taxation-management considerations. The value of a company's shares will depend to a large extent upon the expectation of future dividends. Some shareholders might see a company's ability to pay out dividends as evidence of financial well-being and many companies set financial targets for dividend growth. This may not always be appropriate since it might compromise other financial targets. This is the problem with multiple financial targets: they might be in conflict with each other.

You will notice in the example set by J Sainsbury plc above that it mentioned very few financial targets. Those mentioned were high level and supported the company's overall vision and corporate goal. No doubt the company had many more lower-level operational financial targets and measures, but the key strategic financial targets mentioned show how it wanted to measure its performance and to report to shareholders. To avoid any suboptimal or dysfunctional management decisions it is important that personal management targets are closely linked to these high-level financial targets.

The role of financial management in senior team motivation

In the credit crunch and financial crisis of 2008 there was much public debate about what were considered to be inappropriate performance bonuses due to senior managers of failing financial institutions. One problem of having senior managers and directors who are not shareholders is how to ensure that they make optimal decisions for the organisation and not their own pockets. How do you stop them rewarding themselves with higher-than-deserved remuneration?

In an attempt to close this gap finance managers should be aware of goal alignment whereby the overall organisational objectives are linked to the individual objectives and remuneration of the executive teams. The higher level this linkage is made, the more chance of success there is of encouraging good corporate behaviour and results. However, as individual objectives are cascaded down there is a risk that managers, to protect their bonuses, can end up acting in a dysfunctional and suboptimal manner.

Financial management is concerned, amongst other things, with the efficient use of assets and these include human assets. It is, therefore, a responsibility of the financial manager to advise, evaluate and be aware of the benefits and pitfalls of various incentive schemes, whether through performance-related pay, share options or other means.

It would be nice to think that today's managers were, on the whole, highly ethical and worked for the benefit of all stakeholders fairly. However, threats to ethical behaviour can arise through many sources, including self-interest, conflicts of interest, intimidation, familiarity and acting in two or more roles. If the role of financial management is to support corporate goals and corporate goals are linked to individual performance measurement then finance managers need to monitor managerial performance schemes and ensure that they encourage the achievement of all stakeholder objectives.

Regulatory requirements that assist the achievement of stakeholder objectives

Good corporate governance and institutional requirements such as the Stock Exchange listing regulations help ensure that business is conducted in an ethical, fair and efficient way.

Corporate governance requires that:

- management reduces risk. This might, for example, mean 'not putting all of your eggs in one basket' or matching long-term assets with long-term loans. How many financial institutions have failed to do this? Management should review risk management and internal controls regularly

- management is accountable at all times

- management and supervision are effective

- management is ethical

- management acts not just to the letter of the law but to the spirit (probably the hardest criterion to enforce)

- the board should be responsible for setting policy and strategy

- appointments of directors should be by a nominated committee

- directors should have an appropriate set of skills and be professionally competent. For example, it should not be appropriate for a managing director of a failing bank to claim a lack of understanding of prudential requirements

- directors' performance should be monitored regularly
- independent non-executive directors should play a key role in governance. The roles of chairman and chief executive should be separate
- directors' remuneration should be set by an independent review committee and based upon individual and overall corporate performance
- directors' remuneration should be disclosed in detail in the accounts
- independent non-executive audit committees should review both internal and external audits
- annual reports must show a fair/balanced view and confirm that the organisation has complied with the regulatory and governance requirements and gives full disclosure
- the board should communicate regularly with shareholders.

Stock Exchange regulations require that:

- all listed companies meet the listing requirements. These are laid down by each exchange with the aim of ensuring openness, fairness and efficiency.

The detailed aspects indicated by the above list of governance and Stock Exchange requirements are beyond the scope of this text on financial management. They are mentioned here because compliance with these requirements will assist in the achievement of stakeholder objectives and is a necessary part of good financial management.

THE ROLE OF THE FINANCIAL MARKETS

In order to obtain appropriate sources of funds for an organisation a finance manager needs to understand the financial markets. A financial market, like any market, is a place where buyers and sellers get together. A financial intermediary is an institution, possibly a bank, which links organisations and people with funds to invest together with those who need to borrow. The reason intermediaries exist is to aggregate money and risk and to facilitate different maturity dates between borrowers and lenders. They provide efficiency through an economy of scale and survive through market efficiency. They should be prudent, spread their risks and ensure that their balance sheet is robust. In particular, long- and short-term assets should reasonably match long- and short-term liabilities in accordance with regulatory requirements. Banks across the world are regulated by central banks and bodies such as the UK's Financial Services Authority (FSA) and are required to make regular returns. There is, of course, an ongoing debate as to the effectiveness of regulation.

There are many types of financial intermediary. Some provide short-term finance and some long-term. The finance manager must choose the correct type of finance for his organisational needs. For example, a short-term bank overdraft, which is repayable on demand, might be used to fund debtors or stocks that turn over frequently. A short-term overdraft would not be appropriate for the long-term funding of plant and equipment or buildings. Long- or medium-term finance or lease finance might be appropriate for plant and equipment. Invoice finance might be the best option for funding debtors balances. It is up to the finance manager to determine the most appropriate source of finance and know where to find this in the market. The cost and availability of finance will depend upon market conditions and upon the borrower's financial strength. High risk equals high cost. The most appropriate source of finance for a particular need might not always be the lowest-cost finance available on the market but it might be the safest. The borrowing financial manager needs to understand fully the terms of the lending contract, covenants and conditions in order to assess and manage the risks to his organisation.

There are many types of financial intermediaries. These include:

■ clearing banks
■ invoice discounters
■ asset-based lenders
■ leasing houses
■ corporate banks
■ commercial banks
■ building societies
■ institutional investors
■ government
■ investment banks
■ venture capital houses.

Loan terms are either:

■ short term – up to one year
■ medium term – up to five years
■ long term – up to ten years and beyond.

Short-, medium- and long-term definitions tend to overlap. For example, a twelve-month invoice discounting facility which may be subject to a three-monthly review and has been in place for many years might have become accepted as a source of medium-term finance. This of course is not really the case. Similarly, most overdraft facilities are repayable on demand even though they have been renewed year on year. They are certainly short term. The finance manager must classify sources of finance correctly and be aware of vulnerability in the event that his company breaches certain covenants or financial intermediaries feel the need to call in or cancel renewals. The 2008 financial crisis has made many finance managers much more aware of their vulnerability.

The following definitions provide a guide to the use of short-, medium- and long-term descriptions.

Types of short-term finance include:

- bank overdrafts (repayable on demand)
- short-term invoice finance, both factoring and discounting
- short-term loans
- short-lease finance
- bill discount facilities.

Trade credit and internal finance, which, of course, is not sourced through an intermediary, can be an easy alternative to institutional short-term finance. However, taking excessive trade credit might disrupt supply chains and lead to penalties. It is just one more option open to the financial manager.

Types of long-term finance include:

- long-term loan finance
- long-term leases
- venture capital.

Equity finance through an organisation's shareholders is an alternative to the above sources of external long-term finance.

Types of medium-term finance include:

- intermediate finance obtained through commercial banks for expansion of plant and other assets and material/stock with a slow turnover.

Common types of medium-term finance for capital assets are hire purchase, leasing and asset-based lending. A rolling invoice discount facility might be considered medium term depending upon the terms.

SUMMARY

- Companies set both organisational and individual senior management objectives.
- Financial objectives (such as the maximisation of shareholder wealth or EPS) are set to support organisational objectives.

- Corporate and individual objectives should be clearly linked.

- Specific high-level financial targets are often communicated to stake-holders and the public.

- A strategy (specific actions that will need to be undertaken to achieve objectives) is identified.

- Financial management decisions include investment, risk, financing and dividend policy. These need to be considered along with the financial objectives and targets.

- The reward for management performance needs to be an integral part of the corporate objectives, target and strategy.

- Corporate governance and regulatory requirements assist in the achievement of stakeholder objectives.

- In order to obtain appropriate sources of funds for an organisation a finance manager needs to understand the financial markets and arrange appropriate external and internal finance.

- Financial management is related to objectives, to strategy and to the financial markets. It is concerned with the achievement of the financial objectives of an organisation.

The purpose of this opening chapter is to give an overview of the scope and purpose of financial management. It is a very broad subject and the extent to which a reader of this text needs to have read associated subjects will depend upon his or her professional background and previous reading.

2

Financial accounting and ratio analysis

INTRODUCTION

You might think it strange to start a financial management text with a short lesson in financial accounting and basic ratio analysis. I have done this because I have met many financial managers who have not come from an accounting background, particularly MBA graduates. This has put them at a severe disadvantage when analysing financial statements and understanding ratio analysis and aspects of management accounting.

I will, therefore, introduce you to some basic accounting concepts. If you are an accountant then you can afford to skip this chapter and fast forward to the next.

THE ORIGINS OF ACCOUNTING AND THE DOUBLE-ENTRY SYSTEM

Double entry is indeed a marvellous system but, like riding a bike, it is easier learned than taught. However, once you've mastered it you will never forget it and it will make your business life a whole lot easier.

The first recorded description that I am aware of was in 'Summa de arithmetica, geometrica, proportioni et proportionali' by the monk Luca Pacioli, a collaborator with Leonardo da Vinci in the late fifteenth century. However, earlier records exist to show a double-entry system being used by the merchant venturers of Venice. Other sources suggest that the system was in use by banks as early as the twelfth century and there is evidence that basic accounting systems existed much earlier.

In the twenty-first century accountancy bodies exist throughout the world to develop and define accounting concepts and to regulate accountants. This is done through accounting standards that lay down consistent accounting treatment for financial transactions and through professional and ethical codes for accountants. Generally Accepted Accounting Practice (GAAP) helps to ensure that postulates such as consistency, materiality and matching are adhered to and International Financial Reporting Standards (IFRS) aim to ensure consistency in global accounting standards. However, at the heart of accounting still lies the double-entry book-keeping system and although volumes are increasingly being written on certain aspects of the subject, the core principles remain unchanged. It is simply these core principles that I will be defining in this text.

First we will work through a simple example showing the mechanics of the basic double-entry system. Then we will explore some of the issues that might arise in accounting and discuss a few of the major established accounting 'postulates' that help to ensure that accounts represent a true and fair view of a business's affairs and financial status.

THE BASIC PRINCIPLES OF DOUBLE ENTRY

The double-entry system recognises that every transaction has two aspects, receiving and giving. Both of these aspects are entered into an organisation's accounts for every transaction.

Debit – the account that receives.

Credit – the account that gives.

So, if a debtor pays me £500 in settlement of an outstanding invoice, the accounting entries would be:

Debit	Cash account	£500	
Credit	Debtor account		£500

Note we debit the cash account since this is the account that has received the cash and we credit the debtor account since this is the account that has given.

Now, at this stage many students get confused because when they view their personal bank statements a receipt of money is shown as a credit. I will then explain to the students that they need to remember that their bank statement is only a picture of the bank's account with them and that the entries in the bank's books for a receipt of £500 cash would be:

Debit	Cash account	£500	
Credit	Customer account		£500

The bank statement that the customer receives shows only the bank's account with the customer being credited with £500.

So you need to remember that when you receive cash you debit your cash account and you credit the account of whoever gave you the cash. This is of fundamental importance and is the one thing that causes problems later if it is not accepted and understood at the start. So, do not proceed any further until you have fully understood and accepted this point. Once you have, the rest is easy!

If a business purchases a consumable item of expenditure such as printing ink for £30 cash then it will debit the expenditure account and credit the cash account.

Debit	Expenditure account	£30	
Credit	Cash account		£30

If a business purchases a car (an asset) for £15,000 from a supplier then the entries will be:

Debit	Asset (Car)	£15,000	
Credit	Supplier		£15,000

When the business actually pays the supplier the £15,000 the entries will be:

Debit   Supplier   £15,000

Credit   Cash   £15,000

When a business sells services or goods to a customer for £700 the entries will be:

Debit   Debtor (customer)   £700

Credit   Sales   £700

When the customer actually pays the £700 to the business the entries will be:

Debit   Cash   £700

Credit   Debtor   £700

I hope that by now you understand the basics of double entry. There must be a debit in one account and a credit in another account for every transaction.

From the above it may be deduced that:

Accounts are debited with: assets, expenses and services received.

Accounts are credited with: payments and services rendered.

Please make sure that you understand and accept these basic principles before you move on to the following worked example and remember that Debits are always shown on the left and Credits are shown on the right column of an account.

I said earlier that double entry is more easily learned than taught. It really is best to just get on and do it and then all will naturally follow. So, let's begin with a simple worked example of how accounting entries are made using the double-entry system for a sole trader who starts to trade as a retailer of animal feeds.

This example will show you entries in accounts, the trial balance, the profit and loss account and the balance sheet. It will be followed by an explanation of basic accounting concepts and issues. Work through the entries slowly until you understand them.

Example of basic double-entry book-keeping:

Bob started a business called Bob's Animal Food (BAF) on 1 January 2008. He opened a business account for BAF and paid in £500, being the opening capital of the company. He then undertook the following transactions:

5/1/08   Purchase 100 kg of animal food for £1 per kg. from Jones Ltd

£100

7/1/08	Sell for cash 20 kg of animal food for £1.5 per kg.	£30
8/1/08	Purchase trolley (which has an expected life of 36 months) from Smith Ltd	£360
10/1/08	Sell 40 kg of animal food for £1.9 per kg to Mr Baldock	£76
10/1/08	Remove 40 kg of sold feed from stock at cost (Cost of Sales)	£40
15/1/08	Pay Jones Ltd the balance of their account	£100
17/1/08	Pay market rent direct from bank account	£50
31/1/08	Charge one month depreciation on trolley (straight-line basis)	£10

Show all of the ledger entries, take out a trial balance and prepare a profit and loss account and a balance sheet as at 31/1/08.

Bank account:

1/1/08 Capital	£500	15/1/08 Creditor (Jones Ltd)	£100
7/1/08 Sales	£30	17/1/08 Rent expense	£50

Capital account:

	1/1/08 Bank account	£500

Stock of animal food at cost:

5/1/08 Jones Ltd	£100	10/1/08 Cost of sales	£40

Creditor (Jones Ltd):

15/1/08 Bank account	£100	5/1/08 Stock	£100

Sales:

	7/1/08 Cash	£30
	10/1/08 Mr Baldock	£76

Fixed assets (trolley):

8/1/08 Smith Ltd	£360	

Creditor (Smith Ltd):

	8/1/08 Fixed assets (trolley)	£360

Debtor (Mr Baldock):

10/1/08 Sales	£76	

Cost of sales:

10/1/08 Stock (sold)	£40	

Rent expense:

17/1/08 Bank account	£50	

Depreciation expenditure:

31/1/08 Depreciation provision	£10	

Depreciation provision (reduction in value of asset):

	31/1/08 Depreciation expense	£10

Once you have understood the above double entries you can take out a trial balance. This is simply a list of the above ledger balances. Remember, Debit balances are on the left and Credit balances are on the right. I have deliberately not 'balanced off/totalled' the above accounts since I find that this initially confuses new students. Simply look at the balance and list below. For example, the Bank account has entries totalling £530 Debit and £150 Credit. The balance is, therefore, Debit £530 − Credit £150 = Debit £380. Listing all of the balances below is our trial balance. Note that the Debit balances equal the Credit balances.

TRIAL BALANCE

Debit balances		Credit balances	
Bank account	380		
		Capital account	500
Stock of animal food account	60		
		Sales account	106
Fixed assets account (trolley)	360		
		Creditor (Smith Ltd)	360
Debtor (Mr Baldock)	76		
Cost of sales account	40		
Rent expenses account	50		
Depreciation expense account	10	Depreciation provision account	10
Total debits	**976**	**Total credits**	**976**

The trial balance 'balances' and this proves the arithmetical accuracy of the entries into the accounts. It does not, however, prove that amounts have been entered into the correct accounts.

Using the figures in the trial balance we can now prepare a profit and loss account and a balance sheet.

PROFIT AND LOSS ACCOUNT

Sales	106
Cost of sales	40
Gross profit margin	66
Rent expense	50
Depreciation expense	10
Net profit	6

BALANCE SHEET

Capital account		500
Profit and loss account		6
Equity		506
Fixed assets	360	
Less depreciation provision	(10)	350
Current assets:		
Bank account	380	
Debtors	76	
Stock	60	
Less Creditors	(360)	156
Net assets		506

Our balance sheet shows us that at 31/1/08 BAF has owner's equity of £506 and that this is represented by net assets of £506.

Another way of looking at the position is to say that BAF has assets of £866 (being 350 + 380 + 76 + 60) and that this is funded by the proprietor's capital of £506 and the creditor balance of £360.

Either way the value of the company at this stage would be £506, the owner's equity. This is the original capital injected plus the £6 profit made and retained during the period.

The basic accounting equation can be expressed in a number of ways:

Equity = Assets − Liabilities

or

Assets = Liabilities + Equity

or

Assets − Liabilities − Equity = 0

The capital of a business is sometimes referred to as a liability. This is because it is the amount that the business owes to the owner. This sometimes confuses students but it is quite logical if you remember that the business unit is a separate entity from the owner and the capital of a business is the amount it owes the owner. In the case of a limited company the shareholders' funds is the amount that the company owes to the shareholders. The liabilities of an entity include amounts owed to people/companies/banks that have invested or lent money to the entity (capital/shareholders' funds, loans, creditors). The assets of an entity might include plant, equipment, vehicles, cash, stock and debtors. A summary of the main classification of assets and liabilities is given below.

CLASSIFICATION OF ASSETS

- Fixed assets are permanent by nature and will not be consumed within one year of the end of the accounting period. Examples are buildings, plant and equipment.
- Current assets are those that are readily converted into cash or are acquired for the generation of sales within one year from the end of the accounting period. Examples are cash, stocks, debtors and bills receivable. Some balance sheets show net current assets by using the creditors' balance to partially offset current assets.
- Wasting assets are those which, being of a fixed nature, are slowly consumed in the nature of earning income.

Assets are generally shown in the balance sheet at cost on the assumption that a business is a going concern. It is not prudent to show them at a higher market value since this has not actually been realised. It is prudent, however, to recognise losses immediately. So, for example, stocks should be shown at the lower of cost or net realisable value. The difference between cost and net realisable value should be written off against profits.

CLASSIFICATION OF LIABILITIES

■ Term liabilities are amounts owing by the entity which are not repayable within one year from the balance date. These include capital/retained profits/shareholders funds, term loans and amounts owing where the lending agreement is for more than 12 months beyond the balance date.

■ Current liabilities are amounts owing by the entity which must be met within one year of the balance date. Examples are creditors and bank over-drafts which are repayable on demand.

FUNDAMENTAL ACCOUNTING CONCEPTS AND PRINCIPLES

In addition to the mechanics of double-entry book-keeping there are a few basic principles that accountants should adhere to when preparing accounts. Many of these are covered by GAAP or by the accounting standards that are set by the accounting profession around the world. These are beyond the scope of this simple introduction but listed below are some of the basic principles.

Accruals concept and matching

The income of any transaction should be matched with expenditure of that transaction during the same accounting period. So, for example, if sales revenue has been recorded during the year then the cost of those sales must also be recorded during the same period. If all costs have not yet been billed then they should be accrued for. This is a process (for example) whereby an expenditure account is debited with consumable purchases received but not yet invoiced and a liability account (accrued creditors) is credited. When the invoice finally comes in the accrued liability account is debited and the supplier's account is credited. This process of accruing ensures that the expenditure is recorded in the correct accounting period and is matched with corresponding revenue.

When a supplier invoice is for services not yet received and relates to a future accounting period, the amount of the 'prepayment' is deferred to the future period to which it relates. For example, if an entity receives an invoice for vehicle insurance covering the period April 2008 to March 2009 and its accounting period ends on 31 December 2008 then one quarter of the invoice value relates to the 2009 accounting period and should be deferred to that period. This is a prepayment and is the opposite of an accrual.

The basic concept that needs to be understood is that income should always be matched with its expenditure.

Accounting periods

Business is usually divided up conveniently into accounting periods of 12 months. Accounting periods may not always be the same as taxation return periods. When preparing accounts for comparative periods with previous years it is, therefore, important to be consistent with accounting periods so as to compare like with like. This may not always be possible (start-ups, takeovers, etc.) and often adjustments need to be made and full explanations given so as not to confuse the readers of the accounts.

Consistency

There should be a consistent treatment for transactions between one accounting period and the next. For example, if the method of valuing stocks changes each year then the level of profits reported will change according to the valuation method used. Consistency in valuation method will prevent this happening.

Conservatism

This concept requires that 1) income is not recognised in the accounts until it is certain and 2) expenditure is recorded in the accounts as soon as it is recognised.

Materiality

There might have been an omission or misstatements of an item. Such a mis-statement or omission is material if it influences the overall view of the financial position of the entity and might affect the decisions of users of the accounts. Materiality will depend on both the size and nature of the error.

Going concern

This accounting concept makes the assumption that the entity will continue trading into the future. This presumption has an effect on the business valu-ation and it is therefore important that the directors or owners of an entity assess the organisation's ability to continue into the foreseeable future as a going concern. Failure to do this could mean that people lending money or giving credit to the entity could end up making losses. The owners/directors of an entity who allow it to get into debt knowing that it could not repay that debt are committing fraud. Uncertainties over an entity's ability to con-tinue as a going concern should be reported and the effect of this reported in the entity's financial statements.

Business entity concept

This concept recognises that the business is a separate entity from the owner. In the case of a sole trader this does not, in reality, mean much. However, in the case of a limited company the company is a separate legal person from the shareholder owners.

Full disclosure

It is Generally Accepted Accounting Practice that reporting accountants make as much disclosure as possible in order to enable investors to see everything that is available to be known about the business. Investors need to understand their risks. Whilst full disclosure is essential, it is fair that the essential, and most important facts that investors/stakeholders need to know are not hidden by a mass of information. Full disclosure is necessary and so is clarity.

Substance over form

Financial statements should show the real substance of the entity in addition to the legal form. If an accountant knows of something that materially affects the view given by the financial statements but knows that disclosure is not 'legally' required, he should nevertheless report.

The above example and explanation of concepts explain the basics of how the double-entry system and accounts production work. It is this process that lies behind the financial statements that you will review as a finance manager or banker. From financial statements it is useful to prepare ratio analysis to easily make comparisons between accounting periods and between competitive organisations.

RATIO ANALYSIS

This is concerned with the relationships between values reported in financial statements. Most organisations have key ratios as part of their corporate objectives and goals. An example of this can be seen in the J Sainsbury plc report in Chapter 1.

Ratios help us understand and compare performance in a number of areas, including:

- profits and returns
- efficiency
- gearing

- liquidity
- investor returns.

Some of the more important ratios are explained below.

Gross margin (gross profit) percentage

This is one of the most widely used ratios. It is the ratio of gross profit to sales value expressed as a percentage.

In our previous example for BAF the gross profit was £66 and sales were £106. The gross margin is, therefore, 62%. This is calculated as follows:

$$\frac{\text{Gross profit}}{\text{Sales}} \times \frac{100}{1}$$

$$\frac{66}{106} \times \frac{100}{1} = 62\%$$

The gross margin is a key indicator particularly when comparing the contribution that individual product lines make to the pool of fixed costs and profits.

Net profit margin

This is the ratio of net profit to sales and is calculated as follows:

$$\frac{\text{Net profit}}{\text{Sales}} \times \frac{100}{1}$$

In the BAF example the net profit was £6 and sales were £106. The net profit margin is 5.7%.

$$\frac{6}{106} \times \frac{100}{1} = 5.7\%$$

In addition to the basic net profit margin, ratios may be calculated for net profit before interest (NPBI) and for net profit before interest and taxation (NPBIT).

Administrative costs to sales

The ratio of administrative costs to sales is calculated as:

$$\frac{\text{Administrative costs}}{\text{Sales}} \times \frac{100}{1}$$

For example, if administrative costs were £300,000 and sales were £2,700,000 then the administrative costs to sales ratio would be about 11%.

$$\frac{300,000}{2,700,000} \times \frac{100}{1} = 11\%$$

Current ratio

This ratio compares current assets to current liabilities as a measure of the solvency of an entity. It is usually shown as a single figure and is calculated as:

$$\frac{\text{Current assets}}{\text{Current liabilities}}$$

In the case of a business that is a going concern current assets are cash and those assets that are readily converted into cash such as debtors and stocks. Current liabilities are amounts owing and due for payment immediately or on demand such as trade creditors. A bank overdraft is normally repayable on demand so this might prudently be considered as a current liability.

In our example for BAF we have:

Current assets of: £516 (Cash £380 + Stock £60 + Debtors £76)

Current liabilities of: £360 (Creditors £360)

$$\text{The current ratio is: } \frac{516}{360} = 1.43$$

Liquidity ratio

This ratio shows an entity's short-term liquidity and ability to pay its debts as they fall due. It is usually expressed as a single figure with a ratio of above 1 as being satisfactory as an indication of ability to pay debts. Remember, though, that too high a liquidity ratio might indicate an inefficient invest-ment of funds just as too low a ratio might indicate poor working capital management and inability to continue trading. All ratios need to be con-sidered as part of an overall picture and not only in isolation.

The liquidity ratio is calculated as:

$$\frac{\text{Liquid assets}}{\text{Current liabilities}}$$

Liquid assets are cash, bank and debtors. Note that stocks are excluded since they have yet to be converted and sold into debts. Current liabilities are creditors and amounts falling due for immediate repayment.

In the BAF example we have:

Liquid assets of: £456 (Cash £380 + Debtors £76)

Current liabilities of: £360 (Creditors)

$$\text{The liquidity ratio is: } \frac{456}{360} = 1.3$$

Since the current ratio is greater than 1 we might assume that BAF can pay its current liabilities (trade creditors) when they are due. This is certainly the case, particularly since cash in bank (£380) exceeds trade creditors (£360). However, an entity can still produce a current ratio of greater than 1 but struggle to pay creditors on time. For example, if in the case of BAF cash was less than the creditors balance then it would have to collect from debtors before it could pay creditors. This, of course, would be fine in normal trading conditions and when debts were of a good collectible quality. However, in adverse market conditions the normal liquidity ratio measure might not be stringent enough to provide assurance. It is always important to understand how ratios are calculated and made up and to look beyond the ratio to the underlying figures.

Debtors' days

This ratio shows how efficient a company is at collecting debts.

$$\text{Debtors' days (collection period)} = \frac{\text{Debtors}}{\text{Sales}} \times 365$$

For example, if sales during a twelve-month period were £2,700,000 and debtors' balances were £350,000 then the debtors' days would be 47 days calculated as follows:

$$\frac{350,000}{2,700,000} \times 365 = \textbf{47 days}$$

This means that on average the company collects its debt in 47 days. Analysts will normally like to see debtors' balances classified into the number of days outstanding. The total debtors' balance can be broken down into amounts outstanding over different periods as follows:

Less than 30 days

30 to 60 days

60 to 90 days

Over 90 days

Stock turnover

This is a measure of the rate at which stock moves through a business. Since there is a cost to holding stock (warehousing, interest, insurance, etc.) it is generally more efficient the faster stock is moved on. I use the word 'generally' since, as you will agree, things aren't always that simple. For example, a supplier might be offering discounts to buy in larger quantities or the buyer might be anticipating a particular commodity price rise. Working out the optimal level of stock to be held, whether raw materials, work in progress or finished stock, needs to take into account many variable factors. At this time, however, we are simply concerned with how fast a stock moves and since a high stock turnover indicates a low level of stock it is generally considered better to have a high stock turnover.

Stock turnover can be calculated as:

$$\text{Stock turnover} = \frac{\text{Cost of sales (materials)}}{\text{Average stock}}$$

For example, calculate the stock turnover if the values of material stocks were: 1 January 2009 £840,000 and 31 December 2009 £570,000. The material cost of sales during the period was £2,700,000.

$$\text{Average stock} = \frac{840,000 + 570,000}{2} = £705,000$$

$$\text{Stock turnover} = \frac{2,700,000}{705,000} = 3.8 \text{ times p.a.}$$

It is useful to prepare stock turnover figures for each type of material or stock (raw materials, work in progress or finished stocks). Remember also that the stock turnover ratio is calculated using period-end figures and can conceal significant movements during the period.

Fixed assets turnover ratio

This ratio is a measure of the efficiency of the use of fixed assets. The more sales generated against fixed assets, the more efficient their use. It is calculated as follows:

$$\text{Fixed assets turnover ratio} = \frac{\text{Sales}}{\text{Fixed assets}}$$

For example, if sales are £3,500,000 p.a. and fixed assets are £900,000 then the fixed assets turnover ratio will be:

$$\frac{3,500,000}{900,000} = 3.9 \text{ times p.a.}$$

It is best to use the average fixed assets during the period of sales rather than the year-end balance (balance at beginning of year + balance at year end) /2.

Gearing ratio

This ratio shows the level of external company borrowing compared to equity. In its most simple form:

$$\text{Gearing} = \frac{\text{Loan capital}}{\text{Equity}}$$

For example, if bank loans were £500,000 and total equity (shareholder's funds) were £2,000,000 then the gearing would be 0.25:

$$\frac{500,000}{2,000,000} = 0.25$$

This might be considered as a lowly geared organisation, depending on the industry. Generally a lowly geared organisation is considered to be more robust and, all other things being equal, a safer lending proposition than a highly geared organisation.

The optimal level of gearing will depend upon striking a balance between the efficient use of shareholders' funds and the financial robustness required of an organisation, taking into account interest rates. When loan interest rates are high a company may wish to repay debt and become more lowly geared. When profits are low a highly geared company may have little left after fixed interest to distribute to shareholders.

In the example we have simply used the nominal value of shareholders' funds. However, gearing ratios can also be calculated using market values. An advantage of this method is that future investors in a company might be able to make better judgements against market values.

Example: Calculate the gearing ratio using the following nominal values:

Debentures	600
Preference shares	700
Long-term bank loans	900
Short-term loans	100
Overdrafts	120
Ordinary share capital	1000
Retained profits	900
Share premium account	200

The gearing ratio can be calculated in several ways:

$$\frac{600 + 700 + 900 + 100 + 120}{1,000 + 900 + 200} \times \frac{100}{1} = 115\%$$

$$\frac{600 + 700 + 900 + 100 + 120}{600 + 700 + 900 + 100 + 120 + 1,000 + 900 + 200} \times \frac{100}{1} = 54\%$$

The first method shows the ratio of loan capital to equity. The second ratio shows the ratio of loan capital to the total capital (loan plus equity). There are many other ways of expressing the gearing ratio. The important thing is to be consistent in which method is used and to ensure, particularly when making comparisons with other organisations, that the same methods are used for comparing.

When setting the optimal level of gearing for an organisation the finance manager needs to maximise the return to shareholders subject to a number of constraints, including the need to be financially robust in differing market conditions. It is useful to simply prepare a number of different scenarios using a spreadsheet and work out the sensitivity of each scenario to changes in variable factors such as interest rates. This is done by replacing the value of each variable (one at a time) and comparing the result with previous scenarios.

In the financial crisis of autumn 2008 most analysts remarked that, with competitive pressures to win new business, lending banks became less conservative in their lending criteria with regards to gearing ratios and perhaps pushed their own prudential ratios further than they should have.

Return on equity (ROE)

This shows as a percentage the return that equity investors (shareholders/proprietors) have achieved during the accounting period. It is calculated by expressing the entity's profits before interest and taxation (PBIT) as a percentage of equity (shareholders' funds or proprietorship).

In our example for BAF the profit before interest and taxation was £6 and the total equity was £506. The ROE percentage is, therefore, 1.2%, calculated as follows:

$$\frac{\text{PBIT}}{\text{Equity}} \times \frac{100}{1}$$

$$\frac{6}{506} \times \frac{100}{1} = 1.2\%$$

Return on capital employed (ROCE)

This relates profits to the value of funds used to produce them. It is calculated by expressing the entity's PBIT to the capital actually employed in producing the profits. Capital employed has many definitions. It is sometimes defined as shareholders' funds (equity) plus term loans or total assets less current liabilities or sometimes fixed assets plus working capital.

$$\text{ROCE} = \frac{\text{PBIT}}{\text{Capital employed}} \times \frac{100}{1}$$

Example: A company had profits before taxation and interest of £57,000. Shareholders funds were £600,000 and term loans were £50,000. The ROCE is:

$$\frac{57}{600 + 50} \times \frac{100}{1} = 8.8\%$$

Earnings per share (EPS)

The earnings per share is the profit attributable to each equity share based on the profits for the period after tax and after deducting minority interests and preference dividends. Profits taken are to exclude extraordinary items. The definition of EPS is given in certain accounting standards, but care should be taken to ensure consistency, especially with international comparisons.

$$\text{EPS} = \frac{\text{Net profit after tax}}{\text{Number of ordinary shares}}$$

Example: A company has equity share capital of 300,000 ordinary shares of 70p each, all of which rank for dividend. It has profits after taxation of £150,000. The EPS is 50p. This is calculated as follows:

$$\text{EPS} = \frac{£150,000}{300,000} = 50\text{p}$$

The price earnings ratio (P/E)

This ratio compares the earnings per share with the market price of one ordinary share.

$$PE = \frac{\text{Market price of ordinary share}}{\text{Earnings per share (EPS)}}$$

If the company considered above had an EPS of 50p when the market price of its shares was £3.50 each, the PE ratio would be 7. This would be calculated as follows:

$$PE = \frac{£3.50}{50p} = 7$$

A high price earnings ratio may indicate market confidence in a company. Whether an investment in a company is attractive will depend upon the price asked for the investment. The price earnings ratio shows the relationship between price and return as measured by earnings.

Earnings yield

This is simply the price earnings ratio expressed as a percentage. In the above PE example it would be calculated as follows:

$$\text{Earnings yield} = \frac{\text{EPS}}{\text{Share price}} \times \frac{100}{1}$$

$$\text{Earnings yield} = \frac{50p}{£3.50} \times \frac{100}{1} = 14.3\%$$

This ratio is often used by analysts as a simple expression of return on investment.

Dividend cover

This measure shows us how secure dividend payments are by demonstrating how many times over the dividend could have been paid from profits. The higher the dividend cover, the more robust.

$$\text{Dividend cover} = \frac{\text{EPS (earnings per share)}}{\text{Dividend per share}}$$

If the EPS was 50p and the dividend paid was 20p then the dividend cover would be 2.5 times. This would be calculated as follows:

$$\text{Dividend cover} = \frac{50p}{20p}$$

$$= 2.5 \text{ times}$$

Dividend yield

This compares the dividend paid to the share price. This is the return against the market value of a share.

$$\text{Dividend yield} = \frac{\text{Dividend}}{\text{Share price}} \times \frac{100}{1}$$

If a dividend of 20p is paid when the share price is standing at £3.50 then the dividend yield is:

$$\frac{20p}{£3.50} \times \frac{100}{1}$$

$$= 5.7\%$$

The dividend yield shows the return on an investment using market value.

Using the basic ratio analysis examples explained above will enable you to take a measured view of financial statements, to make comparisons between accounting periods and between companies and to ask questions. There are no hard and fast rules on ratios, but they lead to further investigation and explanations. Different stakeholders might place different emphasis on the importance of different ratios and what their values should be.

Some analysts like to link ratios together. The Du Pont system of ratio analysis constructs what is known as a pyramid of ratios. Details of this pyramid are now widely available for view on the web. For our purposes it is worth noting how ratios are interrelated.

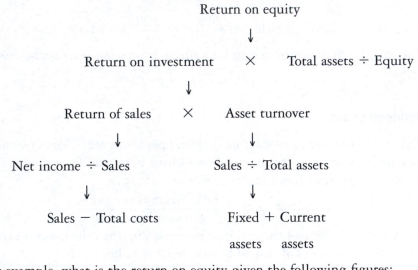

For example, what is the return on equity given the following figures:

Sales	£500
Total costs	£475
Fixed assets	£150
Current assets	£100
Equity	£600

Then, working from the bottom up, we have:

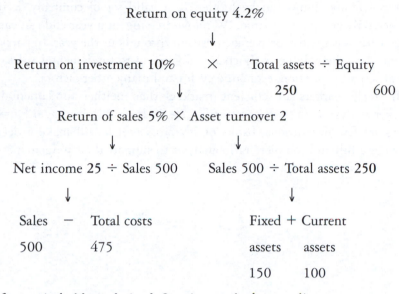

Return on equity 4.2%

↓

Return on investment 10%   ×   Total assets ÷ Equity

250   600

Return of sales 5% × Asset turnover 2

↓   ↓

Net income 25 ÷ Sales 500   Sales 500 ÷ Total assets 250

↓   ↓

Sales   −   Total costs   Fixed + Current

500   475   assets   assets

150   100

The figures in bold are derived. Starting at the bottom line:

Sales 500 − Total costs 475 = Net income 25

Fixed assets 150 + Current assets 100 = Total assets 250

Net income 25 ÷ Sales 500 × 100% = Return on sales 5%

Sales 500 ÷ Total assets 250 = Asset Turnover 2

Return on sales 5% × Asset turnover 2 = Return on investment 10%

Return on investment 10% × (Total assets 250 ÷ Equity 600) = Return on equity 4.2%

The value of the Du Pont system is that given a certain amount of information it might be possible to complete the picture. It is also useful to see that the arithmetic is correct and the picture is complete. It is used by some analysts to cross check their calculations.

SUMMARY

In this chapter we have looked at the fundamentals of how basic accounts are prepared and then looked into some simple ratio analysis. The objective of the chapter was to ensure that the reader understands the basics of accounts analysis, starting with the structure of accounts.

Ratio analysis is used by the finance manager to monitor company performance against strategic financial objectives. It is used by analysts, investors and bankers as an aid to investment decisions. However, ratio analysis does not provide all of the solutions. As we have already discussed it is at the most a means to an end. It helps in our overall analysis and questioning. Many things can be hidden in a valid set of company accounts viewed only at a point in time. 'Window dressing' at a year end can camouflage what was the real or average position throughout the year. In particular financial markets do not only change according to fundamental rules, they are affected by emotion, economic cycles and many other factors.

If stock markets are efficient markets then neither fundamental nor market analysis alone will necessarily give an investor advantage. However, there are few institutions, banks or investors which will make a decision without a full and complete ratio analysis to support their judgement.

Company taxation interface with financial management

OVERVIEW

All business income is shared with the government through taxation and we need to be aware of how this will affect our financial decisions. It is quite likely that taxation will affect alternative projects or investment opportunities differently and we do, therefore, need to take taxation into consideration. Before we can do this we need some basic knowledge of taxation and how it should be brought into financial decision processes.

This chapter is concerned with the high-level principles of taxation that apply to businesses and how these should be considered when preparing a corporate and financial strategy and in the decision-making process. It is not intended to be a practical guide to taxation or to show how to calculate a tax liability. It is simply a global guide showing how to introduce taxation factors into financial management and decision making.

There used to be a clear difference between tax avoidance and tax evasion, tax avoidance being considered to be simply a matter of arranging affairs in a manner that was 'tax efficient' and tax evasion being the illegal act of evading taxation which was due. The position varies from country to country. However, the distinction between tax avoidance and tax evasion has in recent years become somewhat cloudy and some countries now have clear anti-avoidance legislation and consider that any transaction that has been entered into with the primary purpose of avoiding tax can be 'put aside'. This chapter is not concerned with how to minimise taxation and offers no strategies for tax minimisation. It is concerned with understanding the tax implications of financial structures and decisions so that they can be properly taken into account in good strategic financial management and planning. For the purpose of this high-level study we will make reference mainly to the UK system of taxation.

In most countries taxation is split between direct taxes and indirect taxes. Direct taxes are levied directly on the earnings, profits or gains of individuals or companies and indirect taxes are levied on expenditure. Examples of taxes under each classification are:

Direct taxes:

- income taxes and national insurance
- corporation tax
- capital gains tax and inheritance tax.

Indirect taxes:

- value added tax (VAT)
- customs duty.

Different countries may have similar taxes to the above but referred to under different names. For example, in New Zealand and Australia a form of value added tax is called goods and services tax (GST).

A company accountant will need to be familiar with all aspects of taxation which affect the company's employees and the company itself. For the purpose of corporate financial management we will be concentrating on corporation tax and on VAT. The best source of information on UK tax is Her Majesty's Revenue and Customs (HMRC) web site which is www.hmrc.gov.uk

This chapter is intended as a guide to some common elements of that interface with financial management decisions. It is not to be taken or used as a guide to any taxation rules or rates since these are constantly changing. Indeed, many of the taxation rates used in this work are not current rates and those that happen to be current may have changed by the date of publication.

OUTLINE OF CORPORATION TAX

The charge to tax and residence

UK corporation tax is a tax charged on the worldwide profits and chargeable gains of UK resident companies. Similar taxes apply in other countries to the profits and gains earned by companies resident in those countries. UK corporation tax is not charged on the dividends received from companies that are resident in the UK.

A company that is not resident in the UK may also find that its profits and gains are chargeable to UK corporation tax if it carries on a trade or vocation in the UK through a branch or agency.

This latter point is important to multinational companies which have a complexity of overseas subsidiaries and branches carrying out activities which overlap from one country to another. So, what may seem a simple rule to apply can in practice become difficult to monitor and it is an important aspect of cross-border financial management to understand the taxation implications in all countries of operation.

Period of assessment

Corporation tax is charged in respect of a taxation accounting period. This may be different to the period of account for which a company prepares its accounts. This is another important consideration for the finance manager when planning tax liabilities. Where the corporation tax accounting period is different from the company period of account it will be necessary to allocate profits between the relevant periods. This will need to be agreed with HMRC. The following is a guide suitable for planning:

- Allocate trading income before capital allowances on a time basis.
- Calculate capital allowances and any balancing charges for each relevant corporation tax accounting period.
- Chargeable gains are to be recognised in the actual period they are realised.
- Other income to be allocated to the actual period to which it relates.
- Charges on income to be deducted from taxable profits in the tax accounting period in which they are paid.

The main point here is to recognise that both residence and the period of assessment are critical aspects to consider when starting a new operation. The above points are mentioned only to raise awareness of the types of taxation implications that need to be planned for. Tax laws, rates and international treaties covering things such as double taxation are for ever changing and it is clearly beyond the scope of this chapter to provide answers or any detailed analysis of taxation computations. It is, however, intended to raise awareness of the type of taxation considerations that need to be considered. Corporate bankers and finance managers will usually pass on their plans to tax practitioners for advice on taxation consequences and also seek advice from counsel if deemed necessary.

Example of a basic calculation of corporation tax:

Net profit per accounts	100,000
Add back depreciation (not allowed)	8,000
Less capital allowances (instead of depreciation)	−7,000
Profit chargeable to corporation tax	101,000
Corporation tax at small companies rate of 20%	20,200

Payment of corporation tax

HMRC states that for most companies corporation tax is due nine calendar months and one day after the end of the tax accounting period (the normal due date). If the accounting period ends on the last day of a month, the normal due date will be the first day of the tenth following month. For example, an accounting period ending on 31 May 2008 will have a due date of 1 March 2009.

In the case of large companies (those which have profits of over £1.5 million) corporation tax is paid by quarterly instalments. There are also special rules for companies when they become 'large' so that they do not need to pay by quarterly instalments in the first period for which they are 'large' (unless their profits exceed £10 million).

For details of corporation tax go to the HMRC web site: www.hmrc.gov.uk and search for corporation tax.

For our purposes in this text on financial management we need to be concerned with the timing of large tax payments.

■ When a company becomes 'large'.

■ When instalments are due.

These factors need to be built into our cash forecasts and financial plans.

Interest on overdue tax

Interest is charged on overdue tax from the reckonable date to the date of actual payment. This interest is not an allowable deduction for corporation tax purposes. The reckonable date varies according to whether an appeal and postponement application has been lodged. The rate of interest varies according to changes in bank rates.

The main point for the financial manager to be aware of is that, unlike other interest expense, interest on overdue tax is not tax deductible.

Corporation tax rates and allowances

Corporation tax on profits – figures		
Rates, limits, fractions for financial years starting 1 April	2007	2008
Main rate of corporation tax	30%	28%
Small companies rate (SCR)*	20%	21%
SCR can be claimed by qualifying companies with profits at an annual rate not exceeding	£300,000	£300,000
Marginal small companies relief (MSCR) lower limit	£300,000	£300,000
MSCR upper limit	£1,500,000	£1,500,000
MSCR fraction	1/40	7/400
Special rate for authorised investment funds – unit trusts and open-ended investment companies	20%	20%

* For companies with ring-fence profits, SCR on those profits is 19% with an MSCR fraction of 11/400 for financial years 2007 starting on 1 April 2007 and 2008 starting on 1 April 2008. Ring-fence profits mean the income and gains from oil-extraction activities or oil rights in the UK and UK Continental Shelf.

The main rate of corporation tax applies when profits (including ring-fence profits) are at a rate exceeding £1,500,000, or where there is no claim to another rate, or where another rate does not apply.

Capital gains and corporation tax

For limited companies capital gains just form part of the total profits of the company on which they pay corporation tax.

HMRC web site

Taxation is no longer the black art it used to be and most people who can navigate the web can find enough information on taxation to assist with their high-level tax planning. In the case of corporation tax the HMRC site at www.hmrc.gov.uk/ctsa/index.htm provides an excellent background, far better than I have read in any text or work manual. I would strongly recommend that you use this site and similar sites for other taxation regimes and then if in doubt or you need confirmation consult a taxation specialist. HMRC will always be helpful with their interpretation, although they will not provide information regarding avoidance. If you are seeking extreme tax efficiency then you need to seek the advice of a taxation lawyer and counsel.

VALUE ADDED TAX – VAT

In the UK VAT is a tax charged on business-to-business and business-to-consumer transactions. It is also charged on goods, and some services, imported from places outside the European Union (EU) and on goods and some services coming into the UK from other EU countries.

VAT is charged to a buyer by a VAT-registered seller. This VAT is reclaimed by a VAT-registered buyer after goods and services are purchased.

There are three different rates of VAT – standard, reduced and zero – which apply to different types of goods and services. Some goods and services are exempt from VAT altogether, while others are outside the scope of VAT. Businesses registered for VAT usually account for VAT on a quarterly basis by filling in a VAT return and submitting it to HMRC.

At the time of writing (January 2009) a business must register for VAT if its turnover for the previous 12 months is over a specific limit – currently £67,000 – or if it thinks its turnover may soon go over this limit. This limit is often changed. A business may register voluntarily at any time. There are a few exemptions from registration. The rules on registration can be complex and HMRC has provided a helpful guide as to whether or not registration is required in the form of 'yes/no' questions. This can be found on www.hmrc.gov.uk/vat/vat-registering.htm

VAT is charged by someone who is registered for VAT – a 'taxable person' – on:

- goods and services sold or otherwise supplied (eg barter) in the UK
- goods, and some services, imported from places outside the EU
- goods and services coming into the UK from other EU countries.

Note that a business cannot escape VAT by entering into barter contracts.

For items which are standard rated or reduced rated for VAT, VAT is charged to the buyer (output tax) by the VAT-registered seller. This VAT is reclaimed by the VAT-registered buyer (input tax) after goods and services are purchased.

If a business is registered for VAT generally it will charge VAT on business sales and reclaim VAT on business purchases. The difference between the VAT charged and the VAT being reclaimed is the amount of VAT it must pay to HMRC. If the value of the VAT to reclaim is more than the value of the VAT charged, then HMRC pays the business.

If a business is not registered for VAT, it does not charge VAT on sales. It will still pay VAT on purchases and cannot reclaim this VAT.

A business usually accounts for VAT on a quarterly basis by filling in a VAT return and submitting it to HMRC. It then pays HMRC the excess of its output tax over the VAT it can reclaim as input tax. If the input tax it can reclaim is more than the output tax, it can reclaim the difference from HMRC.

Rates of VAT

Different VAT rates apply to different goods and services. Currently there are three rates:

- standard rate – 17.5 per cent (1/1/2010)
- reduced rate – 5 per cent
- zero rate – 0 per cent.

The standard rate of VAT is the default rate for goods and services unless specified otherwise.

Examples of reduced-rate items include:

- domestic fuel and power
- installation of energy-saving materials
- residential conversions
- women's sanitary products
- children's car seats.

Examples of zero-rated items include:

- food – but not meals in restaurants or hot takeaways
- books and newspapers
- children's clothing and shoes
- public transport.

Items not covered by VAT

Some items are not covered by VAT – exempt items and items which are outside the scope of VAT.

Items which are exempt from VAT include the following:

- insurance
- providing credit
- education and training, if certain conditions are met
- fund-raising events by charities, if certain conditions are met
- subscriptions to membership organisations.

The difference between exempt and zero-rated

If you sell zero-rated goods or services, they are taxable for VAT at '0' per cent. If you sell exempt goods or services they are not taxable for VAT. Unlike zero-rated supplies, exempt items are not treated as taxable. No tax is payable, but equally, the person making the supply cannot normally recover any of the VAT on their own expenses. If you sell only exempt goods or services, generally you cannot register for VAT or reclaim VAT on purchases. If you sell some exempt goods or services, you may not be able to reclaim VAT on some purchases. If you sell only zero-rated goods or services you may apply for exemption from VAT registration. If you pay little or no VAT on your purchases this would probably make sense.

Be aware that if you bought goods or services for your business before you registered for VAT you may be able to reclaim the VAT you paid on those items:

- for goods: you can reclaim VAT up to three years before you registered for VAT.
- for services: you can reclaim VAT up to six months before you registered for VAT.

You should include this VAT on your first VAT return.

Clearly the financial plan will need to consider the implications of VAT or similar goods and services taxes in other countries. It will affect cash forecasts and the timing of payments to HMRC can be critical. For example, the

VAT on sales in the last few days of a quarterly return period will have to be paid earlier than the VAT on sales made just after the cut-off period. This can be particularly harmful to a business that has to grant extended credit to its customers for it can find that it has to pay over VAT charged to customers but not yet received from them.

PAYE AND NI

PAYE stands for the Pay As You Earn system. NI stands for National Insurance. If you employ staff you will need to deduct tax and NI contributions (NICs) from their pay. The best sources of information of employers' responsibilities and how the process works are on the HMRC web site which links through to the relevant Business Link site. You will find details of the rules and mechanical process involved regarding record-keeping, forms, returns and making payments.

The PAYE system is the HMRC device for collecting income tax from the pay of employees, including directors. It is done as they earn, for example monthly or weekly. An employer needs to deduct income tax and NI contributions from each employee's pay and submit the deductions to HMRC. The employer has to account for both the employer's and the employee's contributions. The guide on the HMRC web site explains how to deduct income tax and NICs and the processes involved. This includes a guide to:

- employers' responsibilities
- starting a PAYE system
- when to apply PAYE
- employee tax codes
- PAYE forms
- general information and questions regarding PAYE.

GLOBAL TAX PLANNING

The tax laws in different countries vary in a number of ways that affect the financial plan. For example:

- The definition of a resident varies from country to country.
- In some countries a non-resident is taxed.
- The definition of a taxable person/entity varies.
- The definition of taxable income varies.
- Allowances are different in each country.

- Tax-deductible expenses vary.
- Tax rates vary.
- The timing of when tax is due to be paid varies.
- Some countries share double tax treaties, others do not.

The financial planner will need to consider the impact of different taxation regimes on his or her organisation's bottom line and on cash flow. With anti-avoidance provisions he or she will need to ensure that all transactions have a 'physical' reality and are not just dressed up to avoid tax. Financial plans need to recognise the potential for double tax.

Some organisations might attempt global tax planning to help reduce the chances of double taxation and reduce their global taxation through the use of transfer-pricing studies. However, tax authorities counter international tax planning by constantly introducing new laws to reduce the use of companies in low-tax countries/tax havens, by limiting transactions that are not commercially justified and by ensuring that transactions between related foreign companies are at arm's-length values through transfer-pricing rules. Withholding taxes may be required on payments to foreign companies.

The important point to remember is that transactions that have no commercial or real business purpose and are designed to avoid tax will be ineffective and that transactions must be at arm's-length value. Failure to do this will attract the attention of the taxation authorities in one country or another, the transaction will be set aside for the purpose of calculating tax and penalties may be incurred.

The purpose of planning global tax in the context of this book is to understand the taxation implications of the financial plan and to make decisions in terms of international activities and trade. To effectively do this will require a tax plan for expected global activities based upon the tax laws of each country. For example, when preparing a tax plan consider:

- the commercial validity of transactions
- the arm's-length rule for transactions between related companies
- sources of international tax law and the rules of different jurisdictions
- definitions of a permanent establishment
- definitions of residency
- the taxations authorities' views on tax planning
- the difference between tax avoidance and tax evasion
- anti-avoidance provisions and the meaning of the law in addition to the letter of the law
- the relationship of tax modelling to corporate structure, plans and strategy
- the effect of taxation regimes on the supply chain

- what is acceptable taxation behaviour
- double taxation.

HMRC makes clear its view on tax planning through the *International Tax Handbook – ITH103*. This is available online at www.hmrc.gov.uk.

Below are HMRC's comments on international tax planning and avoidance in the international context.

Within the Revenue we do not categorise avoidance in quite the narrow way that the Courts have done. Of course we make a distinction between mitigation and avoidance. However, if a taxpayer takes advantage of the law to get a tax advantage which is not, in our understanding, within the spirit of the legislation, we tend to look on that as avoidance. But unless the prerequisites of the new approach are present such avoidance can only be countered by legislation brought in for the purpose. As an example of mitigation, Lord Templeman instances a taxpayer transferring assets to an Isle of Man company which is outside the United Kingdom tax jurisdiction. In many circumstances we would regard that as avoidance and indeed there is legislation which is designed for such 'mitigation' – for individuals, that is ICTA88/S739 and for companies the controlled foreign companies provisions.

When considering groups operating internationally, the question of whether there is avoidance is perhaps even more difficult to answer than in the purely domestic field, if only because, in their arrangements, the groups have regard to their worldwide tax bill. They may pay little or no tax worldwide and yet, looking at the United Kingdom in isolation, there may be no avoidance. There are some examples of what views we take of some such situations in chapters 10 and 12. Chapter 14 (para 1438) considers the implications of Ramsay and Furniss in the context of the motive test in the controlled foreign company provisions.

This book frequently uses the expression 'tax planning'. This term embraces a wide range of options from those which are merely 'mitigatory' to those which we would regard as 'avoidance'. As already noted, fine distinctions between 'tax planning' and 'tax avoidance' are seen as being of less consequence than the overall effect on the yield to the Exchequer. This is particularly so where the apparent result is not in accordance with Parliament's intentions or which would not have been had Parliament addressed itself to the particular issue. Where cross-border avoidance schemes are involved International Division will always consider the possibility of using the 'new approach' although, as will become apparent later in the book, the appropriate remedy is often by way of legislation.

HMRC, October 2008

OVERSEAS ACTIVITIES

Companies with overseas activities will have to comply with the rules for the taxation of controlled foreign companies, with anti-avoidance provisions and be aware of aspects of double taxation. For the purpose of this section on the taxation of overseas activities we will consider the position from the perspective of a UK resident company and the UK taxation authority (HMRC).

Basic position

A UK resident company that makes overseas investments will be liable to pay UK corporation tax on income received before the deduction of any foreign taxes. This income will be assessed as follows:

Interest received through agents	Schedule C
Profits from an overseas branch controlled from UK	Schedule D, Case 1
Income from foreign securities	Schedule D, Case lV
Dividends from overseas subsidiaries	Schedule C, Case V
Profits for an overseas branch controlled from overseas	Schedule C, Case V

Any gain on disposal of a foreign asset will also be taxed.

In addition to incurring UK taxation on overseas activities there will be foreign taxation liabilities depending upon the jurisdiction of the overseas activity. However, double-taxation relief is available.

There may be a benefit in accumulating income in a foreign country with an effective tax rate that is lower than the UK. However, anti-avoidance provisions may eliminate such benefits. Also, benefits may be lost in repatriation of funds and may be subject to exchange-control regulations.

Controlled foreign companies and motive testing

Most taxation regimes do not like companies setting up 'name plates' overseas in an attempt to avoid taxation. Most major industrialised countries have rules to prevent the avoidance of tax using shell or name-plate companies. The UK has Controlled Foreign Company (CFC) rules that effectively stop multinationals from avoiding UK tax by diverting profits to tax havens and areas of lower taxation. The rules contain a motive test to ensure that CFC tax is only ever payable if a company is involved in UK tax avoidance. The rules are complex and can be obtained from HMRC – refer to CTSA Guidance Notes on the Provisions of Part XVII Chapter IV ICTA 1988, the Motive Test Guidance published in March 2003 and guidance on provisions relating to CFCs in recent Finance Acts, up to and including FA2003.

HMRC will offer guidance but will not help tax avoidance! As I have stated this chapter is not about avoidance or tax efficiency but covers understanding the taxation implications of corporate plans and strategies.

A useful address in the UK for questions of this nature is: HMRC, Revenue Policy International Registry, 100 Parliament Street, London, SW1A 2BQ; or visit www.hmrc.gov.uk/international/technical4.htm

Migration of companies from the UK

If it is intended to transfer a company to another country it is necessary to ensure that all UK taxation up to the point of migration is paid and that appropriate arrangements are made and agreed with HMRC to ensure that it receives the tax due. This is covered on the HMRC web site and an extract of the process is given below:

> When a company migrates after 15 March 1988, FA88/S130 to FA88/S132 impose various requirements on it to ensure that it settles all its tax liabilities in due course.
>
> Notice and arrangements for payment of tax:
>
> 1) A migrating company is required to notify the HMRC Board of its intention to cease to be resident in the UK and to obtain the Board's approval of arrangements for payment of the company's tax liabilities.
>
> 2) A notice under Section 130 (2)(a) should be sent to: HMRC, CT&VAT, International CT Company Migrations, 3rd Floor, 100 Parliament Street, London, SW1A 2BQ. The notice should give the intended date of migration, a statement of tax liabilities, proposals for making payments and other information required by Section 130 (2)(b) and (c). A copy of the notice and the tax computation should also be sent to the company's district tax office.
>
> 3) Information to be supplied will include:
>
> a) The name of the company, UK address and place of incorporation.
>
> b) Its tax district and reference number.
>
> c) A copy of the latest available accounts.
>
> d) A detailed statement of all tax liabilities which are or will be due for periods commencing before the date of migration.
>
> e) The company's proposals for making payment of tax liabilities including the name and address of the proposed attorney and of the proposed guarantor.

f) If a corporate guarantor other than a bank is proposed a copy of its memorandum and articles of association is required.

4) Arrangements for securing payment of tax:

4.1 a) It may be necessary to appoint an attorney to act for the company in tax matters, for example, to receive notices of assessment. The attorney must be resident in the UK and will usually be an individual who is professionally qualified, for example, as a solicitor or accountant. The Board will need to be satisfied that the migrating company has power to appoint an attorney.

4.1.b) The capacity of a migrating company to appoint an attorney may be demonstrated to the Board by an opinion of a lawyer (qualified in the appropriate local law) upon the following matters:

i) That the company has power through its constitution and/or by appropriate local law to appoint an attorney.

There are other requirements regarding arrangements for securing payments through a power of attorney and the migrating company will need to satisfy the Board in these matters.

5) Date of migration:

The intended date of migration should be not less than two months from the date of the notice.

6) Non-compliance

Where a company migrates without the requirements of Section 130 being met, the persons responsible, including individual directors, may be liable for substantial penalties under Section 131. Where tax liabilities of a migrating company remain unpaid those liabilities may also be recovered from related companies, or from certain directors, under Section 132.

DOUBLE-TAXATION RELIEF

In the UK there is relief from double taxation (foreign tax paid by a UK company). This is given by:

■ relief under reciprocal treaties whereby relief is given for tax paid in one country against the tax liability of another

■ unilateral relief in relation to a particular tax where no treaty relief is given

■ the ability to deduct overseas tax from overseas income when treaty or unilateral relief is available.

Double taxation occurs when income is taxed more than once. That is when income is taxed by the taxpayer's country of residence and also in another country where the income was earned. Double-taxation relief removes or partially removes the disincentive that double taxation puts on outward investments. Much of the double-taxation relief that is allowed relates to the underlying tax paid by subsidiary companies on the profits out of which they pay dividends.

The Finance Acts 2000 and 2001 established changes to the way the UK gives relief for double taxation to companies. These changes and guidance notes are available in the *International Tax Manual* (HMRC) and can be found in the section from INTM164210 to INTM164340 which deals with dividends paid to the United Kingdom.

FOREIGN COMPANIES TRADING IN THE UK

A non-UK-resident company will be liable to UK taxation on profits arising in the UK if it has a branch, agency or physical presence in the UK. The first thing to establish is whether the foreign company is actually trading in the UK. Trading may be taken to mean having a branch, agency or physical presence. It is important to seek clarification with HMRC on the taxation status of foreign companies with UK activities. HMRC has tests to decide whether a CFC is exempt or not. The UK CFC rules are intended to stop multinationals avoiding UK tax by diverting profits to tax havens and preferential regimes.

Finance from overseas

A UK company borrowing funds from a non-resident organisation will want to obtain tax relief on the amount of interest paid. The foreign lender will, in all probability, want to receive interest gross without the deduction of any tax. Interest paid on loans not exceeding a year (known as short interest) paid to a non-resident is fully deductible for taxation purposes as long as it is eligible (incurred to earn taxable income). The rate must, however, be commercial, otherwise the relief will be restricted.

Yearly interest that is paid to an overseas lender is normally allowed as a tax-deductible expense. It must be proper business interest relating to earned income and it must have been paid under deduction of tax (or exempt by a double-taxation treaty) or it is paid out of Schedule D Case lV or V income or meets certain other criteria stipulated by HMRC. Again, HMRC clarification is needed before any agreement is concluded.

TRANSFER PRICING

Transfer pricing refers to the price at which goods, services, assets and funds are transferred between one part of an organisation and another. For example, HR might charge finance for recruitment services or the production department might charge finished goods produced to a group selling and distribution company or even a foreign subsidiary. Prices are set within an organisation and the market forces that establish prices for similar 'outside' transactions between third parties are not used. This means that the transfer price chosen will affect the allocation of the profit between various parts of the company, both local and overseas. You can see, therefore, that this becomes a concern for taxation authorities which see transfer pricing as a mechanism that could be used by multinational organisations on cross-border transactions to reduce taxable profits in a taxation jurisdiction where they want to avoid tax. Transfer pricing has now led to increasing global tax regulations and compliance is a particular concern for multinational companies.

Most countries have tax laws that require transactions between different parts of an organisation to be at an arm's-length price. A price that is artificially set to reduce taxation in one regime may be set aside and the transaction, for taxation purposes, be considered at the true arm's-length price. Of course, determining a true arm's-length price is not an easy thing, especially if the goods or services are unique, not a commodity and there are no external yardsticks available. The Organisation for Economic Co-operation and Development (OECD) Transfer Pricing Guidelines for Multinational Enterprises and Tax Administrations assist in determining how transfer prices can be set and help ensure a country gets to tax fairly. In the US guidance on transfer pricing is given under Section 482 of the Internal Revenue Code. Note that pricing for taxation under a regime might be different from customs or border-protection guidelines on process in the same regime.

Different countries have different methods for calculating transfer prices and before transfers are made between foreign-based subsidiaries it is essential to be familiar with the different regimes. For example, the methods used in Japan can be very different to those applicable to the UK.

The following descriptions of ways to determine fair transfer prices are extracted from the OECD Guidelines.

Comparable uncontrolled price (CUP) method

The CUP method compares the price at which a controlled transaction is conducted with the price at which a similar uncontrolled transaction is conducted.

The arm's-length price is determined by the sale price between two unre-lated corporations. However, it might be difficult to find comparable transactions. Comparable transactions fall into two categories: external and internal.

Cost plus method (CP)

The CP method is simply a case of adding up all of the costs and applying a suitable margin. Definitions here can be a problem. What is cost and what is a margin? Have costs been loaded? How much of the cost is the absorption of internal costs and how much is more arm's-length outside costs? What is a normally accepted margin? A company might use actual costs, standard costs, variable costs or marginal costs and the acceptability of these will vary between countries. Key here is to be able to prove that costs are actual arm's length and that margins are normal for the market. However, even with such proof there is no certainty as to how a foreign regime might react and interpret a case. One can be sure, however, that many will want to maximise their own take.

Resale price method (RP)

The RP method is similar to the CP method but is found by working back-wards from a transaction taking place at the next stage up in the supply chain. Subtract a market-based mark-up from the sale price to a third party.

Other methods

Other methods available for determining the arm's-length price include the profit split (PS) method where profits are split between subsidiaries on the basis of some measurable allocation of effort and the transactional net margin method (TNMM) which bases arm's length prices on relative operating profits.

Advance pricing agreement (APA)

An APA is an agreement between the taxpayer and a taxation authority that a future transaction will be based on an agreed price which is based upon an agreed arm's-length price for the period designated. This might, but not necessarily, avoid future unexpected problems. APAs may be unilateral or bilateral/multilateral. A bilateral or multilateral APA obviously provides a better level of confidence.

You will have concluded from this that nothing is certain when planning international taxation and dealing with international taxation authorities.

However, understanding and complying with the OECD guidelines and having a bilateral/multilateral agreement in place will be a good start to bringing some certainty into relations with foreign taxation authorities.

TAX AND DECISION MAKING

Every decision that a company makes will have a taxation implication. For example, taxation will affect:

- cash flow
- the prices of goods and services
- the cost of supplies
- supply-chain decisions
- domicile
- dividend policy
- the evaluation of investment opportunities
- the cost of capital
- project costs.

To bring taxation considerations into financial calculations it is, first of all, necessary to identify how taxation affects the profits and cash flows of financial options. For example, different types of plant and machinery might attract different capital allowances. These can be different in rate and different in timing. Investment may be made in different taxation regimes. In addition to the effect of differing taxation benefits on capital investment there may be the opportunity for certain types of investment to attract investment incentives from certain countries. The financial manager evaluating alternative investment decisions will need to be aware of the taxation options available.

To illustrate how tax benefits affect investment decisions we will use a simple example concerning a choice of investment in standard equipment or 'green' equipment which attracts higher taxation benefits.

Example of taxation implications on financial alternatives

A company has two options available when purchasing new equipment. The options are £15,000 for a standard model or £17,000 for a similar but 'green' model with low carbon-dioxide emissions. Which financial option should it take? The discount factor, that allows for the diminution in the value of money over time, is 6% (see Chapter 4 for an explanation of this). Tax allowances are first year allowance of 40% and a writing-down allowance of

25% p.a. on the diminishing value thereafter for the standard model. In the case of the 'green' model, a 100% first-year allowance is available. Assume corporation tax is 30%.

In this example we will evaluate and compare the net present value (NPV) of taxation benefits available under the two options. This will enable us to see which of the financial alternatives is best although, as we shall see, there are other less obvious financial factors relevant to the decision that we have not recognised in this simple example.

To make a comparison we will first of all value the tax benefits of option one over a ten-year period using the writing-down capital allowances available. Then we will compare this with the 'green' option that attracts a 100% first allowance.

Option one – standard model

Year	Cost	Capital allowance (c/a)	Written-down value	Discount factor (d/f)	Present value of capital allowances
1	15,000	6,000	9,000	.943	5,658
2		2,250	6,750	.890	2,003
3		1,688	5,062	.840	1,418
4		1,265	3,797	.792	1,002
5		949	2,848	.747	709
6		712	2,136	.705	502
7		534	1,602	.666	356
8		401	1,201	.630	253
9		300	901	.596	179
10		225	676	.564	127
					12,207

Present value of capital allowances   12,207

Corporation tax rate   30%

Present value of tax benefit   3,662

Against an initial outlay of £15,000, tax benefits of £3,662 (at present values) give a net after-tax cost of **£11,338**.

Option two – 'green' model

At the end of year one a 100% capital allowance is given. The value of this is:

$$£17,000 \text{ (cost)} \times 100\% \text{ (FYA)} \times .943 \text{ (D/F)} \times 30\% \text{ (CT)} = £4,809$$

Comparison

	Standard	Green
Cost	15,000	17,000
Present value of tax benefit	−3,662	−4,809
Net	11,338	12,191

Therefore, after taxation and allowing for the effect of time on the value of money over a ten-year period it would seem that the standard option has a marginally lower net cost than the green option. However, there are many other considerations. For example:

- In the early years the standard option is not so favourable since the present value of the tax benefits is less than the present value of the tax benefit of the green option. It takes some years for the standard option benefits to exceed those of the 'green' option.

- How would a financial decision to forgo a green alternative reflect on the company's Sustainable Development Report (SDR)? Appealing to the wider interests of stakeholders might attract a lower cost of capital now and increasingly in the future.

Summary

Taxation affects the cost of capital and cash flows of a company and it is, therefore, relevant to financial decisions. In addition to the rate/timing of corporation tax and value added tax the financial manager needs to consider the effects on cash flow of making payments of tax on behalf of others (for example PAYE). Then there are the implications of different taxes on loan interest versus dividends. Tax rules need to be understood and applied to all aspects of financial decision making in the broadest sense.

In this chapter I have outlined some basic taxation principles and how these might be applied to the decision-making process. If this is a topic that interests you then I would recommend *Taxation for Decision Makers* by Shirley A. Dennis-Escoffier and Karen A. Fortin (Prentice Hall, 2006). This work has an emphasis on determining the effect that taxes have on business strategy and planning decisions.

TAX STRATEGY INTERFACE WITH BUSINESS STRATEGY AND FINANCE

Listed below are some of the questions and areas that affect taxation. The implications of business strategy should be considered against their effect on company and personal taxation. Taxation strategy should support business strategy.

Each of the following issues will have an impact on taxation. This needs to be evaluated and considered against the proposed business strategy.

Organisation and incorporation

Incorporate or not?

When to commence trading?

Accounting/taxation periods.

Residence of company?

Residence of shareholders?

Distribution and dividend policy?

Early-year losses, how to utilise?

Prices at which assets are transferred on incorporation?

Disposal of assets.

Whether to acquire or create a subsidiary to carry on another trade?

Advantages or disadvantages to shareholders of grouping companies.

Ownership of shares, individuals and trustees.

Effect of splitting company into a group.

Finance

The Enterprise Investment Scheme.

Equity or debt? Dividend or tax-deductible interest?

Tax deductibility of interest having little use to tax-loss company.

Tax efficiency of derivatives.

Tax implications of converting capitalisation loans into shares.

Payment of interest under deduction of tax.

Whether deep discount bonds will be qualifying corporate bonds exempt from capital gains tax (CGT).

Taxation aspects of foreign-exchange dealing.

Collective investment schemes.

Repos, stock loans, securitisations.

The best source of information for taxation and corporate finance in the UK is the HMRC site page that gives the links into the detailed corporate finance manuals. The web address is: www.hmrc.gov.uk/manuals/cfm manual/index.htm. A summary of the areas covered on the HMRC site is given below.

Introduction to the Corporate Finance Manual

The Corporate Finance Manual is a comprehensive resource for anyone applying corporate finance legislation following FA 2002. For cases where the earlier rules apply, please refer to the Company Taxation Manual at CT12000 onwards.

Guidance

The guidance covers loan relationships, foreign exchange (forex) and derivative contracts. Each subject is considered from three different angles: business understanding, accountancy treatment and taxation. Loan relationships and derivative contracts aspects of collective investment schemes are dealt with separately. Further chapters deal with:

- an introduction to accounting for financial instruments under IAS 39 and IAS 32

- the tax consequences of first-time adoption of IAS 39 or FRS 26

- commercial background to, and taxation of, repos and stock loans

- other provisions relevant to corporate finance.

The legislation covered in the last two bullet points applies for income tax as well as corporation tax purposes, but is more likely to be encountered in the context of companies.

Contents

Loan relationships

CFM3000	Loan relationships home page
CFM3100	Understanding loan relationships
CFM4000	Accounting for loan relationships
CFM5000	Taxing loan relationships

Forex

CFM7000	Forex home page
CFM7005	Understanding forex
CFM8000	Accounting for forex
CFM9000	Taxing forex

Derivative contracts

CFM11000   Derivative contracts home page

CFM11005   Understanding derivative contracts

CFM12000   Accounting for derivative contracts

CFM13000   Taxing derivative contracts

Collective investment schemes

CFM14001   Collective investment schemes

International Accounting Standards (IAS)

CFM16000   Accounting for financial instruments: IAS 32 and IAS 39

CFM16500   Transition to IAS

CFM16600   Hybrid, convertible and share linked securities

Other corporate finance topics

CFM17005   Artificial payments of interest

CFM17030   Funding bonds

Repos, stock loans and manufactured payments

CFM17050   Stock loans

CFM17150   Repos: commercial background

CFM17200   Repos: taxation

CFM17300   Manufactured payments

CFM17360   Manufactured overseas dividends

CFM17500   Repos: FA2007 rules for companies

Securitisations

CFM20000   Securitisations overview

Capital investment

Consider the taxation implications of the capital investment programme.

Distinctions between capital and revenue expenditure.

Replacement versus repair – tax implications.

Lease versus buy decisions.

For details of capital allowances go the HMRC web site and page: www.hmrc.gov.uk/capital_allowances/investmentschemes.htm

Details of the contents showing the principal areas and links are given below:

Capital allowances investment schemes

Since 1997, a number of capital allowances schemes have been introduced to encourage investment in particular assets or by particular sorts of businesses. This site provides a brief description of each scheme and a link to more detailed guidance. It also highlights the established incentive allowances for R&D and enterprise zones. Here is a list of the schemes:

- *40% FYAs for small and medium-sized businesses*
- *100% FYAs for investment by small businesses in ICT (to 31 March 2004)*
- *100% ECAs (FYAs) for energy-saving investments*
- *100% ECAs (FYAs) for water-efficient investments*
- *100% FYAs for low CO_2 emission cars and gas refuelling infrastructure*
- *FYAs for North Sea oil ring-fence plant and machinery and mineral extraction*
- *100% FYAs for SMEs investing in Northern Ireland (to 11 May 2002)*
- *100% Flat Conversion Allowances*
- *100% Research and Development Allowances*
- *100% Enterprise Zone Allowances*

VAT

Registration.

VAT status.

Invoicing and VAT payment dates.

Exempt supplies.

Other issues

Transfer of trade

Understand the taxation implications of a transfer of trade. Legislation prevents transferred trade from being treated as permanently discontinued in the hands of the first company and a new trade starting in the hands of the second company. Instead, ICTA88/S343 treats the second company as succeeding to the trade of the first company.

Close companies

Consider the implications of close company status. In terms of IHTA84/S102 'close company' basically means a company which would be a close company within the meaning of the Corporation Tax Acts. The concept of a close company was introduced by FA65 and ICTA70/S282 as amended by FA72/SCH17 para 1 gives the definition rules. It is subject to specified exceptions:

- a UK company in broad terms controlled by
- either 5 or less participators (individuals or bodies corporate) or
- by participators (however many there are) who are directors. A participator is defined (FA72/S303) as anyone who possesses or is entitled to acquire share capital or voting rights in the company. It can also include a loan creditor.

A company can also be regarded as close if more than half of the income which can be apportioned under a shortfall direction can be apportioned to five or fewer participators.

However, a company is not to be regarded as close if controlled by a company which is not itself a close company, or by two or more companies none of which is a close company, and it cannot be treated as a close company except by taking as one of the five or fewer participators requisite for it being so treated a company which is not a close company.

If a loan is made to a participator of a close company then there might be an additional charge to corporation tax.

Groups and consortia

Consider the taxation implications of group structures particularly with regards to group relief. Group relief is available to companies in a consortium relationship.

From 1 April 2000, a company which:

- is within the charge to corporation tax (CT), and
- has trading losses or other items eligible for relief

can surrender the losses or other amounts as group relief, subject to various conditions. The reference to such a company in the guidance that follows is to 'the surrendering company'.

A company owned by a consortium can surrender the losses or other amounts for set-off against the total profits of a claimant company which is a member of the consortium. Similarly, where the surrendering company is a member of a consortium, it may surrender relief to a claimant company, which is a trading company or holding company owned by the consortium.

Prior to 1 April 2000, both the claimant and the surrendering company had to be resident in the UK. There are transitional agreements.

Overseas activities

Consider permanent establishment definition and rules.

Consider representative offices.

Consider the tax implications of subsidiaries versus branches.

Dual resident companies.

Tax havens and anti avoidance provisions.

Global profits.

Global dividend distribution policy.

COMMITTING TO A TAX STRATEGY

Taxation has a big-item impact on a company's distributable profits. It also carries risks, particularly if a company adopts an aggressive tax strategy. HMRC has an increasingly risk-based approach to tax assessment and corporate executive teams need to give some thought to their approach to tax management and determine appropriate strategies.

A company can do things to minimise global taxation but there are risks associated with this and also costs. This chapter starts from the premise that an executive board will need to know the taxation implications of their business strategies. This text is not concerned with aggressive tax minimisation.

A company might have a high appetite for risk and be willing to try things that may lead to litigation with tax authorities. This can be expensive and the outcome will be uncertain. One should ask, is such an aggressive approach part of a company's core business and can it afford to take the risk? Also, what type of relationship does it want with the tax authorities? Boards are often split in their views regarding the minimisation of taxation. Some executives want to pay as little as possible whilst others see their company as a responsible citizen and value their relationship with the government and taxation authorities. They have choices and the CFO has to advise and find ground upon which all are reasonably satisfied. Tax strategy and decisions carry risk and need, therefore, to be made in the context of shareholder value. There are also ethical and moral issues involved. What is morally due and what is legally due? What is the letter of the law and the meaning of the law? We cover ethical issues broadly in Chapter 23. A company that adopts an aggressive tax policy will be viewed by the public in a particular way. Avoidance is that, avoidance of laws. Does this reconcile with good corporate citizenship? There may be a cost associated with adopting aggressive tax policies.

Once a board has agreed on a taxation strategy it should be documented, communicated and adopted. It should be reviewed each year in light of changes in business strategy and taxation changes.

4

Inflation and the changing value of money over time

OVERVIEW

In this chapter we will define the principal terms used in describing changes in the value of money and then how to apply this to financial decisions.

INFLATION, DISINFLATION, DEFLATION, STAGLATION, HYPERINFLATION

We know that a pound today will probably not have the same purchasing power now as it will have at some time in the future. It will probably be worth less in the future, although there is a chance (I've never seen it) that it might be worth more. This is because of inflation or deflation.

Inflation

This is when the purchasing power of a unit of money is less in the future than it is today. It is basically a rise in the general level of prices expressed as a percentage change in the price index over time. There are many causes of inflation. For example, in the short term prices may increase due to increased demand or reduced supply and in the longer term higher rates of inflation or even hyperinflation may be caused when the money supply increases faster than the growth in productivity of an economy. One measure of inflation in an economy is the price change of a basket of goods and services. In the UK official statistics are available for the Retail Prices Index (RPI) and the Consumer Prices Index (CPI).

Of course, in a free market businesses cannot just raise prices when they want because their competitors will simply win business by offering lower prices. However, if each pound is becoming worth less due to an increase in the supply of money then all businesses will want to increase prices in order to get the same value for their offerings.

Disinflation

Disinflation refers to a reducing rate of inflation. This means that prices are still increasing but at a lower rate. For example, if the rate of inflation in 2009 is 5% but the rate in 2010 is only 4% then we have experienced disinflation.

Deflation

Deflation is an actual decrease in the overall price of goods or services. Whilst I have obviously seen prices of individual goods or services decrease I have never yet experienced an overall deflationary decrease. Probably the last time this happened in the UK was shortly after the 1914–18 war when Britain returned to the gold standard. It can occur by taking purchasing power out of an economy by means of increasing taxation and cutting government spending.

Stagflation

Stagflation refers to a period of inflation during a time of stagnation in the economy.

Hyperinflation

Hyperinflation is inflation where the rate is very high and accelerating out of control. Causes of hyperinflation are the subject of much debate among economists but it becomes visible when a massive and rapid increase in money supply is not supported by appropriate growth in output. The result is an imbalance in supply and demand for money and loss of confidence, possibly leading to the complete breakdown of a monetary system.

OFFICIAL SOURCES OF INFLATION STATISTICS

Most governments produce statistics on inflation. The UK Government produces public information through National Statistics Online showing measures of inflation. These are available through www.statistics.gov.uk and examples for the Retail Prices Index and the Consumer Prices Index are given below:

'Inflation

Sept: CPI up to 5.2%, RPI up to 5.0% (see graph opposite)

Consumer Prices Index (CPI) annual inflation – the Government's target measure – was 5.2 per cent in September, up from 4.7 per cent in August.

Retail Prices Index (RPI) inflation rose to 5.0 per cent in September, up from 4.8 per cent in August.

Notes

CPI is the Consumer Prices Index. It is the measure adopted by the Government for its UK inflation target. The Bank of England's Monetary Policy Committee is required to achieve a target of 2 per cent. Prior to 10 December 2003, the CPI was published in the UK as the harmonised index of consumer prices (HICP).

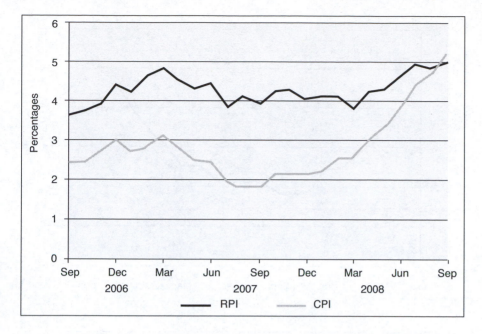

RPI is the Retail Prices Index – the uses of the RPI and its derivatives include indexation of pensions, state benefits and index-linked gilts.

Inflation is the percentage change in the index compared with the same month one year previously.'

(The above information on inflation is an extract from the official government web site www.statistics.gov.uk and is reproduced with permission.)

In the last quarter of 2008 and early in 2009 both the RPI and the CPI took a substantial dive when retailers made price reductions to keep sales alive as the recession took hold and discretionary consumer demand slackened. Added to this was a reduction in the rate of VAT. The graph overleaf is reproduced with permission of the UK National Statistics Office.

The effect of inflation on business decisions

To increase real shareholder value a business needs to ensure that it produces a return on investment that is greater than the rate of inflation. Therefore, inflation has to be allowed for in the appraisal of investment opportunities. Also, the higher the rate of inflation, the more capital will be required to fund real assets. Inflation also means higher costs and selling prices. These factors need to be built into financial models together with accompanying sensitivity analysis. Inflation usually varies between countries so, for example, a company exporting from a location with high inflation may find that it cannot pass on its local inflation without a dampening in demand for its products. Inflation affects the cost of capital and financial gearing. The

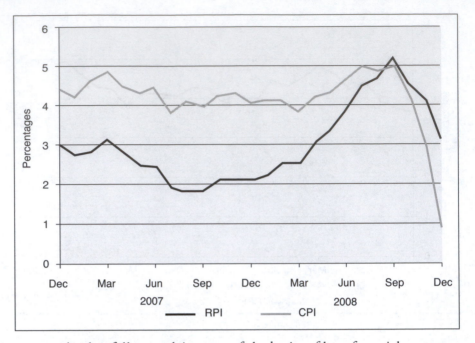

paragraphs that follow explain some of the basics of how financial managers allow for the effects of inflation in their forecast.

THE TIME VALUE OF MONEY AND DISCOUNTED CASH FLOW

The concepts of interest and cost of capital and the price change issues described above all depend upon the idea that money has a time value. Normally the longer we have to wait for our money, the less valuable it is. To work out the future value of money we apply a discount factor. For example, calculate the discounted value of £6,000 in 3 years' time when the rate of inflation is 5% p.a.

$$\text{Discounted value} = P \times \frac{1}{(1 + i)^n}$$

where: P = the principal sum

i = the rate of inflation or interest

n = the number of years

$$\text{Discounted value} = £6.000 \times \frac{1}{(1 + .05)^3}$$

$$= £6,000 \times \frac{1}{1.1576}$$

$$= £6,000 \times 0.864$$

$$= £5,183$$

Accordingly, when inflation is running at 5% p.a. £6,000 received in 3 years' time will buy only what £5,183 would purchase today.

The real rate of return and the nominal rate (money rate)

This is the rate of return after allowing for the effect of inflation. For example, if a company experiences a rise in sales from £100,000 to £110,000 when its prices have gone up by 10% then the real value of its sales has not gone up at all.

Example:

If inflation is 5% p.a. and investors expect a return of 8% p.a., what real rate of return does this equate to?

$$\frac{1.08}{1.05} = 1.029$$

Therefore, the real rate of return is **2.9%** p.a.

Which rate should be used in discounting, the nominal rate or the real rate? If the cash flows represent the actual amounts to be received or paid on future dates then you should use the nominal or money rate for discounting. If the cash flows are given in terms of amounts at time 0 you should use the real rate.

Investment decision and net present value (NPV)

The net present value of a project is the total of the present value of all of the cash flows. The cash flows for each year are first of all discounted using a discount factor (the required rate of return) to give a present value. Then the present values are totalled to give a net present value. If this is positive then the proposed project will give a return which exceeds the required return. If the NPV is negative then the required return will not be met on the assumptions taken. This is best explained by an example.

Example:

A company is considering investing £6,000 in a project which will yield the following nominal income: year 1 £2,000, year 2 £1,900, year 3 £1,800 and year 4 £1,700. It requires a nominal rate of return of 10%. Should it undertake the project?

Year	Cash flow £	Discount factor @ 10% (refer to tables in appendix 1)	Present value £
0	−6,000	1.000	−6,000
1	2,000	0.909	1,818
2	1,900	0.826	1,569
3	1,800	0.751	1,352
4	1,700	0.683	1,161
Totals	1,400		**−100**

The project's NPV (the total of the present values) is marginally negative and on this basis would fail to meet the company's required return.

Internal rate of return (IRR)

The internal rate of return is the interest rate which will produce a net present value equal to zero. If the internal rate of return exceeds the cost of capital then perhaps the investment or project should proceed. I have used the word perhaps because there are, of course, other considerations such as risk and uncertainty. One way of calculating the IRR is to use interpolation as demonstrated below. First of all, find the two discount rates that produce a positive and negative NPV. Do this by judgement and trial and error.

Example of IRR calculation:

Year	Cash flow	9% factor	Present value	10% factor	Present value
0	−27,500	1	−27,500	1	−27,500
1	10,000	.917	9,170	.909	9,090
2	10,000	.842	8,420	.826	8,260
3	7,000	.772	5,404	.751	5,257
4	7,000	.708	4,956	.683	4,781
Totals	6,500		**450**		**−112**

Using a discount factor of 9% produces a net present value of 450 whereas using a discount factor of 10% produces a net present value of −112. Therefore, the discount rate that produces a zero net present value must lie between 9% and 10%.

Now, you will have noticed that an increase in discount rate of 1% (10%−9%) has produced a movement in present value of 562 (450 to −112 = 562).

9% = 450
10% = −112
1% = 562

Therefore, the discount rate that will produce a net present value of zero is:

$$9\% + \frac{450}{562} = 9.8\%$$

If, in our example above, the cost of capital on the investment had been 8.5% then because the IRR exceeded this (9.8%) the investment could, so far as this measure is concerned, go ahead.

Proof of IRR

Year	Cash flow	9.8% factor using $\dfrac{1}{(1 + i)^n}$	Present value
0	−27,500	1	−27,500
1	10,000	.911	9,110
2	10,000	.829	8,290
3	7,000	.755	5,285
4	7,000	.688	4,815
Totals	6,500		0

Using the 9.8% discount factor produces a net present value of 0.

In the example I have given for determining the IRR I have used trial and error followed by interpolation. This is an easy method. However, you can also calculate it by using the following formulae derived from the above method:

$$IRR = x + \frac{LNPV}{LNPV - HNPV} \ (y - x)\%$$

Where x = lower of the two rates of return used

$\qquad y$ = higher of the two rates of return used

$\qquad LNPV$ = NPV using rate x

$\qquad HNPV$ = NPV using rate y

Then in the above example:

x = 9%

y = 10%

$LNPV$ = 450

$HNPV$ = −112

Substituting values in the formulae we have:

$$IRR = 9\% + \frac{450}{(450 - (-112))} \times 10\% - 9\%)$$
$$IRR = 9\% + (0.8\% \times 1\%)$$

$$IRR = 9.8\%$$

The IRR is a short way of expressing whether a project is viable. For example, if a company has a cost of capital of 8% and a proposed investment has an IRR of 9.8% then it will know that the investment will increase shareholder value. Projects may be ranked in terms of IRR and we shall discuss this and other methods of investment appraisal later.

INTEREST CALCULATIONS

Some of the more useful interest rate calculations and their formulae are given below:

Interest calculations and formulae

P = principal

i = rate of interest

n = number of years

m = number of months

M = number of payments p.a.

Basic compounding $P(1 + i)^n$

£10 @ 10% p.a. for 2 years

£10 $(1 + 0.1)^2$

= £12.10

Frequent compounding $P\left(1 + \dfrac{i}{M}\right)^{mn}$

£8 for 3 months @ 20% p.a. credited monthly.

£8 $\left(1 + \dfrac{0.2}{12}\right)^{3 \times 1}$ = £8 × 1.0508

= £8.41

Proof of frequent compounding formulae:

	i	$P + i$
£8 × $\dfrac{0.20}{12}$	0.1330	8.13
£8.13 × $\dfrac{0.20}{12}$	0.1356	8.27
£8.27 × $\dfrac{0.20}{12}$	0.1378	8.41

Effective rate

$$\left(1 + \frac{i}{M}\right)^m - 1$$

1½% per month on balance outstanding.

What is the effective rate?

$$\left(1 + \frac{0.015}{1}\right)^{12} - 1$$

= 19.56% p.a.

(alternative formulae $(1 + i)^m - 1$)

Annuity $P\left(\dfrac{(1 + i)^n - 1}{i}\right)$

£50 p.a. for 3 years @ 10% p.a.

$£50\left(\dfrac{(1.1)^3 - 1}{0.1}\right) = £165.50$

Sinking fund

$$\dfrac{P}{\left(\dfrac{(1 + i)^n - 1}{i}\right)}$$

How much is required to be invested each year to produce £165.50 in 3 years' time when interest is 10% p.a.?

$$\dfrac{165.50}{\left(\dfrac{(1.1)^3 - 1}{i}\right)}$$

$$= £50 \text{ (proof above – see annuity)}$$

Basic present value

$$P\left(\dfrac{1}{(1 + i)^n}\right)$$

What is the present value of £165.50 to be received in 3 years' time when interest is 10% p.a.?

$$£165.50\left(\dfrac{1}{(1.1)^3}\right) = £124.34$$

Present value of annuity

$$P\left(\dfrac{1 - \dfrac{1}{(1 + i)^n}}{i}\right)$$

What is the present value of £50 received each year for 3 years when interest is 10% p.a.?

$$50\left(\dfrac{1 - \dfrac{1}{(1.1)^3}}{i}\right) = £124.34$$

Annual equivalent – repayment

$$\dfrac{P}{\left(\dfrac{1 - \dfrac{1}{(1 + i)^n}}{i}\right)}$$

What annuity is equal to a present value of £6,000 payable over 8 years with interest running at 7% p.a.?

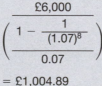

$$\dfrac{£6,000}{\left(\dfrac{1 - \dfrac{1}{(1.07)^8}}{0.07}\right)}$$

$$= £1,004.89$$

Proof: The present value of an annuity of £1004.89 for 8 years @ 7% is:

$$\pounds1004.89 \left(\frac{1 - \frac{1}{(1.07)^8}}{0.07} \right) = \pounds6,000.$$

Perpetuity – present value

A perpetuity is an annuity that goes on for ever. The present value of a perpetuity is found by simply dividing the annual amount by the interest rate. For example, the present value of £100 p.a. in perpetuity when interest rates are 10% p.a. is

$$\frac{\pounds100}{0.1} = \pounds1,000.$$

SUMMARY

In the long term inflation may be considered as essentially a monetary phenomenon. However, in the short term inflation may be affected by everyday supply and demand pressures, commodity prices, the elasticity of wages, product/material prices, interest rates and other factors. Whether the short-term effects mentioned last long enough to affect long-term inflation is the question at the core of the debate between monetarist and Keynesian theories.

For practical purposes we can assume that in an efficient business market inflation occurs when businesses increase prices to counteract the effect of money becoming worth less due to an increase in the supply of money. It happens when all businesses want to increase prices in order to get the same value for their offerings.

Inflation affects every business decision and the discounted cash flow, net present value and internal rate of return techniques help finance managers make better decisions by showing real returns. We will discuss this again in more detail alongside other methods of investment appraisal.

5

Budgeting

BUDGETARY CONTROL AND THE BUDGET PROCESS

A budget is a financial evaluation of the future courses of action set out in a business plan. It is prepared in advance (normally for the year ahead) and reflects the financial consequences of the agreed strategies that are necessary to achieve corporate objectives.

In most companies budgetary control takes the steps shown in Figure 5.1.

The budgeting process fits into the overall planning process, it evaluates the financial consequences of the plan and provides financial feedback so that plans can be monitored and revised.

The budgetary control steps   Figure 5.1

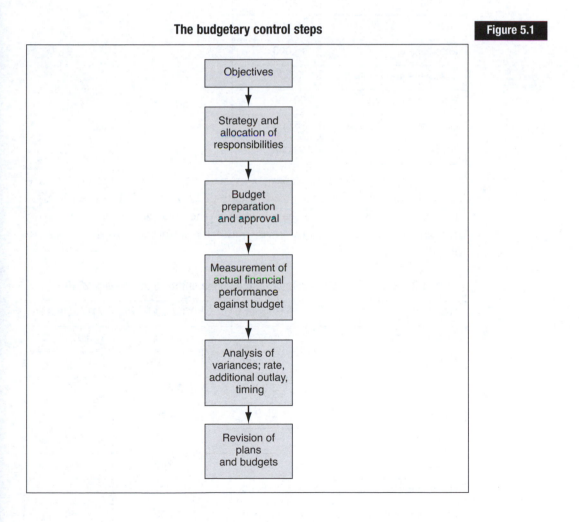

BUDGETS AND VARIANCE ANALYSIS

The simplest form of budget is the departmental resource budget. Here, a departmental manager will assess what he is expected to achieve in the year ahead and determine what resources he needs. These will be listed in terms of resource costs. For example:

HR department budget for 2010

Resource	Budget £
Salaries	250,000
National insurance	15,000
Training	30,000
Travel	25,000
Entertainment	15,000
Stationery and printing	3,000
Recruitment costs	200,000
Share of premises costs	15,000
Total	553,000

Each month the accounts department will produce a statement for the budget holder showing actual year to date (YTD) expenditure against YTD budgeted expenses. If we assume that the budget is spread evenly throughout the year (usually it is not), the statement might appear as follows:

HR department actual versus budgeted expenditure in January 2010

Resource	Budget £	YTD budget £	YTD actual £
Salaries	250,000	20,833	20,000
National insurance	15,000	1,250	1,000
Training	30,000	2,500	0
Travel	25,000	2,083	1,000
Entertainment	15,000	1,250	1,250
Stationery & printing	3,000	250	300
Recruitment costs	200,000	16,667	0
Share of premises costs	15,000	1,250	1,250
Total	553,000	46,083	24,800

Our next step is to analyse the variance. For this purpose we can classify variances into three major categories:

- *Rate*: this is a variance that results from an increase in the rate. For example, if salaries were favourable because the actual pay increase awarded was only 2% compared with a budgeted increase of 3% then the resulting variance would be classified as a rate variance.

- *Additional outlay*: this is where additional or fewer resources have been expended than were budgeted for. For example, if the budget for stationery included five ink cartridges at £50 each but six were purchased at £50 each then the additional outlay variance would be £50.

- *Timing*: a timing variance recognises that the difference between actual and budget is only temporarily due to a difference in the timing of the budget and the actual expenditure. For example, if recruitment costs reflected recruiting a new staff member in January but this had been delayed until March then the resulting favourable variance is only due to timing and will be lost in a few months' time. This type of variance must not be confused with a variance resulting from a failure to accrue expenses incurred and not yet invoiced. For the purpose of our variance analysis we will assume that all accruals have been made.

Applying the rate, additional outlay and timing concepts our variance analysis could look as follows:

HR department variance analysis

Resource	YTD budget £	YTD actual £	Total variance £	Rate	Additional outlay	Timing
Salaries	20,833	20,000	833	833		
National insurance	1,250	1,000	250	250		
Training	2,500	0	2,500			2,500
Travel	2,083	1,000	1,083			1,083
Entertainment	1,250	1,250	0			0
Stationery & printing	250	300	−50		−50	
Recruitment costs	16,667	0	16,667			16,667
Share of premises costs	1,250	1,250	0			
Total	46,083	24,800	21,283	1,083	−50	20,250

Summary for January:

Budget	46,083
Actual	<u>24,800</u>
Variance	21,283 (favourable)

Reasons for variance:

Rate	1,083 (favourable due to reduced pay increases)
Additional outlay	−50 (adverse due to additional print cartridge)
Timing	<u>20,250</u> (favourable – slipped training, travel and recruitment)
Total	21,283 (favourable)

What effect will this variance analysis have on our annual plan and budget estimates?

Original annual budget	553,000	
Rate variance x 12	12,996	(favourable @ 1,083 p.m.)
Additional outlay	−50	(adverse one-off)
Revised annual estimate	**540,054**	

Note: The timing variance is ignored for the purpose of a revised annual estimate because it will be lost before the year end once expenditure is incurred.

BUDGET METHODS AND TYPES OF BUDGETING AND RELATIONSHIP WITH PLANNING

Many types of budgeting have been developed for different organisations. Needs vary greatly, for example the type of budgeting used in the military is likely to be different from that used in a bank. We will discuss the following types of budget and process:

- the fully integrated budgeting process and limiting factors
- simple resource budgets
- zero-based budgets (ZBB)
- flexible budgets
- planning, programming, budgeting systems (PPBS).

An integrated budget

The flow chart in Figure 5.2 shows a typical integrated planning and budgeting process.

A typical integrated planning and budgeting process

Figure 5.2

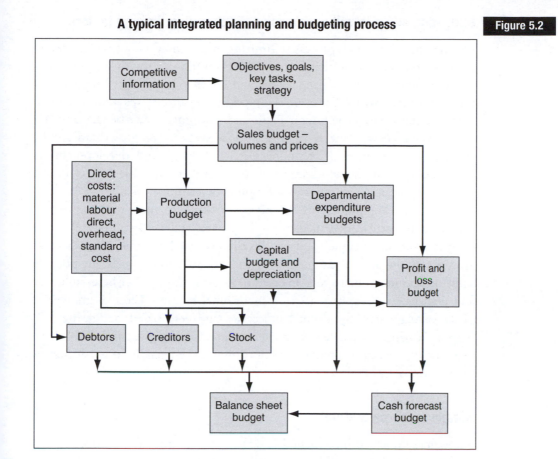

Figure 5.2 shows how from high-level objectives, goals and key tasks a strategy is developed within the competitive environment. From this a sales budget can be prepared in terms of volumes and prices again taking account of competitive and external information. Generally, the sales budget will drive the production budget in terms of volumes where supplier information regarding the price of materials is gathered together with direct labour and overhead costs. The production budget will drive the capital budget in respect of plant and equipment which in turn will produce the budget for depreciation. The production budget together with the sales budget will drive departmental budgets which feed into the profit and loss budget. The production budget also determines creditors and stocks and the sales budget feeds into the debtors' budget. Debtors, creditors, stocks, capital expenditure and the profit and loss budget all feed into the master cash forecast and the balance sheet.

Budgeting as an iterative process with changing limiting factors

During the budgeting process a limiting factor may be identified. Most organisations have a limiting factor which inhibits growth and development. Eliminate one limiting factor and another factor will be identified that will limit growth. For example, production capacity may not be able to meet the sales budget volumes. Plant and equipment may be the limiting factor. When new plant is acquired the next limit to growth might be medium-term finance. This might restrict research and development. A budget process might be iterative whereby different variable factors are fed into the model until an optimal solution is determined.

In a budgeting process we are always looking to maximise the overall shareholders' return identified in the corporate goals and strategy. We will wish to avoid suboptimal solutions. In this regard departmental goals must always support and be aligned with top organisational goals. In practice some departmental managers, in order to increase their power base, influence and perhaps bonuses, may act in a suboptimal manner. Close alignment of goals, management by aligned objectives and zero-based budgeting will help avoid this. Other concepts such as internal charging and PPBS have been used to ensure alignment and optimisation, especially in not-for-profit organisations.

Simple resource budgets

Sometimes known as incremental budgeting this is simply an estimate of the resources and their costs that are needed to complete the tasks required for the coming year. One danger of this type of budgeting is that departmental managers might simply look at the previous year's spend and use this as a base for the coming budget plus an increase to cover the effect of inflation, hence the term incremental budgeting. This could lead to perpetuating tasks that were not required or aligned with the overall corporate goals. To avoid this happening some form of alignment and zero-based budgeting needs to be introduced into the process. However, one advantage of looking at the previous year's spend is to ensure that certain unavoidable costs are not omitted. In reality, few managers would prepare their budgets without looking at the previous year's items.

Zero-based budgeting

In contrast to the simple resource/incremental budget that starts with last year's spend the zero-based budget starts from scratch/zero and each item in the budget is built up and justified in terms of supporting aligned key tasks and goals. In reality a balance is often struck between the ZBB and the incremental approach, taking advantage of the benefits of both methods. Under ZBB each cost has to be justified and it may be run alongside a management by objectives approach (MBO).

Advantages of zero-based budgeting

1. ZBB helps to ensure that departmental goals are aligned with organisational goals.
2. It can provide an efficient allocation of resources since the focus is on what is actually needed to complete aligned key tasks.
3. It forces budget holders to find cost efficiencies and to streamline operations.
4. It avoids budgeting for what was spent in previous years regardless of real need.
5. It can help some departments identify their value and real customers.
6. It helps develop a greater sense of responsibility and perhaps motivation.
7. It will certainly improve departmental coordination within an organisation and help avoid departments working in isolation.
8. It identifies obsolete and inefficient practices.
9. It might help identify opportunities for shared services and outsourcing.

Disadvantages of zero-based budgeting

1. ZBB can be tough and time consuming to introduce and keep running. It is often just a 'one-off', producing some benefits initially until there is slippage back into incremental budgets. Some budget holders might even work back from an incremental budget and fudge ZBB results. It can also be difficult to define what control a budget holder really has over certain costs and decisions.
2. Research, especially pure research, may be difficult to justify and short-term decisions might be made.
3. The training of budget holders in ZBB can be a significant investment in its own right.
4. The ZBB process when fully integrated with the planning process can become complex.

Flexible budgets

Flexible budgets show how budgeted costs vary with different levels of sales and output. In the simple example below we can see how the total budgeted costs will vary with different levels of output. This requires the identification between variable costs (those that vary with different levels of output) and fixed costs (those that do not vary and remain the same within the output ranges).

Item	Variable unit cost	1,000 units	2,000 units
Direct material	£5	£5,000	£10,000
Direct labour	£2	£2,000	£4,000
Total variable costs		£7,000	£14,000
Fixed costs (rent)		£3,000	£3,000
Total costs		£10,000	£17,000

Some costs are considered as semi fixed in that they remain fixed up to a certain point within the budgeted output range and then increase (step up).

With a flexible budgeting system a series of budgets is prepared for differing output levels.

PPBS – programmes rather than departments

PPBS is a planning-based method to develop a programme budget. Programme budgets are budgets whereby expenditures are based on programmes of work. The fundamental strength of PPBS is in the planning process and the making of programme decisions from which budgets are produced. It is a method that is used in some non-profit organisations and has its routes in the US where it was designed to establish control over defence spending. It provides a way of allocating resources to top priorities.

A programme budget is one where an organisation's activities are grouped into programmes supporting a single objective. The budgets are set out for programmes rather than for departments.

TYPES OF BUDGETS

The principal types of budget prepared by an organisation will depend upon the business activities undertaken. For example, a manufacturing company will have a different set of budgets to a marketing agency. Some organizations will have departmental budgets whilst others may have programme budgets. The budgets of for-profit organizations will look entirely different to those of the not-for-profit sector. Set out below are examples of the types of budget that you might expect to see in a manufacturing company:

- sales budget
- production budget
- labour budget
- materials budget

- overhead and departmental budgets
- capital expenditure budget
- cash budget
- profit and loss budget
- balance sheet budget.

Sales budget

The sales budget is central and core to most other budgets since it will determine the level of activities needed to support sales. It will consider the whole market and competitive environment, including the following factors:

- required organisational growth
- demand
- competition
- market trends
- constraints and limiting factors
- distribution
- marketing strategies: offensive/defensive/leader
- resources
- advertising
- pricing.

A simplified example of a sales budget for a company assembling and selling outboard motors is given below:

Sales budget

Product/ service	Sales forecast in units	Expected unit price £	Sales forecast £
4hp motor	1000	500	500,000
6hp motor	500	700	350,000
8hp motor	300	800	240,000
15hp motor	200	1200	240,000
Total			**1,330,000**

Once the sales budget has been agreed the next stage is for the production department to take the budgeted sales volumes and prepare a production budget. This will consider the sales forecast adjusted for any opening and closing stocks required and will calculate the production hours required.

The production budget will feed the direct labour and direct materials budget and will also identify any additional plant capacity required which will in turn feed into the capital expenditure budget.

Taking the figures from the sales budget the production budget is given below:

Production and plant utilisation budget

Product	Production budget = sales less opening stock plus closing stock	Assembly hours 4hp = 2h 6hp = 2h 8hp = 2h 15hp = 3h	Painting hours 0.5h per motor	Testing hours 0.1h per motor
4hp motor	1000	2,000	500	100
6hp motor	500	1,000	250	50
8hp motor	300	600	150	30
15hp motor	200	600	100	20
Total hours		4,200	1,000	200
Plant capacity		5,000	900	400
Spare (shortage)		800	(100)	200

Note that the production budget has identified the following:

Assembly time	4,200 hours
Painting time	1,000 hours
Testing time	200 hours
Capacity shortage	100 hours of painting capacity

The production budget has identified a limiting factor. The paint shop does not have enough capacity to cope with the required level of production to meet the sales budget. This might mean that additional plant is required and this will feed into the capital expenditure budget and also the cash forecast.

Direct labour budget

The direct labour budget calculates the cost of labour and the number of employees required by taking the hours identified in the production budget and applying standard or estimated labour rates.

Direct labour budget

Process	Total hours	Man hours 2 persons on assembly 1 person painting 1 person testing	Labour rate per hour £	Labour cost £	Employee numbers assuming 1,700 hrs p.a. per employee
Assembly	4,200	8,400	9.50	79,800	4.9
Paint	1,000	1,000	7.50	7,500	0.6
Test	200	200	7.50	1,500	0.1
Total	5,400	9,600		**88,800**	5.6

From the direct labour budget we have determined:

the budgeted labour cost for the year will be £88,000

labour rates have been set. These may become the standard labour rates used in a standard costing system. Standard costing is a technique described in Chapter 7.

It seems likely that to make up worthwhile hours for the testing process an option would be to utilise any slack on the assembly process if this can be done without disrupting assembly. The paint shop may require part-time/flexible working.

The direct materials budget

This is the budget that determines what materials and components are required in the production process. This will determine the material costs.

Direct materials budget

Component	Qty for 4hp	Qty for 6hp	Qty for 8hp	Qty for 15hp	Total component usage	Unit cost £	Total material cost £
Carburettor	1,000	500	300	400	2,200	20	44,000
Fuel tank	1,000	500	300	200	2,000	15	30,000
Propeller	1,000	500	300	200	2,000	30	60,000
Fuel pipes	1,000	500	300	400	2,200	10	22,000
Pistons	1,000	500	300	400	2,200	35	77,000
Block	1,000	500	300	200	2,000	40	80,000
Head	1,000	500	300	200	2,000	30	60,000
Other parts	3,000	1,500	900	1,000	6,400	5	32,000
Total							**405,000**

The direct materials budget tells us that the cost of materials in producing products to meet the sales/production budget is £405,000.

At this point, remembering that budgeting is an iterative process, it is worthwhile taking a look at what our estimated gross margin will be:

Sales budget	£1,330,000
Direct materials	−£405,000
Direct labour	−£88,000
Gross margin	£837,000 (63%)

In this case we have shown the gross margin before any direct overheads. In other words, the contribution towards the total pool of overheads and profits (sales less direct variable costs) is £837,000 and this is 63% of sales. Most industries will know whether this is an acceptable and workable margin and it is normal to review this margin before proceeding with the rest of the budget process. Direct overheads, that is those that relate directly to production, may also be allocated to the total direct costs before the gross margin is calculated.

Overhead budgets

So far we have considered only direct labour and material costs. These costs are generally variable in that they fluctuate with the level of production. We will now look at overheads and other departmental costs. Some of these costs may also be variable but most overheads are fixed or semi fixed during the budget period and will not fluctuate with levels of production or sales. Examples of overhead and departmental budgets are:

- selling and marketing
- warehousing and distribution
- research and development
- administrative and support departments
- production overheads.

These budgets typically appear in the following format showing the proposed budget against the previous year's actual budget. Remember, though, that the proposed budget should be calculated on a zero base and not just as an extension of the previous year's spend.

Sales and marketing expenditure budget

Expenditure	Previous year's budget £	Previous year's actual £	Proposed budget £
Sales force salaries			
Sales force commission			
Vehicle expenses (petrol, repairs, depreciation, lease costs, insurance, road tax, etc.)			
Travel			
Entertainment			
Accommodation			
Sales office expenses, etc.			
Sales support salaries			
Sales support bonuses			
Telephone			
Stationery, postage, printing & other office support costs			
Marketing salaries			
Marketing bonuses			
Brochures			
Exhibitions			
Advertising and communications: • New media and web • Press • Radio • TV • Direct mail • Agency fees • PR			
Marketing office and expenses			
Totals			

Note that some of the sales and marketing costs are variable and some are more of a semi-fixed nature. Clearly the sales and marketing resource costs will vary with the volume of sales required. However, the cost of salaried people may be more of a fixed nature within the budget period given notice periods required and redundancy payments. Some office costs are certainly fixed (rent, business rates, etc.). These have not been shown in the sales and marketing budget but are included in the central administrative and support department's budget. This is because, in this case, control over these items is central. Generally, there is little point in allocating costs to a budget holder that are not controllable by the budget holder. However, there is some argument in allocating centrally controlled costs to the departments that enjoy the benefits so as to see the overall true departmental costs. At this time, we have not allocated such costs and they remain in the central control budget.

In arriving at a sales budget it is necessary to calculate how much selling activity is required to meet the sales budget. For example, to make a sale it might be necessary to meet a prospective customer and this will require time and travel costs. To arrange one meeting might require (for example) ten phone calls and to make a phone call will require research time probably by the marketing department. It might also be necessary to meet with many prospective customers before a single sale is completed. Then there is the activity required to retain and extend existing customers' business. Knowing these activities will enable the sales and marketing director/s to prepare a sales and marketing expenditure budget.

Warehouse and distribution costs

Expenditure	Previous year's budget £	Previous year's actual £	Proposed budget £
Warehouse salaries			
Warehouse wages			
Warehouse materials – cases, tape, paper, etc.			
Warehouse equipment costs			
Warehouse premises costs			
Logistics staff salaries			
Driver wages			
Vehicle costs			
Totals			

Note in this simplified example of warehousing and distribution costs that some items are variable and some not so variable (semi fixed or fixed). For example, warehouse material usage will vary with levels of production and sales since finished goods will be packed and stored in the warehouse and sold goods may require additional packaging. Within vehicle costs some items are very variable, such as fuel, which will vary with the number of miles covered during distribution.

Research and development budget

	Project 1 £	Project 2 £	Project 3 £	Project 4 £	Project 5 (Pure) £	Project 6 (Pure) £
Salaries						
Wages						
Materials						
Laboratory costs						
Totals						

The research and development budget, in addition to having columns for previous year's budget and actual as shown in the other department budgets, will have columns for each project being undertaken. I have kept it simple here by showing the resources and projects only. Note that projects 5 and 6 have been classified as pure research, that is, research where there is no specific current application. Projects 1 to 4 are applied research where the work relates to a specific product offering.

Research and development costs may have a different treatment for taxation than other costs which are directly incurred in earning income. For example, in the UK research and development tax credits are a company tax relief which can either reduce a company's tax bill or, for some small or medium-sized companies, even provide a cash sum.

The purpose of these tax credits is to encourage more research and development spending that will encourage investment in innovation. The majority of claims are from small and medium-sized enterprises.

The research and development tax credit scheme in the UK allows companies to deduct up to 150% of qualifying expenditure on research and development (R&D) activities when calculating their taxable profit. Small and medium-sized companies may, in certain circumstances, surrender this R&D tax relief to claim payable tax credits in cash from HMRC.

Tax rules are forever changing and, of course, vary from one country to another. The important point to note is that for taxation purposes R&D costs are often treated differently from costs chargeable directly against income and this will have a roll-on effect for the cash forecast and other budgets. In addition, the accounting treatment of R&D costs varies from country to country, particularly in the definition of what can be classified as R&D expenditure.

Administrative and support department expenditure budget

Expenses	Previous year's budget £	Previous year's actual £	Proposed budget £
Salaries and remuneration			
Contractors			
Premises costs: • Rent • Rates • Light • Heat • Insurance • Repairs and maintenance			
Telephone			
Postage			
IT			
Office equipment			
Depreciation			
Office supplies			
Professional services			
Travel Entertainment			
Other expenses			
Total			
Charged out to other departments	( )	( )	( )
Net total budget			

There will be a budget for each administrative department (HR, Accounts/Finance, Buying, etc.). If a system of internal charging is introduced then an amount of the administrative department's budget will be charged out to those departments that have agreed to use the services. For example, if the Finance department has asked the HR department to recruit new finance staff then the costs of that recruitment will be charged out to the Finance department. This will reduce the HR net budget and the Finance department must remember to pick up the cost in the finance budget. Of course, the Finance department might decide to recruit its own staff, in which case HR will not need to budget or incur recruitment costs for finance people. Normally, for internal charging to work, the 'customer department' must have choice of where it shops. This can cause problems if it is not possible for the service department to shed costs. A clear distinction needs to be made between fixed and variable costs and also between those that are controllable and those that, realistically, are not.

The budget formats shown above are typical of those found in the major areas of business activity. Each department will be a cost centre and each item of expenditure will be classified by an expense code. The examples given above are highly simplified. Typically an organisation will have many more cost centres and line-of-expense codes.

The capital expenditure budget

Capital expenditure normally refers to items of a permanent nature that will not be consumed or used up entirely during the budget period. Examples of capital expenditure are:

- buildings
- plant and equipment
- vehicles
- large computer installations
- furniture and fittings
- improvements.

Expenditure on items that are not permanent but are consumed during the budget period are not capital expenditure but are classified as revenue expenditure. Examples are salaries, travel, entertainment, materials use, repairs, consumable supplies, printing ink, recruitment, etc. An improvement or extension that increases the value of an existing asset is capital expenditure whereas a repair is revenue expenditure.

It is important to understand the difference since it will affect the accounting treatment, taxation and cash flow.

Capital expenditure is not written off in the budget period but is carried in the balance sheet as an asset for its expected useful life. The amount of the asset that is used is charged in the accounts as a depreciation charge. So, for example, if an asset costing £10,000 has a life of 10 years with a nil residual value then the annual depreciation charge against profits would be £1,000. Depreciation may also be charged on a diminishing value basis. In most taxation regimes depreciation is allowed for by way of a capital allowance, which may be a different amount to the depreciation charged in the accounts.

There are a number of stages in capital budgeting. Budget holders will submit their capital projects and estimates for approval by the budget committee and the board, with an investment proposal which will include the rational and expected return on investment.

The procedure for capital investment decisions is somewhat different to those of revenue expenditure budgets in that the organisation is being asked to consider a long-term investment decision. Paul King of Queen's College Cambridge wrote several papers which explained the decision process ('Capital Investment Decisions', 1967 and 'Is the Emphasis on Capital Budgeting Theory Misplaced?', 1974). He identified the following six stages:

- triggering
- screening
- definition
- evaluation
- transmission
- decision.

Capital budgeting relies on sound capital investment and financial decision-making. The above stages identified and classified by King are sound and are core to most decision-making processes used in large organisations. For the purpose of this work on financial management it is enough to apply these stages; however, readers interested in this subject might like to take a glance at *Capital Investment and Financial Decisions* by Haim Levy and Marshall Sarnat (Prentice Hall, 1994).

The principal stages in capital budgeting identified by Paul King are given in Figure 5.3.

At all six stages it is necessary to ensure that the item of capital expenditure proposed is fully aligned with business goals. During this process the proposer is likely to involve other departments and obtain their buy-in and sponsorship.

Once a decision has been made an item may appear in the capital budget, but it is normal that a final sanction is obtained during the actual budget year before the project can be commenced. This is because events may well have changed between the time that the budget was approved and when a commitment is about to be made. For this reason the capital budget might have items carried forward from previous years that have not yet started or that have started but have not yet completed.

Stages in capital budgeting

Figure 5.3

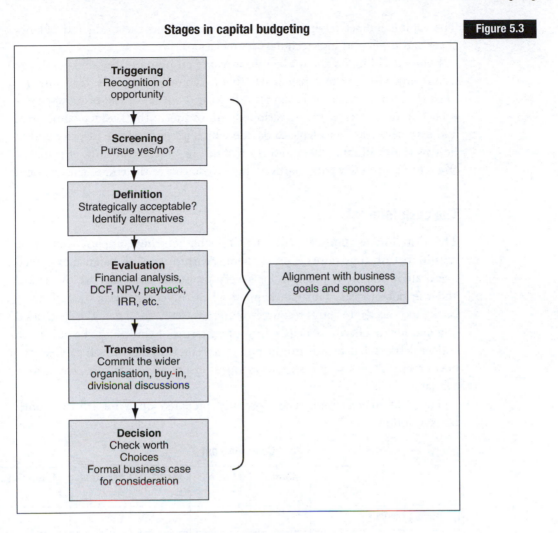

The capital expenditure budget

	January £	February £	March £	April–December £	Total £
Prior year projects not yet started					
Prior year projects started but not completed					
Current year projects • Project 1 • Project 2 • Project 3					
Total					

The capital budget feeds into the cash forecast and the budgeted balance sheet and profit and loss account (depreciation).

Before deciding on the budget approval of an item of capital expenditure a company will need to consider whether it can raise the funds. It might also need to consider whether it can afford to carry out all of the proposed projects. Capital is scarce and is rationed. Accordingly the budget committee and executive team will have to decide which projects have a priority and to do this they will rank them and try to find the best overall mix of projects. We will devote a few paragraphs on how to do this at the end of this chapter.

The cash forecast

The cash forecast/budget will identify whether the company can trade within its cash constraints. Can it operate within its bank balance or agreed overdraft limits? It is possible for a very profitable company to 'overtrade' and run out of cash. This can happen when the company has a full order book and needs to buy resources/materials, etc. to meet the increased demand for its offerings. Depending upon terms of trade and the ability to collect debtors' balances it might find it starts to run out of cash to meet the new orders. This is why cash forecasting is essential – to ensure that cash is available.

The cash forecast/budget is normally prepared on a month-by-month basis as follows:

Cash forecast

	Month 1 £	Month 2 £	Month 3 £	Month 4 £	Month 5–12 £
Opening balance					
Receipts:					
Receipts from debtors					
Receipts from sale of assets					
Other receipts					
Payments:					
Payments to trade creditors:					
Payments of salaries and wages					
Payments of tax and NI					

	Month 1 £	Month 2 £	Month 3 £	Month 4 £	Month 5–12 £
Payments of VAT					
Capital expenditure					
Other payments including loan repayments					
Closing balance (deficit)					

The budgeted profit and loss account

Using the figures from the budgets for sales, production costs, departmental overheads and other revenue items it is possible to construct a profit and loss budget:

Profit and loss budget

	£
Sales	
Less Cost of sales: • Direct materials • Direct labour • Direct overheads Selling and distribution costs Administrative department costs Research and development costs written off Loan interest Other costs including depreciation	
Budgeted profit (loss)	

The budgeted balance sheet

To prepare this take the opening balance sheet and project the closing balance sheet by using values taken from the previous budgets. For example:

Fixed assets will be the opening balance plus items in the capital budget less any expected disposals.

Depreciation provision is the charge calculated and debited to the profit and loss account plus any opening provision and adjusted for any disposals.

Cash will be the closing figure shown in the cash forecast.

Debtors will be the opening balance plus expected sales invoices less cash receipts expected under normal terms and also less any expected bad debt write-offs.

Stocks or raw materials, work in progress and finished goods is calculated by estimating the optimal amount of materials required to maintain production and meet sales.

Creditors are taken as the opening balance plus purchases less payments.

The overdraft is taken from the cash forecast.

Short-term and long-term loans will be in accordance with the loan repayment schedules.

Equity/shareholders' funds are calculated by taking the opening balance and adjusting this for any additional retained profit/loss from the profit and loss account and for any other expected movements – issues/repayments.

Balance sheet budget

	Opening balance £	Closing balance £
Fixed assets: • Cost • Less depreciation		
Current assets • Cash • Debtors • Stocks		
Current liabilities • Creditors		
Short-term loans and overdrafts		
Term loans		
Equity – shareholders' funds including retained profits		

The above are simplified examples of the types of budget seen in most organisations. In describing these we have naturally crossed into certain cost-accounting concepts such as fixed and variable costs, marginal costing, absorption costing and standard costing. These subjects and their usefulness in financial management are described in subsequent chapters.

It will have become apparent that the budgets described above are all interrelated and naturally lend themselves to the use of spreadsheets. For example, a change in the capital budget will also change the cash budget, the depreciation budget, the profit and loss budget and the balance sheet. It is essential to set up a robust spreadsheet for budgeting or to use one of the many excellent budgeting software packages available. However, before doing this it is useful to understand how the budgets are interrelated and to have at least the basic knowledge of accounting that is set out in Chapter 2.

Many budgeting software solutions have been developed to simplify the task of budgeting. However, choosing the right one is not easy. Many provide solutions that are simply beyond a user's requirements and can be cumbersome to use. Others may not provide the overall solution that a user needs. The ability to customise for the particular needs of an organisation is essential. This may be why many users prepare their own spreadsheets.

Software that allows the company to connect and integrate budgeting with other functions that drive the company can be useful but might become inflexible and difficult to use. Often the higher level of integration, the greater the opportunity for perpetrating an error and the less flexible the system becomes. Perhaps it is best to initially prepare an overall budgeting model on a spreadsheet and then, when it is tested and working, look for a systems integrator that can select and install budgeting software that will integrate with other key functions.

CHOICES, PRIORITIES AND CAPITAL RATIONING

The executive team and budget committee will have to make choices throughout the budget process and prioritise scarce resources. They will want to maximise the return to their shareholders and other stakeholders whilst making responsible investment decisions. In addition to the measures concerning return on shareholders' investment there will be wider socio/economic, environmental and corporate governance issues to be taken into account. This paragraph will discuss how these choices are made in the budget process.

Capital rationing

Capital is scare and it is not always possible to undertake all of the projects in a budget. Regardless of cost, finance may not be available to undertake all of the projects identified in a plan and budget. It is, therefore, necessary to select the mix of projects that yields the highest return whilst also considering other factors such as risks and environmental, social and corporate governance. When there is a limit on available capital, choices have to be made between projects. This is best explained by an example:

	Project A	Project B	Project C
Cost/outlay in year '0'	£1,000	£300	£1,500
Net present value	£500	£240	£900
Net present value as a percentage of cost/outlay	50%	80%	60%

Although Project C produces the highest NPV, Project B provides the highest return on investment and will, therefore, be subject to maximisation.

If we assume that only £2,500 is available for investment and that all of the projects are divisible then the optimal investment will be:

	Outlay	NPV	Return %
Project B	£300	£240	80%
Project C	£1,500	£900	60%
Project A	£700	£350	50%
Totals	£2,500	£1,490	59.6%

Since the projects are divisible it is simply a matter of maximising both the NPV and the return by prioritising the projects in the order of highest NPV and return first. We have maximised our NPV to £1,490 and our return to 59.6%.

However, often projects are not divisible in this way. It is a case of either undertake the whole project or not at all. If this were the case then we might wish to maximise the NPV by selecting the projects with the highest NPV:

	Outlay	NPV	Return %
Project A	£1,000	£500	50%
Project C	£1,500	£900	60%
Totals	£2,500	£1,400	56%

Here we have sought to maximise our return within the constraints of the capital limitation and inability to divide projects. This has resulted in a total NPV of £1,400 and a return of 56%.

One important point to remember in making project choices is that capital rationing is only one factor. Also, the conditions that are limiting capital might change or be lifted. Is it real capital rationing or simply a ration of funds available at certain costs? If it is the latter then we can model different scenarios of investment mix with appropriate capital costs.

The term capital rationing may be used to describe the situation where some projects are not taken up due to an artificial internal limit being placed on the amount of finance available rather than a market limitation. For example, a family-run business wishing to retain control and not introduce additional external funds would be imposing an internal constraint on funds available. This may be considered inconsistent with value maximisation.

Capital rationing that is brought about by internal factors is sometimes referred to as soft capital rationing. Capital rationing brought about by external factors may be referred to as hard capital rationing. Examples of each are given below.

Soft capital rationing (caused by internal factors):

- Owner/managers being reluctant to introduce additional external capital that might dilute their influence and control over the business.

- A reluctance to introduce additional debt capital that commits the company to fixed repayment schedules.

- An unwillingness to issue additional share capital that might dilute the existing earnings per share.

- A desire to restrict investment and grow only through retained earnings.

- An inability to take on too much at once or a desire to focus on core business.

Hard capital rationing (caused by external factors):

- Banks may be reluctant to lend due to a shortage of funds through the money market or for other reasons (for example, the credit crunch of 2008).

- The raising of money through the stock market may not be possible during depressed times.

- Financial institutions may find a particular business or even a business sector too risky for investment at a particular time.

- The government might be restricting bank lending.

Ways to remove the constraints of capital rationing

An organisation that is restricting growth through soft rationing may be rejecting projects with a positive net present value that could have increased the organisation's value. These are really choices for the owners to address and will depend upon their propensity to invest and their attitude towards risk. However, a company that has a desire to undertake more projects but is constrained by hard capital rationing may have ways to circumvent the constraints. These will include:

- contracting out part of a project to reduce the investment required
- finding a joint venture (JV) partner
- improving internal capital management
- entering into licensing agreements for the project with another organisation
- selling and leasing back property
- releasing the value of debtors through invoice finance.

(However, remember that it is necessary to match long-term projects with long-term finance. Short-term finance is not suitable for long-term investments.)

Profitability index

During a time of single-period capital rationing one convenient method of ranking projects is by their profitability index (PI). The profitability index is the ratio of present value (PV) of future cash flows to investment required to produce the cash flow.

$$PI = \frac{PV \text{ of cash flow}}{Investment \text{ required}}$$

Consider the following example of a capital-rationing optimisation using the profitability index

Project	Investment £	Present value of cash inflows (PV) £	Net present value (NPV) £	Profitability index (PI)	Ranking using NPV	Ranking using PI
A	20,000	22,500	2,250	1.13	2	1
B	25,000	26,000	1,000	1.04	4	4
C	29,000	31,000	2,000	1.07	3	3
D	39,000	43,000	4,000	1.10	1	2

If capital was rationed to £70,000 and projects were divisible, then using NPV ranking as the method of selection we would have:

Project		Outlay	NPV
D	100%	£39,000	£4,000
A	100%	£20,000	£2,250
C	37.9%	£11,000	£758
		£70,000	£7,008

Using the PI ranking for selection the result is:

Project		Outlay	NPV
A	100%	£20,000	£2,250
D	100%	£39,000	£4,000
C	37.9%	£11,000	£758
		£70,000	£7,008

Note that the results in this case are the same whichever method is used. However, this will not always be the case, it depends upon the level of capital rationing. For example, if capital was rationed to £20,000 and projects were divisible then the results would be:

Using the NPV ranking:

Project		Outlay	NPV
D	51.2%	£20,000	£2,048

Using the PI ranking:

Project		Outlay	NPV
A	100%	£20,000	£2,250
Increase in NPV			£202

Choosing the project according to the PI (when capital is constrained to £20,000) results in a greater NPV. The NPV has increased by £202.

Of course, when projects are not divisible the PI method cannot be used and the decision will be made by obtaining the best combinations of NPVs that fit within the capital constraint.

SUMMARY

In this chapter we have discussed budgetary-control processes and their link with corporate plans. We have shown how to undertake variance analysis, explained the different budgetary methods and types of budgets and discussed methods of dealing with capital rationing. In the following chapters we will take things a little further and explain some costing techniques, including an explanation of fixed and variable costs, absorption and marginal costing.

Marginal costing and pricing

OVERVIEW

In the previous chapter on budgeting we made reference to fixed and variable costs. We will now discuss these in greater depth and explain how they are used in marginal costing and pricing. Marginal costing is a technique used to show the effect on costs and profits of changes in volumes of sales or output. Whilst selling prices are, of course, determined by market forces, marginal costing information can be a valuable aid to pricing and sales volume/mix decisions.

FIXED COSTS

Fixed costs are those that do not change in the budget year with changes in the volume of output or sales. Examples of fixed costs are:

- business rates
- insurance premiums
- management salaries
- rent
- taxes
- depreciation.

Of course, all costs can change over time, but the above are examples of fixed costs that are unlikely to change much during the budget period with changes in output. It is likely that these types of cost are committed for the year ahead. Even if salaries are shed as a result of redundancy it is likely that redundancy payments will offset or partially offset any saving during the budget year.

The fixed cost remains constant during a specified period of time and over a specified range of output. This means that when the level of output is decreased the fixed cost per unit of output increases, and conversely when the level of output increases the fixed cost per unit decreases. This is the problem with allocating fixed costs to unit product costs. The fixed cost per unit will depend upon the number of units produced.

VARIABLE COSTS

Variable costs change in relation to changes in the level of output or sales. Examples of variable costs are:

- direct material
- direct labour
- plant power usage.

These types of cost will vary with any change in production. If the factory stops production it will not use materials or power for the plant. The direct labour costs will also fall away, although perhaps not in direct relationship with a change in production.

The variable cost per unit of production will essentially remain unchanged whatever the level of production.

SEMI-VARIABLE COSTS OR SEMI-FIXED COSTS

Many costs change only at certain levels of changes in output or at certain points in time. These are named semi-variable or semi-fixed costs. Some costs go up in 'steps' when a certain level of production is reached. For example, warehouse rent may be a fixed cost during the budget period but only up to a certain level of inventories stored. When stocks increase above that level there will be an increase in warehouse rent because additional space will need to be used. The total rent cost will, therefore, step up to a higher level. This is known as a stepped increase.

TOTAL COST

This is the total of all costs, fixed and variable, at a certain level of output. For example, if a factory has fixed overhead costs of £200,000 p.a. and the cost of direct materials and labour is £9 per unit of production then the total cost when the level of production is 35,000 units will be:

Fixed costs	£200,000
Variable costs (£9 × 35,000)	£315,000
Total cost	£515,000
Unit cost (£515,000/35,000)	£14.71

If product is increased to 40,000 units then:

Fixed costs	£200,000
Variable costs (£9 × 40,000)	£360,000
Total costs	£560,000
Unit cost (£560,000/40,000)	£14.00

Note that when production is increased fixed costs remain the same and variable costs increase. This means an increase in total costs. However, the unit cost has actually decreased.

CONTRIBUTION

Contribution is the value of sales less the variable cost of the sales. For example, if a company sells 20,000 units for £15 each when the variable cost of sales per unit is £7 and fixed costs are £90,000 p.a. the result would be:

Sales (20,000 × £15)	£300,000
Variable costs (20,000 × £7)	£140,000
Contribution	£160,000
Fixed costs	£90,000
Net profit	£70,000

The contribution towards overheads and profits is equal to 20,000 × unit contribution. That is 20,000 × (£15 − £7) = £160,000. Since the fixed overheads are only £90,000 the net profit is £70,000.

BREAK-EVEN POINT

Working out the volume of units that needs to be sold to cover the fixed costs is called the break-even point.

In the example above we have a unit contribution of £8. Therefore, to 'break even' and cover the £90,000 of fixed costs we would need to sell 11,250 units. This is simply the fixed costs divided by the unit contribution (£90,000/£8 = 11,250).

By selling 11,250 units with a unit contribution of £8 we will make a total contribution of £90,000 towards fixed overheads. Then, since fixed overheads are also £90,000, we will make neither a profit nor a loss but will break even. Proof below:

Sales (11,250 × £15)	£168,750
Variable costs (11,250 × £7)	£78,750
Contribution	£90,000
Fixed costs	£90,000
Profit/(loss)	£0

The break-even point occurs when 11,250 units are sold. If more units than this are sold then the company will make a profit of £8 per unit (unit selling price less unit cost). For example, if another 10,000 units were sold (21,250 in total) the profit would be £80,000 (10,000 × £8). Proof below:

Sales (21,250 × £15)	£318,750
Variable cost (21,250 × £7)	£148,750
Contribution	£170,000
Fixed costs	£90,000
Profit	£80,000

Understanding the unit contribution and the level of fixed overheads can be useful in pricing decisions. Of course, price is a function of the total market, not just a company's own costs. However, knowing that a certain selling price makes a contribution towards overheads and profits is valuable information when deciding whether or not to accept a price.

The break-even point is illustrated in Figure 6.1.

Figure 6.1

The break-even point

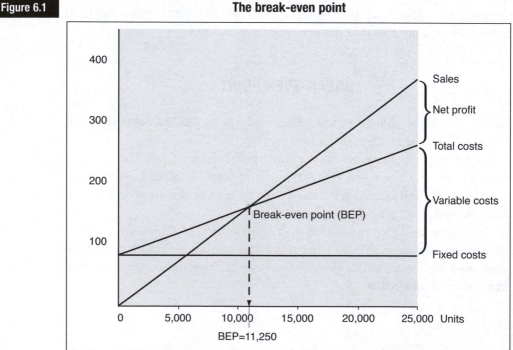

THE USE OF MARGINAL COSTING IN PRICING DECISIONS

Selling prices are determined by the interaction of the market forces of supply and demand. When setting selling prices the sales director will be mindful of competitive prices and the choices that customers have in terms of alternative suppliers and products. However, knowing the unit contribution that a certain selling price brings can help an organisation make better pricing and business decisions.

For example, if the total cost of a product is £10 per unit and the variable cost is £6, should a company accept an order to buy the product at £9 per unit? Well, the full-cost argument will be simply that to sell a product at less than its total cost will result in a loss, in this case a loss of £1 per unit. However, it might also be argued that the company should accept the order since it will in fact make a contribution towards fixed costs of £3 per unit sold (£9 − £6). It could be argued that the company would be better off accepting the order at less than full cost recovery since it does at least make a contribution that would otherwise be lost. Such a marginal decision will of course depend upon other options and the sales of other products. Clearly a company cannot afford to sell all of its products at less than fully absorbed cost and a company that is trading and ordering when in loss is in danger of breaking laws if it incurs costs when insolvent.

It is important to know marginal costs in addition to full costs so as not to automatically dismiss orders at prices that are at less than full cost but would at least make a contribution.

There are weaknesses in the argument for the use of marginal costing as a basis for deciding whether or not to accept an order. For example, no costs are fixed for ever. Capacity ceilings will be met when there will be a stepped increase in certain fixed costs. Selling prices cannot disregard fixed and total costs since to do so might result in overall losses. The true cost of a product is not disclosed by marginal costing as it is by full absorption costing (we will discuss this in the next chapter).

In spite of its disadvantage, marginal costing is widely used because it is simple to understand.

Example

It is close to the end of the year for a company that has so far made sales of £500,000 against variable costs of £300,000. Fixed costs for the year are £90,000, so it will make a profit of £110,000. It has just received an order for 10,000 units of a product that has a variable cost of £6 and a full/total cost of £10. The best price the salesman can get is £9. Should it accept the order?

In this case the answer is yes, it should accept the order. This is because it will obtain a contribution of £30,000, being 10,000(£9 − £6). It will be

£30,000 better off even though it is selling each unit at less than its total costs.

The conclusion that the order should be accepted is based on the assumption that the company has no other orders to accept before the year end. Even though the unit selling price of £9 produces a fully costed loss of £1 per unit, it does nevertheless produce a contribution towards overheads of £3 per unit. Accordingly, the company is better off accepting the order than declining it. At this point any selling price above the variable cost of £6 will improve the bottom line.

During a business recession it is often wise to accept orders at a price that is less than full cost if by so doing the variable costs are covered and the price obtained will make a contribution to a portion of overheads and fixed costs that would otherwise be uncovered.

THE ADVANTAGES AND DISADVANTAGES OF MARGINAL COSTING

Advantages:

1. Shows the relative contributions of products.
2. Shows clearly the exact relationship between cost, selling price and volumes.
3. Helpful in pricing and outsourcing decisions.
4. Shows how the overall profit can be maximised.
5. Separates variable and fixed costs so that better business decisions can be made.
6. Does not arbitrarily allocate fixed or indirect overheads to products in an unrealistic way.

Disadvantages:

1. Does not show the full (fully absorbed) cost of a product.
2. Does not enable the profit (after all costs) of a product to be determined.

Standard costing, which is covered in the next chapter, gets over some of the disadvantages but does not provide the advantages offered by marginal costing. Marginal costing can be applied to standard costing methods to good advantage and we will see how this works in the next chapter.

Absorption costing, standard costing and activity-based costing

ABSORPTION COSTING

In the previous chapter we explained the concept of marginal costing where only variable costs are allocated to a product. We will now discuss the concept of absorption costing where all costs are absorbed into the product cost. Absorption costing is a technique in which all overheads and indirect costs associated with the production of a product are charged to that product. It is a method that will tell us all of the costs associated with a product. Standard costing is a major form of absorption costing and we will use this method to help explain how absorption costing works.

For absorption costing to work we need to find a way of relating overhead costs to products so that the overheads can be absorbed by the products. One of the problems in doing this is that the level of activity upon which absorption is based can fluctuate, giving rise to an over- or under-absorption of overheads and inaccurate product costs. To get over this, absorption costing systems measure the variances and reasons for over- or under-absorption and these can be built back into product costs, stock valuations or pricing calculations.

A properly designed and run absorption costing system is indeed a very elegant and accurate way of calculating product costs. Absorption costing systems, especially those that are fully integrated, can become complicated and perhaps cumbersome to operate. This is a major criticism of them. However, for some industries they are essential and run alongside marginal costing information it is possible to have the best of both absorption and marginal costing systems.

THE FULLY INTEGRATED STANDARD COSTING SYSTEM

This is, perhaps, the ultimate in costing systems. It is a system that uses predetermined standards for every element of cost. Standard rates, allowances and times are used in costing products and variances from these standards are measured and explained so that remedial action can be taken. It shows a total product cost and also helps management concentrate on important variances from the budget and plan.

The components of costs that are absorbed into the manufacture of a product are:

- Materials
- Labour
- Overheads.

Standards will be set for each of these as follows.

Materials

Standard price.

Standard allowance for materials used in manufacture.

Labour

Standard labour rate.

Standard time allowed for the completion of a job.

Overheads

Standard absorption rate based upon capacity of overhead unit and time taken by a product in that unit.

Having set standard rates the costs of products manufactured will be calculated using those rates. This will give rise to variance because the actual costs will invariably be different to the standard rates. The following variance will be measured:

Material price variance: this measures the difference between the actual price paid for a quantity of materials and the standard price paid for the same quantity. Actual less standard price multiplied by actual quantity.

Material usage variance: this measures the difference between the actual quantity used and the standard quantity allowed at the standard rate. Actual less standard material multiplied by standard rate.

Labour rate variance: this is the difference between the actual and standard rate of pay for the actual hours worked. Actual less standard rates multiplied by actual hours.

Labour efficiency variance: this is the measure of efficiency and is the difference between the standard and actual times taken to complete tasks multiplied by the standard rate.

Overhead budget/expenditure variance: the difference between the actual and budgeted overheads spent. It is a measure of the efficiency of buying.

Overhead efficiency variance: this measures the effect of labour efficiency on overhead absorption. For example, if labour is inefficient it will not absorb the overheads of the factory. Standard efficiency (time) less actual efficiency (time) multiplied by the standard overhead rate set.

Overhead volume variance: overhead absorption rates are set using the known capacity of plant. If it is not utilised as expected then there will be an overhead volume variance. Actual level of activity (not output) less the standard level of activity at the standard rate.

As materials are purchased and goods manufactured they move through the production process and are costed always using standard rates and allowances. When the standard costing system is fully integrated with the financial accounts, all entries into the accounts are at standard. As a consequence variances from standard are recorded in the accounts.

For example, if a company had a standard cost for bolts of £0.20 per bolt and purchased 3,000 bolts at £0.21 per bolt, the entries in the accounts would be as follows:

Debit Materials Account	£600	
(with 3,000 @ £0.20 standard)		
Debit Material Price Variance Account	£30	
(with 3,000 @ £0.21 − £0.20)		
Credit Supplier (Creditor)		£630
(with 3,000 @ £0.21 actual)		

Similar entries are made for each element of cost so that costs reflected in the work in materials, work in progress, finished stocks and the cost of sales accounts are all shown at standard rates. The variances from standard are shown in variance accounts and the business can be managed by concentrating on the variances.

This is not a text on cost or financial accounting but an understanding of the fully integrated costing system at a high level is useful in financial management. Figure 7.1 overleaf shows how standard costing entries are made in the accounts for materials, labour, overheads and their associated variances.

Standard costing has most use in organisations where a product and its components can be standardised. This is most likely in a manufacturing organisation, although many other commercial undertakings use a degree of standard costing or a derivative system. Because of its complexity, the full use of standard costing processes may not be practical, although, it might be argued, full integration may reduce overall costing and accounting work. Certainly concentrating on variances provides management with a 'dashboard' approach to monitoring performance.

The cost of sales will reflect the standard costs of goods removed from the finished stock account and sold. The cost of sales and the variance accounts will all be taken into the profit and loss account. Stocks at year end will generally be valued at their standard cost, although it is argued by some that this is not in fact their true actual cost and that some part of the variances incurred during the accounting period should be apportioned back into the stock value. Whichever method is used it is important to maintain a consistent approach between accounting periods so that profits are true.

Figure 7.1   **Integrated standard costing**

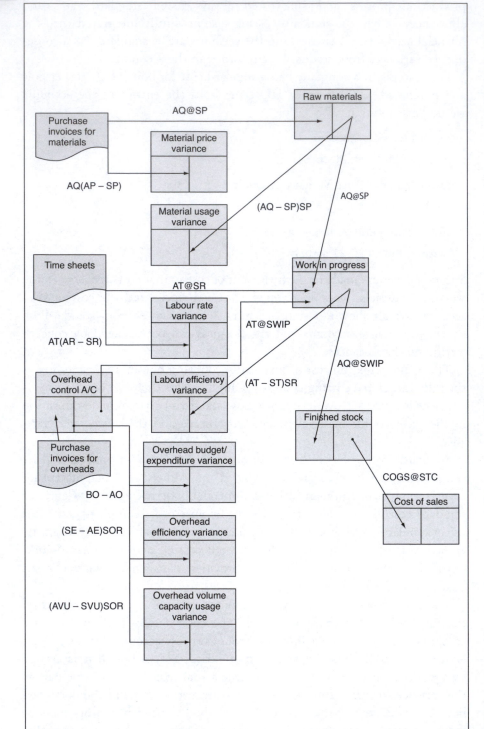

Key to abbreviations used in Figure 7.1

AE = actual overhead absorption efficiency (hours)

AO = actual overheads

AP = actual price

AQ = actual quantity

AR = actual labour rate

AT = actual time

AVU = actual volume used (capacity usage)

BO = budgeted overheads

COGS = cost of goods sold

LEV = labour efficiency variance

LRV = labour rate variance

MPV = material price variance

MUV = material usage variance

OBV = overhead budget variance

OEV = overhead efficiency variance

OVV = overhead volume variance

SE = standard overhead absorption efficiency (hours)

SOR = standard overhead rate (budgeted overheads/budgeted capacity usage)

SP = standard price

SQ = standard quantity

SR = standard labour rate

ST = standard time allowed

STC = standard total cost

SVU = standard volume used (budgeted capacity usage)

SWIP = standard work-in-progress rate for material, labour, overheads

Key formulae

MPV = AQ (AP − SP)

MUV = (AQ − SQ)SP

LRV = AT(AR − SR)

LEV = (AT − ST)SR

OBV = BO − AO

OVV = (AVU − SVU)SOR

OEV = (SE − AE)SOR

A summary of the principal reasons for standard costing variances is given below:

Cost	Variance	Reason
Material	Price	A change in actual compared with standard prices
Material	Usage	More or less materials being used in a production process
Labour	Rate	An increase or decrease in actual pay compared with standard pay rate
Labour	Efficiency	An increase or decrease in the actual time taken to complete a task compared with the standard time
Fixed overheads	Expenditure	An increase or decrease in actual versus standard price
	Capacity usage	An increase or decrease over the budgeted output
	Volume efficiency	A change in the actual compared with budgeted output for the time spent

Other measurements include mix, yield, wastage, idle-time and calendar variances. In choosing the level of standard costing to apply, select the most important areas that managers need to concentrate on and develop a 'dashboard' approach to reporting. Avoid overcomplicated reports where important issues can be hidden and management time spent on items that are not key to organisational success.

THE PRINCIPAL ADVANTAGES OF STANDARD COSTING SYSTEMS

Standard costing, and in particular the fully integrated standard costing system, provide a comprehensive product cost taking into account all elements of cost and absorbing fixed costs into the cost of a product. By using standards for material prices, materials used, labour rates, production times, capacity usage and overhead rates a company can be managed by exception. What this means is that by having set standards at the commencement of a period the organisation then concentrates on the variances from these standard rates. This can quickly focus management attention on key areas that are not proceeding as planned so that corrective action can be taken. Management can focus on those areas that need attention and not on areas that are going well.

SETTING STANDARDS

Setting standard costs for manufacturing processes requires consideration of:

- quantities
- prices
- times
- rates
- quality.

When setting standards care must be taken to ensure that they are realistic and attainable. Like objectives, they may be demanding but they must also be achievable, otherwise they can have a negative influence on motivation. This is particularly important when setting standard times which may be used to measure labour efficiency and used as a base for performance bonuses. Often standard times will be set and left unchanged for many years when all around has changed in terms of equipment and efficiency. Sometimes a standard time will be too demanding and tight and an operative, however efficient, never earns a bonus.

When setting standard times the work processes must be observed and measured with various levels of experience in operational staff. Often three types of time can be considered:

- tight time
- realistic and attainable time
- generous or lax time.

In selecting standard times for a standard costing system it might be appropriate to set them between 'realistic' and 'tight'. However, in terms of standards that are used for performance payments other considerations need to be addressed, including union and trade concerns. Most organisations set standard times in their costing systems at the 'realistic' level and then graduate bonuses upwards from that level.

Standards for labour rates are usually set from current pay levels by grade and adjusted for expected rate increases during the year.

Material price standards are set by the buying department who consider the materials budget for the year ahead in addition to current stock levels and buying levels. Current supplier prices and quantity/cash discounts are taken into account along with market trends, new supplier and commodity/material price movements.

ACTIVITY-BASED COSTING (ABC)

Activity-based costing, commonly known as ABC, is a costing approach that identifies activities in an organisation and assigns the cost of each activity resource to end products and services. It enables an organisation to determine the true cost of its individual products and services for the purposes of identifying their profitability.

The ABC method assigns an organisation's resource costs through its activities to products made and services provided. It is used to help determine both product and customer cost and profitability. ABC is mainly used to help with strategic decision making in areas such as selling prices, processes and outsourcing.

ABC tries to be more accurate than some other methods of costing that use arbitrary methods for allocating indirect costs to products. It looks more closely at how activities and equipment relate to products and services provided so that management can make better decisions. ABC seeks to identify cause-and-effect relationships to more accurately allocate costs to products/services.

Activities are identified and the cost of each activity is attributed to each product or service according to usage of that activity. Areas of high overhead cost per unit are identified and alternatives can be considered. ABC is used in a variety of industries.

THE USE OF MARGINAL COSTING IN CONJUNCTION WITH STANDARD COSTING

In the previous chapter we discussed the use of marginal costing techniques. Marginal costing can be applied in conjunction with standard costing. Standards are prepared in the usual manner but in a system of 'marginal standard costing' only variable costs are included in the standards. The variable costs included would be direct materials, direct wages and variable direct overheads. These costs would enter the standard product costs. This system has the benefits of both standard and marginal costing.

8

Pricing and costs

SETTING SELLING PRICES

In an efficient market the function of price is to equate supply with demand. Setting a selling price for a product or service is fundamentally about determining the best that can be obtained and knowing the lowest price that is acceptable. To do this requires knowledge of the market place, the competition and product costs/contributions.

A company must first of all decide where to position its product in terms of quality and price. For example, is it selling on the basis of high quality or just on basic low price functionality? Positioning the offering within the range of strategies will help understand the market reaction to a price. Below are some examples:

Price v quality strategies

	High price	Medium price	Low price
High quality	Premium	High value	Marvellous value
Medium quality	Overpriced	Middle value	Bargain
Low quality	Not worth it	Overpriced	Economy/Cheap

Equilibrium price

Figure 8.1

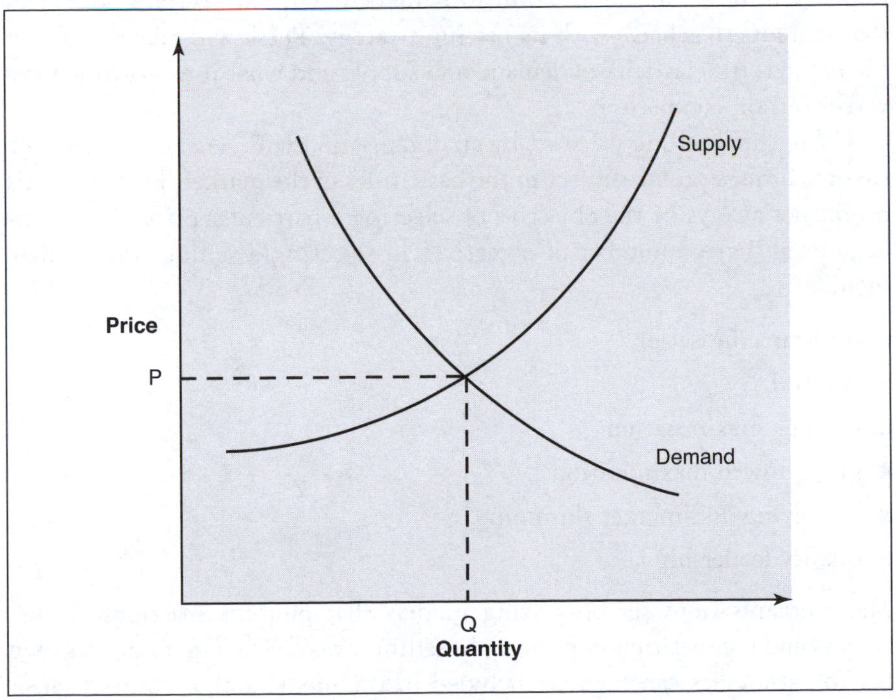

127

When setting prices the interaction of the forces of supply and demand will ultimately find the equilibrium price. As prices increase, demand will fall off. Supply will increase if the price obtainable increases. This is demonstrated in Figure 8.1.

An example of a market demand and supply schedule for a product

Price	Quantity demanded	Quantity supplied
£30	150,000	380,000
£29	160,000	350,000
£28	170,000	310,000
£27	180,000	260,000
£26	**200,000**	**200,000**
£25	220,000	140,000
£24	250,000	80,000
£23	290,000	20,000
£22	340,000	10,000

In this example, the equilibrium price for this product in the market is 200,000. This is a useful starting point in price determination, but a particular selling organisation within this market will have certain objectives that it wants to achieve with its pricing strategy. These will take account of the market, the elasticity of demand and supply and what it wants to achieve versus certain competitors.

The optimal selling price set by an organisation will generally be the one that maximises profits subject to the basic rules of the market. However, this might not always be the objective of selecting a particular price. An organisation can have a number of objectives in selecting a selling price. These include:

- profit maximisation
- survival
- revenue maximisation
- sales growth maximisation
- kite flying and market skimming
- quality leadership.

Many organisations set up pricing models that plot the reactions of customers and competition to changes in selling prices. The organisation's own pricing strategies can then be included in the model and various scenarios run showing the sensitivity of the result to changes in each variable. The variable factors include the following:

■ Demand – this can be determined through research into consumer buying reactions to differing prices either in a 'laboratory' setting or through sampling.

■ Costs – these can be calculated from the organisation's own product-costing systems. Competitor costs can be estimated according to the comparative size of their plant.

■ Competitor's prices – these can be obtained through research and tested in 'laboratory' studies.

■ The economic value to the customer of an offering can be determined by comparing the selling price of a product against the value of benefits to the customer.

■ Other variable factors may include social and legal factors that affect prices. These will be considered later in this chapter.

Once the budgeted selling price for a product has been established it will be included in the calculations for the sales budget and product-mix calculations.

SOCIAL AND LEGAL ISSUES IN PRICING

Pricing does have social and legal consequences that have to be addressed. These should be taken into account in the price-determination model as constraints. Before we move on to the sales budget we will consider some of these issues.

Price fixing

This is illegal in most countries. It is illegal for sellers to collude and to fix prices. This would be anti-competitive. Therefore, sellers must set their own prices without talking to each other.

Deceptive prices

There is a raft of legislation concerning deceptive prices in the US and other countries. Basically, a seller should not deceive a buyer into thinking the price he is paying is anything other than what the price truly is. For example, to say that prices are reduced when they were artificially set higher in the first place is deceptive.

Price discrimination

Some countries have laws to ensure that sellers offer the same prices to a certain level of trade. Differences are allowed, of course, if the seller can prove different levels of cost for different buyers.

Predatory prices

Some countries will not allow sellers to sell at lower than cost with the purpose of destroying competition. This normally refers to the situation of a large company attempting to put a small competitor out of business and to destroy competition.

These and other practices are outlawed in certain countries and it is as well to be sure that your pricing strategies are fair and honest. Of course, it can be difficult to prove bad practice at times, especially since product costing has many variables and can be approached from different perspectives. However, it is as well to stick with the meaning of the various laws on pricing that are designed to protect the consumer and ensure fair trade and competition.

SALES MIX

When an organisation sells a number of products, each of which makes a different contribution to costs and profits, the mix of product sales will have an impact on the total profit. If more of the products that yield a higher contribution are sold then total profits will be higher. Of course, there may be other reasons why an organisation wishes to have a certain mix of product sales, for example new market/product penetration.

Example of a budgeted sales mix

Product	Budget mix	Unit contribution	Total contribution	Fixed costs	Net profit
A	200	£20	£4,000		
B	100	£10	£1,000		
C	100	£5	£500		
	400		£5,500	£5,000	£500

The company budgeted to sell 400 units with the mix of, A 200, B 100, C 100. Assuming the company actually sold 400 units in total as per the budget but that the mix was A 150, B 150, C 100, the results would now be:

Actual contribution and profit

Product	Actual mix	Unit contribution	Total contribution	Fixed costs	Net profit
A	150	£20	£3,000		
B	150	£10	£1,500		
C	100	£5	£500		
			£5,000	£5,000	0

A change in the product mix has meant that the overall contribution has gone down to £5,000, eliminating the profit. This was caused by an overall sales volume mix variance of –£500.

The effect of sales volume variances on contribution is:

Product	Budget volume in units	Actual volume in units	Variance in units	Unit contribution	Variance £
A	200	150	−50	£20	−£1,000
B	100	150	+50	£10	+£500
C	100	100	0	£5	
					−£500

The overall effect of the adverse sales volume mix variance on contribution and profits was £500 adverse.

When the objective of pricing is to maximise profits, the volume mix needs to be monitored. This can be done on unit volumes and contributions and also on sales and gross margins:

Product	Selling price	Variable cost	Contribution £	Gross margin
A	£100	£80	£20	20%
B	£80	£70	£10	12.5%
C	£50	£45	£5	10%

Maximising the sales of product A (with the highest gross margin) would maximise overall profits.

Example of the effect of sales mix on gross margins and profit:

Although overall sales may be looking fine and on target, a hidden adverse sales mix variance could be reducing profits substantially.

	Sales budget £	Actual sales £	Sales variance £	Gross margin %	Gross margin variance £
Product A	50,000	20,000	−30,000	45%	−13,500
Product B	30,000	25,000	−5,000	35%	−1,750
Product C	10,000	45,000	+35,000	5%	+1,750
Total	90,000	90,000	0		−13,500

In this example the actual total sales achieved were £90,000, which compared to the budget of £90,000 produced a total variance of £0. However, because the actual mix of products sold had changed adversely from the budgeted mix, the total gross margin achieved was £13,500 less than budgeted.

USING LINEAR PROGRAMMING TECHNIQUES TO SOLVE PROBLEMS OF SALES MIX WHEN THERE ARE RESOURCE CONSTRAINTS

Clearly a business would wish to sell more of those products that provide a higher unit contribution and profit. However, there may be constraints that prevent selling too much of any one product. In these circumstances the business will wish to maximise the sales of the most profitable products subject to a number of constraints. A linear programme model will help solve this type of problem. This is best explained through an example.

Example

A company produces two products, Product 1 and Product 2. Details of the processing times and unit contributions are given below:

	Product 1	Product 2
Processing time machine A	2 hours	2 hours
Processing time machine B	1 hour	2 hours
Unit contribution	£2	£3
Maximum possible sales	130 units	160 units
	Machine A	Machine B
Time available	400 hours	280 hours

What are the quantities of products 1 and 2 that should be sold in order to maximise profits?

Solution:

Let x be the quantity of units of product 1 and y be the quantity of units of product 2 that are made and sold.

Then constraints are:

Machine A	$2x + 2y$	$\leq$ 400 hours
or	$x + y$	$\leq$ 200 hours
Machine B	$x + 2y$	$\leq$ 280 hours
Sales of 1	x	$\leq$ 130 units
Sales of 2	y	$\leq$ 160 units

The objective is to maximise the value of $2x + 3y$ subject to the following constraints:

$$x + y \leq 200$$
$$x + 2y \leq 280$$
$$x \leq 130$$
$$y \leq 160$$
$$x \geq 0$$
$$y \geq 0$$

The above axis and constraints can be shown on a graph (see Figure 8.2) from which we can determine the point where the product mix yields the maximum contribution/profit.

Linear programme

Figure 8.2

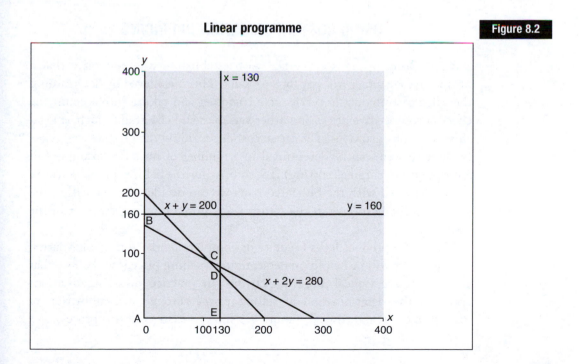

The point on the graph that produces the maximum contribution is the point farthest away from both the x and y axis. This is at point 'C' and is demonstrated below:

Point	x	y	2x + 3y
A	0	0	0
B	0	140	420
C	120	80	480 (maximum)
D	130	60	440
E	130	0	260

The maximum contribution/profit obtainable within the constraints defined is £480 and this is achieved with 120 of product 1 (x) and 80 of product 2 (y).

The value at point C can also be found through the following equation:

$$x + 2y = 280$$
$$x + y = 200$$
$$y = 80 \text{ (by subtraction)}$$
$$x = 120 \text{ (by subtraction)}$$

USING COST INFORMATION IN PRICING

Setting selling prices is concerned with establishing the best price that a prospective customer will pay for a product. This is achieved by determining the value of a product or service to a customer and taking into account the effect of competitive prices and other variables and constraints such as legal and social considerations. The actual cost of providing the product or service, as we have seen, can be determined in a number of ways (for example full absorption or marginal costing). By comparing the selling price we think can be achieved with the budgeted costs we can decide whether selling the product is likely to give us the return we require on our investment in the business.

Where the product lacks accurate or complete market-price information our own costs will be helpful in determining a selling price if we believe that these costs are typical and competitive. In practice most organisations approach the determination of selling prices through a combination of market research and costing. Figure 8.3 shows the steps in this process.

Costing and price determination

Figure 8.3

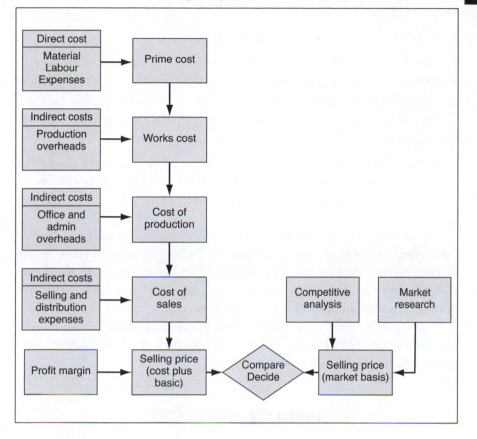

Steps in product cost and price determination

- Determine the **prime cost**. This is the combined costs of direct material, direct labour and direct expenses.

- Determine the **works cost**. This is the prime cost plus the indirect costs of production overheads.

- Determine the **cost of production**. This is the works cost plus the indirect costs of office and administrative overheads.

- Determine the **cost of sales**. This is the cost of production plus the indirect costs of selling and distribution expenses.

- Determine the **cost plus selling price**. This is the cost of sales plus the required profit margin that is needed to provide the required return on investment.

- Determine the **market selling price**. This is the selling price indicated by the results of competitive analysis and market research.

- Compare and decide on an appropriate selling price.

If the market selling price is lower than the cost plus derived selling price then we will need to decide whether to:

- accept a lower price, margin and return on investment
- explore ways of reducing our costs
- price on the basis of cost plus and accept the possibility of lower margins
- explore ways to differentiate our product in terms of quality, etc. and obtain a better price. This is in effect changing the offering and/or market positioning.

When looking to reduce cost it is a matter of going through each element of costs and exploring ways of increasing labour efficiency, material usage, buying efficiency, stock holding costs, etc. Some costs will be more controllable than others.

If a company is confident that its cost information is accurate and that its production and distribution processes are highly efficient then it might accept that its competitors who are selling at lower prices are willing to accept a lower return on investment. It will then have to decide on its own business strategy and position in the market.

Price decisions are a combination of market research, competitive analysis and cost information. Having a structured approach to product costing will enable better price decisions.

MARKETING STRATEGIES

Having determined selling prices at various volumes through both market and internal cost methods an organisation will have various marketing strategies available. A detailed examination of these is outside the scope of this text on financial management. However, some principal marketing strategies are mentioned here to conclude our chapter on pricing in so far as marketing strategies affect prices.

Three categories of marketing strategies are:

- offensive
- defensive
- rationalisation.

Offensive strategies are concerned with increased penetration, expansion and market leadership. Defensive strategies are all about protection and maintenance of the existing market position. Rationalisation strategies are concerned with reducing costs.

Offensive strategies

Expansion	New branches, outlets and channels to market.
Penetration	Win new customers in existing markets. Increase existing customer purchases and usage.
New market	Find and establish new markets
Challenger	Be innovative. Sell new ideas. Outsell minor competitors. Take on higher-risk business. Seize new opportunities.
Leader	Best-price leadership. Better distribution networks. Powerful advertising campaigns. Take over smaller competitors.

Defensive strategies:

Follower	Take lower risks.
Niches	Concentrate on specialisation and serving existing customer/product niches well.

Rationalisation strategies

Cost reduction	Eliminate high-cost low-return activities. Cut costs wherever it will improve return on investment.

Selecting a strategy, appraisal and review

Having considered the various marketing strategies available the next step is to select one or a number of strategies. The process for this will include the appraisal of different strategies, the formulation of preferred strategies and their evaluation. The optimum strategy will be selected and implemented and the actual results will then be monitored and the appraisal process started over again. During this process the marketing director will consider service/product differentiation and market segmentation. These may affect both costs and selling prices available and will be fed into the costing and budgeting process.

Strategy selection and review is a circular and continual process. The following steps may be followed:

Step 1. Determine relevant internal factors, including goals, resources available, costs, cost-plus prices.

Step 2. Determine relevant external factors, including market prices, demand, market size, socio-economic considerations and legal constraints.

Step 3. Identify all relevant strategies that are realistically available, including offensive, defensive and rationalisation strategies.

Step 4. Appraise all of the strategies available, run through options and formulate best-fit strategies.

Step 5. Consider shareholder and stakeholder requirements.

Figure 8.4   **Marketing strategy selection, prices and costs**

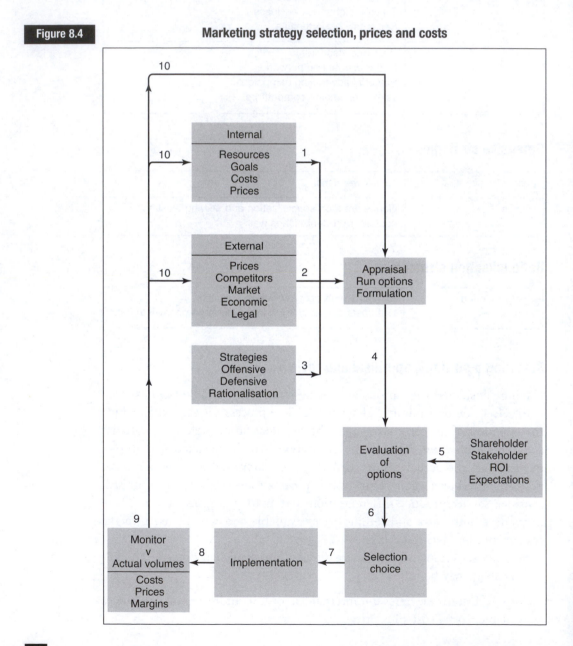

Step 6. Evaluate options, discounted cash flow (DCF) analysis and sensitivity analysis.

Step 7. Select the best options.

Step 8. Implement selection.

Step 9. Monitor actual results in terms of volumes achieved, prices, costs and margins.

Step 10. Feed the information collected during the monitoring process back into the model and go through the process again.

Figure 8.4 shows these processes.

SUMMARY

Sales are dependent upon a wide variety of factors. Pricing policy is just one of these factors. Determining the optimum selling price is important to success.

In this chapter we have put some structure around the process of determining and monitoring selling prices using both market and internal cost information. In determining selling prices we are attempting to achieve our corporate goals and return on investment through maximising our market share, taking into consideration such factors as our own resources and capabilities, competitive prices, market demand, strategies available, social and legal issues. Sales volumes/mixes and actual performance are continually monitored and the information collected is fed back into the pricing model.

Encouraging performance through goal alignment and congruence

GOAL ALIGNMENT

One role of financial management is to ensure that all assets provide the greatest possible return. This includes the return on human assets. Of all the assets in an organisation it is the human asset that can provide returns far greater than expected.

Shareholders and other stakeholders want to ensure that they obtain the best value they can for their investment or interest. One way to help make this happen is to ensure that the employees and management have personal company goals that are aligned with higher goals. The most obvious form of this would be that of a sales person who receives commission on sales made.

Types of rewards that are designed to encourage maximum results and goal alignment include:

- works and production bonuses
- sales commissions
- management bonuses
- indirect incentives.

Apart from rewards, performance and loyalty can be enhanced through the broader incentives of corporate social responsibility, sustainable and environmental policies.

Methods of rewards and incentives are discussed below.

REWARD SCHEMES

Works and production bonuses

These schemes reward efficiency in terms of quantity and quality of output. Typically they are based upon output measured against standards set for time, quantity/output, rejects and materials used. This often goes in line with a fully integrated standard costing system where, for example, production staff might share in a labour-efficiency variance.

This type of reward is based upon the setting of accurate and reasonable standards in the first place and this is no easy task. Standard times are set for each production process through detailed work study/measurement and in light of previous times taken. Actual times taken as measured in timesheets and output reports are then compared and efficiency variances measured.

This type of measurement sets clear expectations and can encourage good performance as long as the standards are set correctly in the first place. This is not easy and is the cause of much discontentment when, for example, an operative has been working to maximum efficiency but receives no bonus.

However, wages and labour costs offer a great scope for cost reduction and management should endeavour to improve efficiency and quality and encourage staff to do this.

Paying staff for production by results rather than just by the time worked will not only encourage greater output but will also enable the company to enjoy the benefits of a greater use of its assets and a lower cost per unit. For example:

	Pay by time	Pay by results
Daily production per operative	50 units	75 units
Labour cost per operative	£80	£120
Fixed overheads per operative	£110	£110
Total	£190	£230
Unit cost	£3.80	£3.07

Few operatives would agree to being paid entirely by results but the above example shows how both the employee and the company can benefit perhaps by a scheme that has part pay by time and part through results. In this example paying by results has enabled the company to lower its unit cost of production through increasing output without an increase in fixed costs. Of course, this may not be possible; if there is a capacity ceiling an additional investment is required.

Operatives can be rewarded through:

- time rate
- piece rates
- piece rates with a guaranteed minimum daily rate
- differential piece rates that vary with production levels.

When proposing a scheme it is normal to model on a spreadsheet the results for operatives and the company at different levels of efficiency and output taking account of any stepped changes in overheads and costs. For example, as the production efficiency increases, the total amount of wages (with bonuses) will increase whilst the wages cost per unit will decrease. Fixed costs will remain constant to a point and will eventually (upon reaching a capacity ceiling) take a stepped increase. These variables are best plotted on a spreadsheet and can be demonstrated in Figure 9.1.

Production bonus schemes that work usually have the following characteristics:

- Effort and reward are fairly matched.

How production bonuses might affect unit costs | Figure 9.1

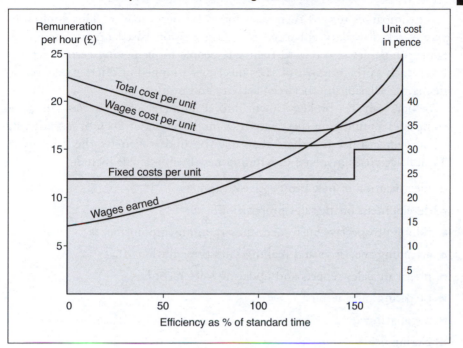

- The incentive bonus should be high enough to motivate improved performance.
- The company must benefit from the scheme and the value of production gains should be shared fairly between the company and employees.
- Operatives, management and unions must collaborate, share, agree to and buy into the scheme.
- The benefits of improved efficiency must be rewarded to operatives as soon as possible after measurement. If there is a lag then performance and reward will not be linked in the mind of the operative and the purpose of the scheme will be lost.
- The scheme rules must be clear.
- Standard times set must be achievable by an efficient operative.
- There should be no limit placed upon the amount of bonus that can be earned within normal working hours.
- There should be no changes without the operative's agreement.
- Quality measures should be integrated into the scheme.
- An operative should be assessed only on tasks within their control.
- The scheme should be fully integrated with any system of standard costing and budgetary control.

Sales performance bonuses

Most companies reward their sales forces for performance. This is often by way of a basic salary enhanced by a commission based upon closed sales. Some companies also reward their sale people for achieving certain activity levels such as the number of sales meetings arranged or offers made, recognising the relationship between activity and results.

Selling can be broken down into a number of activities. In some companies a number of these activities might be undertaken by a marketing department whilst in others they may be undertaken by the sales force. Typical activities involved in winning new business will include:

- identification of new prospective customers
- development of the sales proposition
- calling prospective customers and arranging appointments
- attending meetings and making sales presentations
- preparing sales reports and updating sales records
- preparing offer letters
- negotiating
- closing deals
- preparing contracts/invoices
- managing the relationship.

The above activities relate to entirely new prospective customers. In the case of existing customers where the sales person is looking to extend or retain business the list may be shorter. Many companies give their sales forces targets for the retention and extension of existing business. This is because it is generally far less expensive to retain a customer than it is to win a new one. In the case of a company with a new business closure rate of one in five meetings it might be simplistically argued that new business costs four times more to win than retaining/extending existing business.

In setting sales targets the primary focus is on completed sales, although the encouragement of good sales activity levels is normally recognised. Listed below are some of the more usual sales targets:

- total sales value achieved
- total gross margins achieved
- number of new customers won
- number of existing customers retained
- percentage of existing customer turnover extended
- spread of new business across various offerings
- number of telephone calls made

- number of meetings attended
- number of offer letters made
- value of offers made.

Sales people tend by nature to be independent and like a fair amount of freedom to undertake their activities. Accordingly, too many controls might be counterproductive. However, recognising all of the activities in the sales process and to some extent incorporating these into the sales reward scheme will not only encourage good behaviour it will also demonstrate an organisation's understanding of what selling is all about. At the other extreme is the commission-only sales person who is paid only on completion of a sale. Of course, it will be argued that no sales person can continue to be paid if there are no sales and this basic reality is understood by all enduring sales people. It can also be argued that whilst sales people are easy to measure (sale or no sale), they are also the most difficult to manage. A clear and regularly monitored sales scheme is most likely to help sales force management and align sales effort with goals.

Common problems with sales incentive schemes include:

- Difficulty in setting realistic sales targets. Knowing the value of sales wanted is one thing but knowing how this relates to an individual's sales target requires a detailed knowledge of the market and of the sales activity processes required.

- Choosing the correct territorial split between sales people. Should it be geography, size of client, business sector, etc.? This may also be dictated by trying to optimise the use of existing sales resources.

- Avoiding suboptimal practices that may occur when a sales person concentrates only on a personal goal to the detriment of the team.

- Holding back sales to a future period when maximum personal targets have been achieved or in order to help next year's personal results.

- Poaching and rule bending.

- Heavily incentivised sales people may damage a company's reputation through sharp and inappropriate selling practices.

Setting sales targets should encourage professional behaviour whilst encouraging maximum achievement and is, therefore, a question of striking the right balance.

Management bonuses

In the credit crunch of 2008 there was much publicity and criticism of the 'huge' bonuses paid to senior executives of failing organisations. It was felt that whilst the bonuses might be due according to the letter of a contract they were certainly not according to the meaning and spirit of the executive's relationship and position in the organisation. Failing banks came under close scrutiny and so did some government agencies.

Why do organisations feel the need to pay huge bonuses? The answer is simple. If an executive offers to increase profits by £10 million in exchange for a bonus of £1 million when this greatly exceeds shareholders' normal expected return on investment then why would they not take up the offer? The arguments arise when the measure of success of an executive is too narrow and gives rise to payments resulting from success in one area when overall an organisation can be failing. So, perhaps the fault lies with the setting of performance measurement and goal alignment. This chapter is all about goal alignment and reward schemes that help avoid the types of issues brought to light in the 2008 credit crunch.

The most important feature of an incentive scheme is goal congruence. This is achieving accord between the personal and departmental objectives of executives and the overall organisational objectives. The most important personal feature of an executive is arguably ethics, without which the risks of personal gain and organisational loss are great.

Goal congruence is normally best achieved by performance rewards that encourage loyalty rather than just short-term gains for an individual. Share options, promotion and recognition in addition to performance-related pay when combined are more likely to achieve goal congruence than simply providing performance-related pay based on narrow measures.

Taxation aspects of management incentive schemes

In the UK companies paying bonuses will treat the payment as a tax-deductible cost and employees receiving the bonus will pay tax and NICs on it through the PAYE system. However, there may well be special implications for both the company and the employee depending on their status. For example, in the UK HMRC operates a scheme called Enterprise Management Incentives (EMIs).

EMIs are designed to help small companies recruit and retain employees who have the scarce skills needed to help growth. They are also a way of helping reward employees for taking what may be a higher level of risk by working for a smaller company.

Tax-advantaged share options up to a certain limit may be granted to a qualifying employee of a qualifying company subject to certain limits (refer to the HMRC web site search facility for details of current limits and requirements).

The grant of the option is tax free and there will normally be no tax or NICs for the employee to pay when the option is exercised. There will normally be no NICs charge for the employer.

For companies or groups to qualify they must have maximum gross assets of less than a specified limit. The company whose shares are the subject of the option must be independent, and the company or group must be trading. Companies carrying on certain trades will not qualify.

To qualify for EMI an employee has to be employed by the company whose shares are the subject of the option, or by a subsidiary, and must spend a certain specified amount of time working in that company.

The options must be granted for commercial reasons to recruit or retain employees in a company and not as part of an arrangement of which one of the main purposes is to avoid tax. Full details of the scheme are given on the HMRC site.

Before deciding on a particular incentive scheme it is necessary to explore the taxation implications applicable to the 'tax country' of the company and of the employee (these could be different).

From a financial management perspective the taxation aspects of incentive schemes need to be understood in order to:

- ensure that adequate provision is made for taxes due
- give consideration to the net after-tax value to an employee of a bonus payment
- ensure that taxation incentives such as EMIs are obtained where appropriate.

BROADER INCENTIVES

Broader incentives might encourage improved performance, goal congruence and loyalty. These types of incentives will exist in some organisations more than in others and are often features of the type of organisation. They might include:

- sustainable business processes
- environmental responsibility (waste, energy, emissions and pollution controls)
- economic value added and local impact
- social contribution to health, training, equality, etc.
- cultural sensitivity
- working environment
- new ideas, cutting edge, research commitment
- reputation of organisation and public respect.

It is hard to put a value on these types of attributes, which incentivise an employee to join and stay with a company. Much development work has been done in recent years with various forms of sustainable development reporting. These reports demonstrate an organisation's impact in a much broader sense than financial and stock market reporting. Companies that prepare SDRs are more likely to attract prospective employees who are interested in and value the environment and sustainability.

The New Zealand accounting profession has, perhaps, led the way with SDR. Typically SDR incorporates the triple bottom line reporting of the economic, environmental and social aspects of an organisation's activities plus reporting on cultural issues and values. The benefits of SDR include:

- motivated staff
- aligned staff and goal congruence
- the ability to attract and retain staff.

SDR has an important part to play in the provision of broader incentives for staff.

More information on sustainable development can be obtained from the World Business Council for Sustainable Development (WBCSD). This association has a membership of 200 companies and deals exclusively with business and sustainable development. The WBCSD provides a place for companies to explore sustainable development and to share knowledge.

SUMMARY

In this chapter we have examined the significance of goal congruence from a financial management perspective. This is to ensure that human assets provide the greatest possible return to the organisation.

There are two routes to goal congruence:

1. an employee's voluntary acceptance of an organisation's goals (this is referred to as a principal–agent alignment)
2. an employee's considered agreement with the organisation's strategy (referred to as an agent–agent alignment.

Indications are that employees are motivated not only by individual gains and that goal congruence does not depend only upon selecting the right job performance measures. Broader incentives play an important part in goal congruence.

Working capital management

THE NEED FOR WORKING CAPITAL, THE WORKING CAPITAL RATIO AND CYCLE

Working capital is the operating liquidity available to a business. It is basically current assets less current liabilities. If current assets are less than current liabilities the business has a working capital deficiency.

A business needs positive working capital to be able to continue its operations. It needs sufficient funds to meet short-term debts and ongoing operational costs.

Management of working capital is required to ensure that a company can continue to trade and meet its obligations. Working capital management involves stock control, debtors' control, cash control and the management of accounts payable.

Working capital management involves managing the relationship between current assets and current liabilities. This requires efficient short-term decisions. These decisions are based on cash flows.

A measure of cash flow is the cash-conversion cycle. This is the number of days taken from the outlay of cash for component parts and raw materials to receiving payment from customers for the finished product. This number represents the days that a business's cash is tied up. Obviously the lower this is, the better.

Working capital cycle **Figure 10.1**

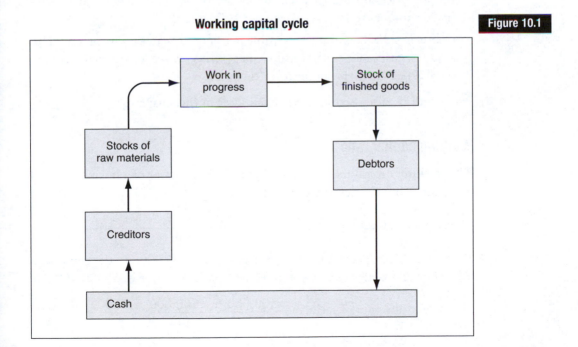

Working capital management is concerned with cash management, debtor/creditor management, stock management including economic order/production quantities, supply chain management, just-in-time (JIT) ordering, short-term finance management of overdrafts, invoice finance facilities and other short-term facilities.

Working capital pressure points

A business will collapse without cash. Profit does not necessarily equal cash and it is vital to manage cash flow and ensure an adequate and efficient balance of working cash is available. The working capital cycle shows how cash is generated (see Figure 10.1). Creditors are paid to provide raw materials which are transformed into stocks which are delivered to debtors who eventually pay. The cash flow pressure points are, therefore, creditors, stocks and debtors.

Creditors: wherever possible use suppliers who allow generous credit terms. It might even be better to forgo discounts for early payment, it all depends on the cost of finance and the cash position. However, it is not a good policy to upset important suppliers by taking credit in excess of agreed terms.

Stocks: these should be kept at an optimal level – just enough to meet demand and to not interrupt manufacturing processes but not too much so as to have cash tied up in excessive stocks. Ensure that maximum volume discounts are received. Make use of economic batch/order quantity techniques to help arrive at the optimal levels.

Debtors: collect as fast as possible without upsetting customers. This requires tact and skill. Ensure that terms strike a balance between attracting customers and putting them off.

These will be discussed in more detail later in this chapter.

Working capital ratio

The working capital ratio is a useful efficiency indicator of a business's management of inventories, debtors and creditors.

$$\text{Working capital ratio} = \frac{\text{Stocks} + \text{Trade debtors} - \text{Trade creditors}}{\text{Sales}}$$

Example: A company has average stocks of £500,000, trade debtors of £300,000 and trade creditors of £200,000. Sales turnover is £2,500,000 p.a.

$$\text{Working capital ratio} = \frac{£500,000 + £300,000 - £200,000}{£2,500,000}$$

$$\text{Working capital ratio} = 0.4$$

This actually means that the business needs 40p of working capital for every £1 of sales. If sales increase by £500,000 then an extra £200,000 of working capital will have to be found (500,000 × 40p).

Some businesses generate cash so quickly that they operate on negative working capital and are funded by suppliers. For example, many retailers buy on credit but sell for cash, knowing that they can quickly turn stocks into cash and pay creditors. However, as we have seen in 2009, some have perhaps pushed this concept too far and it has been a contributing factor in their demise.

The working capital cycle

This is the time taken to convert cash which has been spent into cash collected from a customer. It is the average time raw materials are in stock, less the period of credit taken from suppliers, plus the time taken to produce and sell the goods, plus the time taken to collect cash from customers.

For example, a company takes 2 months' credit from its suppliers. Raw materials remain in stock for 1 month and it takes 3 months to produce and distribute a finished product. Customers take on average 2 months to pay.

The working capital cycle is:

Time raw materials are in stock	1
Trade credit taken	−2
Production and distribution time	3
Debt collection time	2
	4

The working capital cycle is 4 months.

OVERTRADING

Overtrading occurs when a business accepts orders but finds that it cannot fulfil them because it has insufficient working capital or other resources needed to produce and deliver. This may be a result of poor cash flow and working capital management.

It is an imbalance between sales, production, delivery capacity, finance and working capital and is more common in new, growing businesses. It can result in business failure, which is particularly frustrating when a business has a full order book. The risk of overtrading can be reduced by knowing the likely causes and through good financial management.

Common problems and symptoms include:

■ poor cash flow management

- paying over VAT output tax on invoices close to the end of the VAT period which have not yet been settled by the customer. For example, VAT on a sales invoice dated 29 March may become payable in a few weeks whereas the customer may take 60 days or more to pay

- a mismatch between the sales and production cycles. This can be helped by better supply chain management and improved stock turnover, enabling a manufacturer to hold fewer parts and components for shorter periods, making the manufacturing process more efficient. JIT techniques may help match sales and production better. This is a system where materials and components are delivered just in time to use, helping to shorten the manufacturing cycle, reduce stock holding costs and reduce the demands on working capital

- a rapid increase in sales turnover

- a rapid increase in debtors and stocks which is not matched by adequate funding

- constantly reaching bank overdraft or other facility limits

- being constantly close to invoice finance (discounting and factoring) facility limits

- a reduction in liquidity indicated by liquidity ratios

- high gearing

- high levels of interest

- lack of bank standby facilities

- Slow-moving stocks (poor stock-turnover ratio) or stock levels too high/increasing.

Balancing sales and marketing with investment is a basic requirement to avoid overtrading. On the one hand investors will not want to leave large sums of their funds 'sloshing around' waiting for orders that might or might not materialise. On the other hand the sales and marketing managers will not want to lose an order simply because the finance manager has not organised funds to be available. A bank standby facility to accommodate rapid increases and fluctuations in sales will help avoid either losing sales or overtrading.

STOCK TURNOVER AND OPTIMAL STOCK LEVELS

Stock levels should be optimal. They should be large enough to meet production and sales needs but low enough so as not to attract high levels of stock holding costs. Investors do not want their funds tied up in slow-moving stocks that attract only a low return on their investment. It is a matter of striking the optimal balance.

Stocks at too high a level may result in:

- unproductive use of investors' funds
- high stock holding costs such as finance, warehousing, insurance
- obsolescence and redundancy of stock
- deterioration of quality over time.

Stocks at too low a level may result in:

- inability to meet sales and production requirements
- loss of economies of scale from high-order levels. Loss of volume discounts
- higher administrative and other costs associated with frequent ordering.

To ensure optimal levels requires a proper system of stock control and then striking the right balance for stock volumes and economic order quantities.

Basic stock control system

Figure 10.2

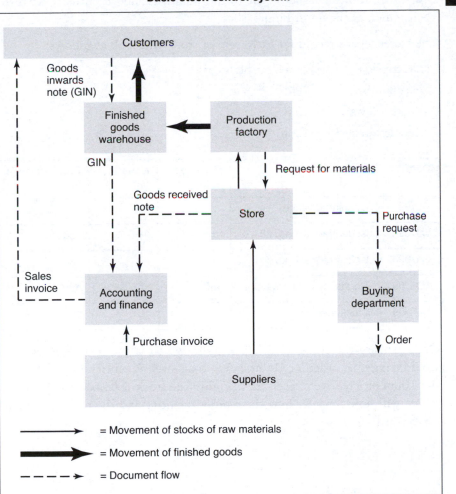

A basic stock control system has the elements shown in Figure 10.2.

1. The factory requests raw materials from the stores.

2. At this point stores may decide to order more materials. If they do they will raise a purchase request to the buying department.

3. The buying department will raise an order to the chosen supplier.

4. The supplier will despatch the materials and raise an invoice.

5. When the stores receive the materials they will raise a 'goods received note' and send a copy to the accounts department. The materials received will go into stock to be available for the factory.

6. The accounts department will compare the copy of the goods received note with the purchase invoice received from the supplier and if they match will make payment to the supplier.

7. Materials received in the factory will enter the production process and end up within finished goods sent to the warehouse and eventually with the customer, as shown in Figure 10.2.

The storekeeper's record for each item of stock will look as follows:

Description: 2cm clear plastic tube

Part number: 7842

Reorder level: 50m

Reorder quantity: 100m

Date	Transaction	Received 'm'	Issued 'm'	Stock balance 'm'
1/3/09	Opening balance			70
5/1/09	Issued request no. 687		20	50
6/1/09	Issued request no. 791		20	30
10/1/09	Goods inward note 342	100		130
14/1/09	Stock loss		10	120

On 5 January the stock level fell to 50m, which is the reorder level. This would trigger an order for 100m, being the reorder quantity. On 10 January the 100m ordered were received, bringing the stock level back to 130m.

We will now consider how the reorder quantity and the reorder level are established.

Economic batch quantity

The economic batch/order quantity is calculated from the formula:

$$EBQ = \sqrt{\frac{2cd}{ip}}$$

where c = delivery cost per batch

d = annual demand

i = stock holding cost (as a % of value or interest)

p = cost price per item

derivation:

stock holding cost $= \dfrac{ipQ}{2}$ [where $Q = EBQ$]

ordering cost $= \dfrac{cd}{Q}$

total relevant costs $(T) = \dfrac{ipQ}{2} + \dfrac{cd}{Q}$

differentiating $\dfrac{dT}{dQ} = \dfrac{ip}{2} + \dfrac{cd}{Q^2}$

set to zero and $\dfrac{ip}{2} - \dfrac{cd}{Q^2} = 0$

$\therefore \dfrac{ip}{2} = \dfrac{cd}{Q^2}$

$\therefore Q^2 = \dfrac{2cd}{ip}$

and $Q = \sqrt{\dfrac{2cd}{ip}}$

The total costs are minimised when the 'holding cost' equals the 'delivery cost'.

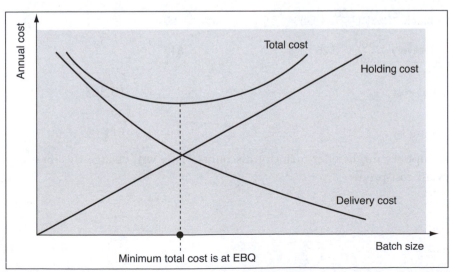

Minimum total cost is at EBQ

Example Canisters cost £4 each. They are normally ordered in batches of 200. Demand is constant at 2,500 p.a. Ordering cost is £25 per batch. Inventory carrying cost is 12½% of the cost of a canister. What is the EBQ and what saving will this make over the normal batch quantity of 200?

$$EBQ = \sqrt{\frac{2cd}{ip}}$$

$$c = £25$$

$$d = 2{,}500$$

$$i = 12\tfrac{1}{2}\%$$

$$p = £4$$

$$EBQ = \sqrt{\frac{2 \times 25 \times 2{,}500}{12\tfrac{1}{2}\% \times 4}}$$

$$EBQ = 500$$

Comparison of total costs using EBQ v normal quantity

EBQ

Canisters 2,500 @ £4	10,000	
Interest @ 12½% on average stock: $12\tfrac{1}{2}\% \left(\dfrac{500}{2} \times £4\right)$	125	
Delivery $\dfrac{2500}{500} \times £25$	125	
Total cost using EBQ	————	10,250

Normal order quantity

Canisters 2,500 @ £4	10,000	
Interest @ 12½% on average stock: $12\tfrac{1}{2}\% \left(\dfrac{200}{2} \times £4\right)$	50	
Delivery $\dfrac{2{,}500}{200} \times £25$	313	
Total cost	————	10,363
Saving by		£113

A supplier might offer quantity discounts. This will change the total relevant cost profile.

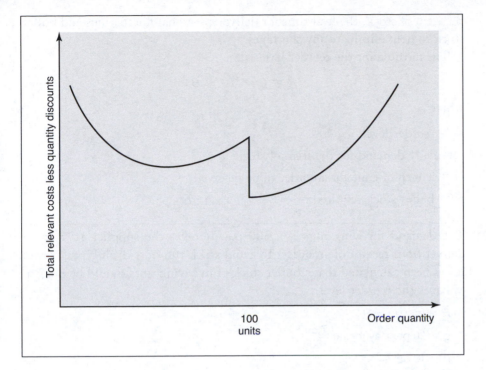

In the graph above a quantity discount is given for orders over 100.

A quantity discount produces two cost savings and one cost increase.

The savings are:

1. Lower price.

2. Fewer delivery costs.

The cost increase is:

1. Higher stock holding cost.

Therefore, a quantity discount is a benefit only if the savings exceed the cost increase of holding the stock. To determine whether a quantity discount produces an overall benefit, run the options through a spreadsheet model or use one of the excellent inventory software packages available.

Compare the total cost using EBQ with the total cost using the minimum order quantities that qualify for the discount.

Reorder level

This is the level at which an item of stock is considered for reordering. The objective is to always have enough stock to meet production demands without having too high a level of stock that ties up capital unnecessarily. In computing a reorder level it is necessary to consider the annual demand for the item of stock, the lead time for delivery, seasonal fluctuations and buffer stock to help eliminate any shortages.

The formula for the reorder level is:

$$R = (q \times L) + B$$

where:

R = reorder level

q = daily demand for the item of stock

L = length of time for an order to be received

B = buffer stock required.

Example

The demand for wing nuts is 7,300 p.a. It takes the supplier 10 days to deliver from receipt of an order. To avoid stock run-outs during peak times it has been calculated that a buffer stock of five wing nuts should be carried. What is the reorder level?

$R = (q \times L) + B$

$q = 20$ per day (being $\dfrac{7,500}{365}$)

$L = 10$ days

$B = 5$ units

$R = (20 \times 10) + 5$

$R = 205.$

The reorder level is when the stock is at 205 wing nuts.

Buffer stock

The buffer stock mentioned above is a safety margin included in the reorder level to allow for fluctuations in demand and to avoid run-outs. The level of buffer stock required is the level at which the combined stock run-out costs and the buffer stock holding costs are minimised.

The process for calculating this is as follows:

1. Calculate the stock run-out cost. This will include loss of sales and disruption. Multiply this by the probability of a run-out for various levels of buffer stock. Obviously the lower the level of buffer stock, the higher the probability of a run-out and the higher the predicted run-out cost.

2. Calculate the additional stock holding cost for the buffer stock at the various levels.

3. Select the buffer stock level which has the lower total cost.

Buffer stock units	Stock run-out costs £	Holding cost £	Total cost £
1,000	0	100	100
800	30	80	110
600	40	60	100
400	50	40	90
200	60	20	80 optimal level
100	70	20	90

In this example the optimal level for buffer stock is 200 units since the total expected cost is at its lowest (£80).

In practice it may be decided that a run-out of a particular item of stock is simply not acceptable for reasons that are not so easily quantified (brand value, reputation, etc.) and regardless of a low probability of a run-out a totally safe level is kept and the cost of this is considered necessary to protect the brand value, etc.

DEBTORS

In some businesses, retail for example, customers often pay immediately for their purchases. In others it is normal and necessary to allow a certain amount of time between invoicing and collection of the debt. This means that a business may have funds tied up in debtors and a financial objective is to keep this to a minimum whilst maintaining good relations with customers. Trade credit might be seen by customers as part of the value of the transaction and it could be a source of competitive advantage. A business with few but close customers might adopt a more lenient approach to debtors than a business with many smaller customers. Therefore, a business's credit policy and the length of time it allows customers to settle their debts might be based upon an optimal solution to the equation that:

- minimises debtor balances
- maximises customer satisfaction and retention.

Ageing and analysis of debtors

Most debtors' systems are able to sort outstanding invoices by date to provide an analysis of debtors by days outstanding. It might look like this:

Debtor	Up to 30 days £	31–60 days £	61–90 days £	Over 90 days £	Total £
A Garden Design Ltd	30,000	1,000			31,000
B Business Advisers	5,000	5,000			10,000
C Illustration Ltd	5,000	4,000	6,000	8,000	23,000
D Tutors	1,000	1,000			2,000
E Electrical Contractors	1,000	2,000	9,000	7,000	19,000
Totals	42,000	13,000	15,000	15,000	**85,000**
Percentage	49%	15%	18%	18%	

This shows how much of the total debtors' outstanding balance of £85K is current and how much is becoming or has become overdue. The debt-collection officer (credit manager) will focus on the older balances first. The percentages can be compared with the credit policy targets as a measure of efficiency as follows:

Days outstanding	Actual %	Target %
0–30	49%	50%
31–60	15%	25%
61–90	18%	25%
91+	18%	0%

Day sales outstanding (DSO)

Another rule-of-thumb measure is the day sales outstanding (DSO). This is simply the total debtors divided by the daily sales. For example, if total debtors were £85,000 when daily sales were £2,500 then the DSO would be 34 days.

$$DSO = \frac{\text{Debtors balance}}{\text{Daily sales}}$$

$$DSO = \frac{£85,000}{£2,500}$$

$$DSO = 34$$

Control of debtors

As sales increase debtors will also normally increase and so will the potential for increased long-outstanding debtor balances and possibly bad debts. To control debtors we need to:

- have a clearly defined credit policy that covers the rules regarding the granting of credit, the length of the credit period granted and the bad debt recovery policy
- have a system of credit checking
- have controls over the quality of goods and services and how this is reflected in customer agreements
- have effective administration and control systems in place.

Credit policy

The credit policy will define the rules for the granting of credit by defining the quality of customers and their credit rating. It will nominate an officer for approving credit or possibly a credit committee. The policy will normally define the contents of a 'request for credit' form, who should authorise the form and when it should be submitted to the credit officer or committee.

The credit policy will also define the length of time that credit will be granted for different levels of business and categories of customer. This will normally be expressed in terms of days. A definition will be given of what constitutes a doubtful or bad debt and what measures will be taken to collect. In summary the credit policy will include:

- periods of credit offered
- cash discounts for early payment
- creditworthiness checking
- late payment and bad debt actions.

Credit checking

There will be different levels of credit checking for different categories of customers. It will also depend upon their history as customers.

Most businesses use one of the established credit-checking agencies through a monthly subscription for a number of users. The credit-checking agency will enable searches for individuals and for companies and will give a credit score. A credit score is normally expressed as a number based upon a statistical analysis of an individual's or company's credit details and is mainly based on credit information normally sourced from credit bureaus. Lending institutions may use credit scores to determine the risk by lending to certain consumers and to determine who qualifies for a loan, risk/interest rate levels and credit limits.

The amount of credit checking will depend upon what is required under the credit policy. Normally it will include:

- an overall agency credit rating
- an analysis of accounts with satisfactory financial performance, position and key ratios
- parentage
- ability to pay
- references
- legality of business
- county court judgments (CCJs)
- checks against directors including CRB (Criminal Records Bureau) and CCJs.

Quality of goods and services

Clearly there need to be controls over the quality of goods and services and how this quality level is built into customer contracts so that there can be no disputes over payment arising from issues of quality. To ensure prompt payment, customer expectations have to be met.

Effective administration and control systems

These cover invoicing and the issue of statements, debtor analysis, customer query handling and overdue debt follow-up.

CASH CONTROL AND MANAGEMENT

A business needs a level of cash to meet its daily payments, to meet unexpected payments and to have available to take advantage of opportunities requiring a quick cash response such as favourable movements in rates of exchange. It needs an availability of cash. However, cash available would normally earn less than the equivalent sum invested in the business and it is, therefore, necessary to strike an optimal balance.

Cash controls and management include:

- cash forecasting (Chapter 5) and funds statements
- bank reconciliations
- internet-based banking systems
- transmission services
- security and armoured car services
- payment services such as BACS/VOCA, CHAPS
- balance reporting services
- cash concentration, offset and consolidations
- lockbox services
- sweep accounts
- electronic funds transfer
- currency.

Cash in the form of notes, coin and cheques can be expensive to process. Banks usually charge so many pence per hundred pounds of cash deposited (known as P%) or so many pence per cheque deposited. They may also charge on the value or volume deposited. Then there is the cost of security couriers. To minimise these charges many companies use the Post Office network as a transmission into their principal bank account. Set up by Girobank when it was owned by the Post Office (before being sold to the A&L), the system may help reduce the cash-processing charge to a customer who deposits via the Post Office because of the demand in the Post Office for cash and the huge economy of scale by using the PO network. Both of these factors to some extent can flow through to the depositing business. Many small and very large organisations deposit their cash and cheques this way in the UK. It works like this:

- A business deposits its cash and cheques into a Post Office.
- The business's transmission account is credited.
- A BACS or CHAPS payment is made to the business's principal bank account for the total deposited.
- The charge for depositing this way may be lower than making the deposit directly into the business's principal bank account.
- There are many more Post Offices than there are branches for a particular bank. This may help reduce courier costs and improve the ability to deposit in certain locations.

Cash management models

Since cash available would normally earn less than the equivalent sum invested in the business it is necessary to strike the optimal cash balance. There are many ways of doing this, including the Baumol Model and the Miller–Orr Model.

The Baumol Model

This is similar to the inventory/stock level model.

$$Q = \sqrt{\frac{2CS}{i}}$$

where:

S = cash to be used in each time period

Q = total amount to be raised to provide for S

C = cost to obtain new funds

i = interest cost of holding cash.

Example

Baldock Ltd requires £35,000 cash each year. The fixed cost to obtain new funds is £7,000. The interest cost of new funds is 7% p.a. The interest earned on short-term deposits is 5% p.a. How much cash should be raised and how often?

Solution

The cost of holding cash is 2%. This is the difference between the cost of funds and the interest earned on short-term deposits (7% − 5%).

Then:

$$Q = \sqrt{\frac{2 \times £7,000 \times £35,000}{0.02}}$$

$$Q = £156,525$$

The optimal amount of cash that Baldock Ltd should raise is £156,525.

Since Baldock requires £35,000 of cash each year it should raise the £156,525 every 4.47 years.

The Baumol Model is simple to use, but it might be difficult to accurately predict cash required over future periods. Also, there is no allowance for a 'buffer' of cash. Running out of cash could be expensive in many ways or even damaging to the business. Also, the cost of holding cash may increase with the amount held. However, it is an easy model to use and understand and when used in conjunction with a 'buffer' is a preferred method of many finance managers.

The Miller–Orr Model

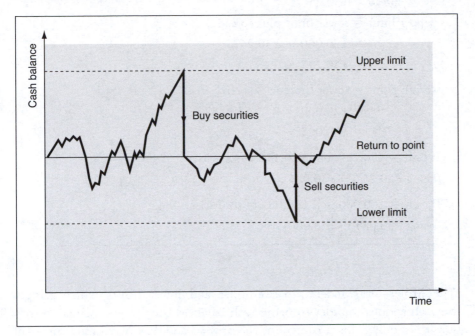

In this method the organisation buys or sells securities for cash to return its cash balance to a normal 'return point'. It will buy securities when the cash balance reaches a pre-defined upper limit. This will lower the cash balance to the 'return to point' and produce more interest income. If the cash balance falls to the predefined lower limit the organisation will sell securities, thereby increasing the cash balance to the 'return to point'.

This method is best explained by using an example.

Example

- The minimum safe cash balance is £20,000.

- The daily cash flow variance is £3,000,000.

- The transaction cost for buying securities is £75.

- The transaction cost for selling securities is £75.

- The interest rate is 0.016% per day (6% p.a.).

First calculate the spread between the upper and lower limits.

$$\text{spread} = 3\left(\frac{3}{4} \times \frac{\text{transaction cost} \times \text{cash flow variance}}{\text{interest rate}}\right)^{\frac{1}{3}}$$

$$= 3\left(\frac{3}{4} \times \frac{75 \times 3,000,000}{0.00016}\right)^{\frac{1}{3}}$$

$$\text{spread} = £30,257$$

$$\text{Upper limit} = \text{lower limit plus spread}$$

$$= £20,000 + £30,257$$

$$= £50,257$$

$$\text{Return point} = \text{lower limit} + \tfrac{1}{3}\text{ spread}$$

$$= £20,000 + \tfrac{1}{3} \times £30,257$$

$$= £30,085$$

If cash $= £50,257$, buy $£20,172$ of securities (being $£50,257 - £30,085$).

If cash $= £20,000$, sell $£10,085$ of securities (being $£30,085 - £20,000$).

The Miller–Orr Model imposes upper and lower limits which trigger buy/sell actions in order to bring cash balances back to an optimal 'return point'. In doing this it constrains the upward and downward movements of cash to within 'acceptable' limits.

WHAT TO DO WITH SHORT-TERM SURPLUS CASH

In the Miller–Orr Model we talked about buying and selling securities to keep cash balanced close to an optimal level. If an organisation has a long-term surplus of cash and no investment opportunities then it should consider returning this to shareholders. However, if a company has short-term surpluses then it will want to obtain the best possible return on this cash while retaining liquidity and of course security. The objective of investment of short-term surplus cash is therefore to:

- ensure security
- maintain liquidity
- maximise interest/return.

Security and liquidity are key to the investment of short-term cash surpluses. It is particularly appropriate to reinforce this point in light of the 2008 credit crunch and crisis. When investing surplus funds the credit rating of the institution is all important. Remember that the purpose of investing surplus cash is to retain security and required liquidity at a good rate of interest. It is not to seek to obtain the highest rate of interest at the cost of a reduction in liquidity or security. This would be taking on additional risk (gambling), which is not what working capital and cash management is all about.

In 2008, more than 110 UK local authorities and other bodies deposited a total of £944.07 million in Icelandic banks. The questions that need to be asked are:

- When the rating of the Icelandic bank was downgraded, why did those authorities that were able to do so not withdraw their funds?
- Should UK public funds (including short-term surpluses) be invested in more risky overseas institutions?
- Were the guidelines to local authorities correct?

The debate on this loss of UK public cash to an Icelandic bank will continue for some years. However, what is clear is that greater interest brings greater risk and the whole point of investing short-term cash surpluses is not to substantially increase the risk of security and liquidity.

Investment guidelines

When an organisation regularly has cash surpluses it requires investment guidelines agreed by its governing body, board and executive committee. These guidelines will include:

- security – credit rating and domicile of bank
- liquidity – term of deposits, ability to liquidate early and penalties for early liquidation
- interest rates – fixed or floating rates
- ease of realisation
- minimum and maximum amounts to be invested in certain types of investments
- types of investment
- cash convertibility
- risk policy.

Short-term investment options

Taking into account the investment guidelines an organisation will be faced with a number of investment options for its temporary cash surplus. These will include bank deposits, treasury bills, certificates of deposit and short-term debt instruments. Remember to:

- stick with investment guidelines
- ensure that security and liquidity are maintained.

WORKING CAPITAL FUNDING STRATEGIES

The working capital requirement of an organisation can be determined in simple terms by calculating the forecast average values of current assets less current liabilities. This requirement can be provided by a mixture of short- and longer-term funding. Having determined the requirement it is then necessary to establish the risks associated with a shortage of working capital and the attitude towards the level of risk that will be adopted. The strategy adopted is a trade-off between risk and return.

The play-it-safe and keep-options-open approach

This is adopted when an organisation feels that the cost of a working capital shortage is simply too high to risk. It will, therefore, aim to hold high levels of working capital. It might also decide that there are opportunities available for which it needs available cash. Keeping too high a level of cash available will, of course, reduce the profitability of the business.

The tight approach

An organisation adopts this approach to increase profitability and get the best return from assets. It may be adopted where there is more certainty over trading patterns and where cash can be forecast accurately. It involves keeping stock levels low, speeding up collections from debtors and delaying payment to creditors for as long as possible, as well as keeping surplus cash to a minimum. The down sides include greater risk and perhaps a loss of goodwill with suppliers resulting in higher prices for purchases. It might also upset customers and cause a reduction in sales.

The in-between approach

This adopts a mid-way approach between the above two strategies.

The relationship between assets and funding is shown in Figure 10.3.

Whatever working capital strategies are adopted they may be tempered by factors not easily controlled. For example, an organisation may decide to adopt a tight strategy where it allows short credit on receivables. However, if this period is different from that being offered by competitors it might be difficult to enforce without losing sales. Then there is the attitude of individual managers towards risk. Some may want to safeguard their departmental efficiency at the cost of keeping high levels of working capital – a possible suboptimal approach. There are many industry and competitive factors which will to some extent dictate what practices are acceptable in the market.

Assets and funding

Figure 10.3

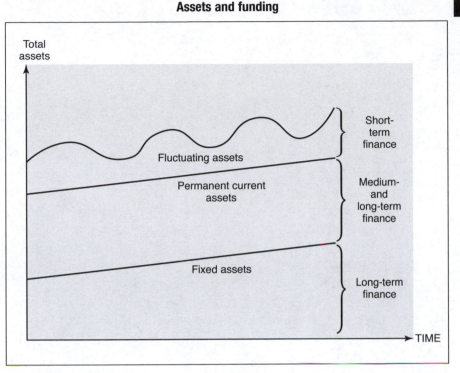

SUMMARY

Cash is vital and the key to this is management of the working capital pressure points of creditors, debtors and inventories. The control of cash and the selection of an appropriate working capital strategy to support the overall business strategy will help prevent unexpected cash problems. However, equally important is the relationship of a company with its bankers and in the next chapter we will discuss strategies for banking relationships.

Business finance, long-term versus short-term finance, gearing and capital structure

THE USES OF LONG-TERM AND SHORT-TERM FINANCE

An organisation should not use a source of short-term finance for its long-term needs. This is because a short-term availability of funds may not be long enough to fund a capital asset. An organisation should always match the term of the funds with the term of the asset they are funding. Therefore:

- use long-term funds for the finance of property, plant and equipment, for example, a term loan or mortgage to fund a freehold building
- use short-term funds to provide for stocks, debtors and other short-term current and fluctuating assets.

By now this statement will seem obvious to you, but it does not appear to have been so obvious to those banks and financial regulators that failed to notice the risk of lending long and borrowing short, that is using short-term sources of funds for long-term assets with the inevitable risk of a run on the bank. This fundamental principle was overlooked by regulators and banks in a rush to win market share and culminated in the 2008 credit crunch.

Sources of short-term finance

Sources of short-term finance suitable for funding stocks, debtors and other working capital needs include:

- bank overdrafts
- short-term loans
- creditors (delaying payment)
- invoice finance, both factoring and discounting (this may be considered medium term depending on the agreement)
- forfeiting.

Sources of long-term and other finance and derivatives

Some of the more common sources of long-term finance suitable for funding capital assets are listed below together with relevant derivative products that might be used to hedge them.

- Debt
- Equity – ordinary shares
- Preference shares
- Venture capital
- Commercial mortgages

- Debentures
- Derivatives
- Forward/futures
- Options
- Swaps
- Bonds
- Deep discount bonds
- Zero coupon bonds
- Convertible loan notes
- Unsecured notes and exchange-traded note (ETNs)
- Subordinated debt
- Eurobonds.

SHORT-TERM FINANCE

Overdraft

This is a short-term facility whereby a bank allows a customer to draw down on a current account and take it into deficit up to an agreed limit. The amount of the overdraft is set according to the size and credit rating of the customer. This type of facility provides the flexibility of short-term borrowing.

The charges for operating an overdraft will include:

- interest on the overdrawn balance – this is normally expressed as a percentage margin over base
- a facility fee or commitment fee
- penalty fees for exceeding the limit without authorisation.

Repayment:

- An overdraft is usually repayable on demand.

Term:

- Facilities usually run for 12 months and are subject to review. Bear in mind that overdrafts are repayable on demand and that if the bank considers the risk to have changed or its own liquidity has diminished it may 'pull back' at any time and reduce the limit or require repayment. There may be financial covenants in place that the customer has to adhere to.

Security:

- This will depend upon the amount of the overdraft but may include fixed or floating charges over assets. It very much depends upon the amount of the overdraft, the credit rating and the track record of the customer. The bank may also require guarantees.

Amount:

- The limit set is usually based upon proven income and cash flow and on knowledge that the bank has gained regarding the customer's trading pattern and ability to repay.

Purposes:

- To cover short-term trading deficits.
- To cover seasonal fluctuations.
- To enable a customer to win opportunities such as price reductions on buying materials at certain times or by paying early to obtain discounts.
- To bridge the gap between trading payments and receipts.

While overdrafts are one of the most popular sources of short-term finance it is clear that since they are repayable on demand and are also normally renewable annually they are not suitable for long-term finance. If a bank notices that an overdraft is becoming a permanent feature and that the customer is seeking an increase then it should require an explanation for this in terms of how the request is supported by increased trade. If it seems that the customer is using the overdraft for long-term needs then the bank should discuss alternative sources of finance with the customer.

Short-term loans

These are loans with fixed repayment schedules, usually for several years. The principal sum is drawn down at the beginning of the loan period and repaid along with interest over a number of instalments, usually monthly. The advantage to the customer is that he knows where he stands for a period of time. The bank can also monitor the repayment easily.

The loan will usually be secured over certain assets and will most often have covenants that the customer is required to adhere to or be in default.

The loan repayment is calculated by the following formula:

$$R = \frac{Pi\,(1 + i)^n}{(1 + i)^n - 1}$$

where:

R = annual repayment
P = principal
i = interest
n = period.

For example, what is the annual repayment on a £35,000 loan for 5 years at an annual rate of 12%?

Using the above formula:

$$R = \frac{£35,000 \times 0.12 \times 1.7623}{1.7623 - 1}$$

$$R = £9,710$$

Trade credit

Short-term finance is taken through the time that creditors allow between delivery of goods and services and when they expect payment. This is normally between 30 and 90 days. In addition to the normal terms of trade a business might take longer to pay its creditors, although this might damage the relationship and may invoke late-payment fees depending upon the terms of the contract. Taking trade credit might also result in a loss of discounts.

Finance of book debts – factoring and discounting

There are two main ways of providing finance for book debts: factoring and invoice discounting (receivables finance). These services are provided by factoring and invoice discount companies, both independent and those owned by banks. In the UK the trade association for invoice financiers is the Asset Based Finance Association (ABFA), which was formerly known as the FDA. This association states that it has 54 members providing finance to 46,000 businesses and transact over £173 billion of clients' invoices each year. The industry is also very significant throughout Europe, Australia, New Zealand and the US where it all started more than 200 years ago.

In any debt-finance transaction there are three parties involved. These are:

- the client – the party who is owed money and wants to raise finance on the debt
- the factor or the invoice financier – the intermediary who will provide finance to the client
- the debtor – the person who has received a valuable service or product from the client and who should pay the invoice.

Factoring

In factoring the book debt is effectively sold to the factor. The debtor will normally be aware that the client is using a factor (financier).

A typical factoring transaction works like this:

- The client raises an invoice to the debtor for services or goods provided.

- The client sends a copy of the invoice to the financier.
- The financier advances up to 90% of the gross invoice value to the client.
- The financier sends out statements and with assistance from the client collects the debt from the debtor.
- The financier then pays the client the balance of the invoice less charges for providing the service and funds.

The charges will typically include:

- an interest charge, normally expressed as a percentage above the bank base rate
- an administration charge expressed as a percentage of the gross invoice value
- an arrangement fee
- audit and debtor survey fees.

There may also be other charges and penalties for late payments and bad debts.

Discounting

Invoice discounting works a little differently from factoring. The book debts are effectively given as security for an advance. The client retains responsibility for collections. With an invoice-discounting facility the debtor will not normally be aware that the client is using an invoice financier.

- The client raises an invoice to the debtor.
- The client then sends the financier a sales day book listing.
- The financier then advances typically up to 90% of the gross debts.
- The client sends out statements to the debtor and collects cash in as he would usually do.
- The client receives payment from the debtor and banks this cash into a trust account.
- The client then receives the balance of debtor receipts less charges.

Charges include:

- a discount rate expressed as a percentage above the bank base rate
- a commission fee (administration charge) expressed as a percentage of turnover
- a CHAPS money-transfer fee.

General conditions in most invoice finance deals

In both factoring and discounting the amount that an invoice financier will advance against a debt will depend upon the quality of the debt and the spread of debtors. Generally the greater the spread, the lower the risk and the higher the concentration into fewer debtors, the greater the risk.

The financier will normally impose operational conditions upon the client and may require additional security. Examples are:

- debtor funding limits
- ongoing debtor surveys
- first ranking all asset debentures
- director warranties.

There may be penalty charges for non-compliance with operational and other conditions.

Bad debt insurance and non-recourse services

Invoice finance deals will often provide insurance against bad debts. This is called a non-recourse service. In the case of a factoring facility with non-recourse it will be the financier (the factor) who takes action to recover the debt against non-payers. This may be an area of tension between the client and the financier where the client will be mindful of protecting business relationships.

The benefits of debt finance are:

- improved cash flow
- ability to obtain better discounts from suppliers for earlier payments as a result of improved cash flow
- possibly less administration and ledger work
- possible insurance against bad debts
- growth finance through the release of sales value
- linking finance to sales performance
- less management time spent chasing slow payers.

The disadvantages of debt finance are:

- in the case of factoring the debtor will be aware that his supplier is using an invoice financier and this may create a negative impression in terms of customer relations and financial stability. However, this need not be justified and as the industry grows it will become a more accepted method of efficiently managing time and an aspect of working capital
- the client needs to be very aware of any penalties and ensure that these are manageable.

Comparative efficiency with other sources of finance

To accurately compare the efficiency of debt finance with other methods of shorter-term finance, such as an overdraft facility, it is necessary to evaluate not just the cost but also the benefits derived from the accelerated cash flow gained by debt financing and possibly savings in management time. Invoice finance can accelerate cash flow and if this had previously been a limiting factor in a company then care needs to be taken as to how to deal with more business activity once the cash-flow constraint has been removed.

The invoice financier's security

In the case of a factoring transaction (asset securitisation), there is an outright sale of a debt to the finance company. The financier is responsible for the collection of the debt and when things go wrong will take action against the debtor to recover the amount owing. The client will have little influence on events at this stage. The financier's ability to collect will depend largely on the quality of the debt and the ranking of the security on receivership. Invoice discounting, which is the provision of invoice finance against debtor balances, does not involve the outright transfer of ownership of the debt and the management of debtors and collections does not move to the financier. The client is still responsible for management of the debtors' ledger. These fundamental differences between factoring and discounting affect the financier's position in a receivership and whether they look to the debtor or the client for recovery.

To help protect the financier's position most invoice finance contracts will require an all-assets debenture over the client company or a first-ranking charge over other acceptable assets, cross-corporate guarantees, the personal warrantees of directors and other securities. The securities may help the financier's position when things go wrong but their many pitfalls emerge when trouble starts. Financiers must be fully familiar with security documents and be able to understand the implications of advice from their lawyers.

Invoice finance mechanics – factoring and discounting (short term or long term?)

I have included invoice finance under short-term finance. To an extent it is perhaps closer to medium-term finance. Some people even consider it to be long-term finance. It all depends upon the devil in the detail of the contract. The main thing to remember is why you are using invoice finance (to finance debtors which are a current asset) and to ensure that the invoice finance scheme reflects your needs.

Many providers of invoice finance belong to ABFA, but the industry, as it is referred to, is not regulated and the ABFA is not a regulatory body. Details of ABFA and its members can be found on www.abfa.org.uk.

As discussed, the two principal types of invoice finance are factoring and discounting.

Why use factoring?

Factoring is where a business sells its invoices to a factoring company. The business gets cash quickly and does not have to collect the debt. This is done by the factor. The cost of this to the business is that it will lose some of the value of the invoice.

The factoring company takes on the debt and has to collect it. Its profit comes from paying the business that raised the invoice less than the face value of the invoice.

Factoring can be useful to:

1. Get funds quickly.

2. Save the effort and time of having to collect debts.

3. Smooth out cash flow.

4. Provide funds secured by debts.

Some businesses, however, are not comfortable in letting the management of sensitive debtors be controlled by a third party.

Why use invoice discounting?

Invoice discounting is a form of invoice finance but is different to factoring. The business that raises the invoice receives finance based on the invoice and also retains control of the debtor and collections. For this reason discounting is usually offered to better-quality credits.

With invoice discounting a business will receive advances of funds against outstanding sales invoices. Up to 90% of the value of sales invoices may be paid out within 24 hours of invoices being raised. Funds advanced can be more when quality assets are available as security.

The discounter checks the business and surveys the debtor/customers. It then sets an advance limit to a certain percentage of the total outstanding sales ledger.

The business pays a monthly fee to the discounter and pays interest on the amount advanced. Each month, more money is advanced by the discounter or repaid by the business, it depends on whether the total amount owing has gone up or down.

If the invoice discounter agrees to advance say 75 per cent of the total owing and the total of outstanding invoices is changing, so will the amount advanced. If the outstanding debt falls, the business will repay 75 per cent of the fall. If the debt rises, the business will receive 75 per cent of the increase.

Features of invoice discounting are as follows:

- The business collects the debts and manages credit control.
- In the case of confidential discounting a business's customers do not need to know about the invoice discounting.
- The annual turnover for a discounting arrangement is often set to be at least £500,000; however, often smaller businesses are being accepted for invoice discounting. Discounters will review the credit history and profit record of the business and will have requirements regarding the quality of sales ledgers and procedures.
- The invoice discounter will audit and check regularly to see that the ledgers accurately reflect invoices and that the procedures are effective.
- The business may choose between recourse and non-recourse discounting facilities. This determines who is responsible for recouping unpaid invoices.

Many companies use discounting rather than factoring since it can offer a degree of confidentiality.

Invoice finance is not necessarily short-term or long-term finance. I have included it under short-term finance since it is used to fund current assets based on debtors' balances and because the facilities are normally subject to 3-monthly audit reviews. However, many organisations have invoice-discounting facilities in place for many years and consider them to be long term. It is really a question of the terms of the facility. Invoice finance is provided by the commercial banking arms of the major banks and also by specialised and independent invoice finance companies. At the time of writing the industry is not regulated in the UK. When choosing an invoice financier the quality of service and relationship management are all important. It is also necessary to examine the contract very closely, especially regarding default penalties and facility closure terms. These vary enormously between providers and a business will want to ensure that it obtains the type of deal it can manage. Rate and price are just two factors. The arrangement must be workable within budget.

Leasing

A lease is an agreement, which confers a right on one person (called a tenant or lessee) to possess property of another person (called a landlord or lessor) to the exclusion of the owner landlord. The relationship between the tenant and the landlord is called a tenancy. The right to possession by the tenant is sometimes called a leasehold interest. A lease can be for a fixed period of time but may be subject to termination sooner. Consideration for the lease is called rent. Types of lease arrangements include finance leases, operating leases and sale and leaseback agreements.

Leases are offered by specialised leasing organisations including banks, insurance companies and other financial intermediaries.

The decision as to whether to buy or lease an asset and the decisions regarding the type of lease (finance, operating or sales and leaseback) are investment appraisal decisions and are covered in Chapter17.

TERM AND LONG-TERM FINANCE AND FUNDS

Long-term finance and funds are for long-term needs such as fixed assets and major investments.

The first decision is whether long-term funds are to be equity or debt and what the ideal level of gearing (debt to equity) should be. Gearing will be covered later in this chapter.

Equity finance – ordinary shareholders

Equity finance is raised through the issue and sale of ordinary shares to people who wish to invest in the company. This can be done through either a new issue or a rights issue.

Ordinary shares in the UK and usually in the US have a nominal value (sometimes called a face value). The nominal value is usually the price at which the shares were first issued, however it usually bears no relationship to the current market value. Dividends on shares are expressed as a percentage of their nominal value. In a company's accounts share capital is recorded at its nominal value and any excess over this is recorded in the UK as 'share premium' or in the US as 'paid in surplus'. In some countries it is not uncommon for shares to have no nominal value.

Sometimes a company may issue bonus shares to existing shareholders in proportion to their existing shareholding. This is not a direct source of finance as is a direct issue of shares for cash.

The shares in a quoted company may change hands frequently through the stock market and this exchange has no direct financial effect on the company.

Ordinary shareholders are the owners and risk takers of the company enjoying the final profits and enduring any losses. The amount of profits distributed to shareholders is a matter for the directors to decide. Distributing profits reduces cash funds available and by reducing shareholders' funds increases the gearing of the company.

The cost of equity should be more than the cost of debt. This is because equity shareholders take the greatest risk and therefore expect the highest return.

A company will seek a stock market listing for its shares through a public offer or through a placing. The reasons and advantages for seeking a stock market listing include:

- improved ability to market shares
- better access to a wide pool of finance
- to obtain a better public image
- to free up funds of original owners
- easier acquisition and growth potential.

There are certain disadvantages in a stock market listing. These include:

- more investors and perhaps a loss of control
- greater reporting and public accountability
- a requirement to comply with stock exchange rules
- additional costs in making shares issues.

There are three ways in which an unquoted company can obtain a listing on a stock market. These are:

- IPO (initial public offering)
- placing
- introduction.

IPO

An IPO is an invitation to buy shares based upon information supplied in a prospectus. It is used to sell shares to the general public and is also known as 'going public'. Usually, an IPO will occur when an issuing house (a merchant bank or stockbroker) acquires a large number of shares and offers them to the public and institutional investors. The issuing house may obtain the shares from existing shareholders or from the company by way of a direct allotment.

Placing

This is where shares are placed with a small number of specific investors such as pension funds or insurance companies. A placing has certain advantages over an IPO in that it may cost less, it is likely to be faster and disclosure may possibly be less arduous. The disadvantages are fewer shareholders and more control by a large holder. This may not be desirable. When a company first comes onto the market in the UK the maximum number of shares that can be placed is 75%.

Introductions

An introduction is a quotation on a stock market without shares being made available on the market. This may happen where shares in a large company can be seen to exist to increase marketability or to obtain a valuation.

Costs of a share issue on a stock market

These will include:

- underwriting costs where an institution may be required to underwrite by buying a percentage of the issue that is not subscribed for by the general public in order to reduce the risk of under subscription
- advertising and PR costs
- prospectus costs
- stock market listing fees
- issuing house fees
- auditors' and solicitors' fees.

The pricing of shares for a stock market issue

When deciding upon a price the company will want to ensure that it does not overprice and end up under-subscribed. Neither will it want to under-price and miss the opportunity for raising more cash with fewer shares. Normally the issue price will be based on the price earnings ratio of the company's last reporting period and this will enable the potential investors to compare and contrast with their other investment opportunities. When deciding on a price it is normal to take the following factors into account:

- the price earnings ratio
- current market conditions (bull or bear market)
- the prices of similar companies
- shareholder requirements
- the present and future trading prospects of the company.

Rights issues

This is an offer to existing shareholders to exercise their right to buy more shares, usually at a price that is lower than the market price at the time of the issue. The invitation to subscribe is in proportion to existing shareholdings and as such is likely to retain a similar ownership ratio. Generally rights issues are cheaper than IPOs to the public at large because there is no requirement to issue a prospectus, underwriting costs will be less and

---

A rights issue price determination

The normal profit after tax for Heritage is 15% on capital employed.

Capital structure is:

100,000 ordinary shares of £2 each	£200,000
Retained profits	£80,000
Shareholders' funds	£280,000
Present earnings at 15% on capital employed	£42,000

Directors want to raise £100,000 from a rights issue when the current market price per share is £3.30.

Earnings per share £42,000/100,000   42p

Earnings after rights issue 15% (£280,000 + £100,000)£57,000

What effect would different issue prices have on earnings per share and how would EPS be diluted?

Rights issue price £ (less than market value)	Number of new shares £100,000 divided by rights issue price	Total number of shares after the issue	EPS £57,000/total number of shares	Dilution against current EPS of 42p
3.10	32,258	132,258	43p	+1p
2.70	37,037	137,037	42p	0
2.40	41,667	141,667	40p	−2p
2.20	45,455	145,455	39p	−3p
1.80	55,556	155,556	37p	−5p
1.70	58,824	158,824	36p	−6p
1.60	62,500	162,500	35p	−7p
1.50	66,667	166,667	34p	−8p
1.40	71,429	171,429	33p	−9p

The current market price is £3.30 per share. If the new issue is at £2.70 there will be no dilution in earnings per share.

general administrative costs will be less. A rights issue is obviously more beneficial to the existing shareholders of the company and if all existing shareholders take up their rights the relative voting rights will remain unchanged. A rights issue will reduce gearing and this may be beneficial.

The issue price will have to be less than the market price to attract buyers and more than the nominal value so as not to contravene aspects of company law. The price should be set to attract shareholders to buy but not too low or it will result in an excessive dilution of the company's earnings per share. The following is an example of how a rights issue could affect earnings per share. This type of analysis provides useful information when deciding upon the price of a rights issue.

Once a rights issue has been announced the existing shareholders will become entitled to the right to subscribe for extra shares. Their shares are then called 'cum rights' and are traded as such. Once the new shares are actually traded on the exchange the rights will no longer exist and the old shares become 'ex rights'.

Example   A company offers the right to subscribe for one new share for £2 for every five shares held. The cum rights price is £2.50. What is the theoretical ex rights price?

5 shares @ £2.50	=	£12.50
1 share @ £2	=	£2.00
6 shares	=	£14.50

The theoretical ex rights price after the rights issue is £14.50/6 = **£2.42**

Note that the value of the rights issue to the shareholder is 42p (£2.42–£2.00). This is because the price being asked for the new shares is £2 but the value after the issue is expected to be £2.42. Of course, this is only theoretical because the actual market price after the rights issue could be different.

Preference shares

Preference shares have preferential rights over ordinary shareholders to profits and also to assets on winding up. Like ordinary shares they are risk taking and are in a sense part of equity capital. However, they are much lower risk than ordinary shares and are often considered as part of loan capital. Preference shareholders are usually entitled to a dividend on their shares at a stated level before any dividend can be paid out to ordinary shareholders. In the event of the company winding up, any surplus assets after prior claims (taxation, salaries, creditors, lenders, etc.) will be used to repay the preference shareholders up to their full nominal value before any final surplus funds are released to ordinary shareholders.

Venture capital

Venture capital is a type of private equity capital provided to high-growth companies in order to provide a return to the venture capitalist through an eventual realisation such as an IPO or company sale. Venture capital is generally provided as cash in exchange for an equity stake in the company. It may come from either institutional investors or rich individuals. Venture capital may be an option for new companies that are too small to raise capital through the stock exchange market and that do not have the track record to raise a bank loan.

A venture capitalist (VC) is a person or investment firm that provides venture capital and normally also provides technical or management expertise. Because of the higher risk taken on by a venture capitalist they will require significant equity and control over the company they invest in. They are very selective and this is rightly an expensive source of finance. However, since they are selective and want to ensure the companies they invest in are successful they provide a good test for aspiring new businesses.

Venture capitalists are generally interested in:

- start-ups
- management buy-outs (MBOs)
- new markets and business development
- exit strategies for proprietors.

A proposal to a VC should have a clearly defined market, strategy, product innovation, unique selling point (USP)/competitive advantage and competent management team in place. Each VC will have a different capability and turnover requirement. This is often in the £1 million to £100 million range; some cover the higher end while others only have the capacity for smaller deals. Some VCs specialise in a business sector – airlines and transport, for example.

The British Venture Capital Association (BVCA) has over 210 full members and more than 200 associate members. It can be found on www.bvca.co.uk.

Commercial mortgages

Commercial mortgages are available from the commercial banking arms of major banks and from specialist commercial lending institutions. They are a good way to finance property for business purposes and provide a flexible and finance solution. With a commercial mortgage the lender has a legal charge over the property until the full amount of the loan (principal and interest) has been repaid. The property charged is at risk if the loan or interest is not repaid on time. They are usually tailor made for purchasing factories, warehouses, shops, offices and other fixed business assets that offer valuable and enduring security.

The advantages of commercial mortgages in the UK include:

- repayment terms of between 2 and 30 years
- normally the ability to borrow up to 75% of the purchase price or valuation, whichever is the lower
- either a fixed or a variable interest rate
- principal amounts generally from £25,000 upwards
- monthly or quarterly repayment plans
- often the ability to take capital repayment holidays
- rate may be LIBOR-linked – generally for loans above £100,000
- can be tailor made to customer needs
- simple to arrange.

Some commercial mortgage providers impose restrictions on the uses of the charged premises such as the ability to sublet and restrictions on use. The details in the terms of the loan agreement need to be fully understood and considered in relation to both present and possible future uses of the charged property.

Debentures

A debenture is a certificate of loan agreement given under the company's seal that has an undertaking that the debenture holder will get a fixed return when the debenture matures. The debenture deed will state the rights of the holder in terms of the redemption date and value and of interest. In corporate finance it is a long-term debt instrument used by governments and large companies to obtain funds.

Normally debentures are secured over the assets of the company by a mortgage deed which would enable the debenture holder to force a company, through the court, to sell secured assets in the case of a default in repayment. Some debentures are 'convertible'. This means that at a certain time they can be converted into ordinary shares. Some are irredeemable. In the US a debenture refers to a debt security which is not specifically protected by assets. Different countries may have different meanings for the term. It is important to understand the details of a debenture deed for there is no universal generic meaning.

In the UK debentures can be bought and sold once they have been issued. The market price will be determined by the debenture's rate of interest compared to the general rates of interest of other instruments in the market. This will mean that as general interest rates rise in the market, the value of a debenture will fall. Once a debenture approaches maturity its value will become closer and closer to the redemption value.

A debenture may carry a fixed charge, a floating charge or no charge (a naked debenture) over the assets of a company.

- Fixed-charge debenture – this carries a fixed charge over specific assets such as freehold property, leasehold property or other assets.
- Floating-charge debenture – this carries a floating charge over some or all of the assets of a company. A floating charge does not deprive the company from dealing with assets until a default occurs. A floating charge 'crystallises' once a company defaults on the terms in the debenture deed.
- A simple naked debenture carries no charge over any assets of the company.

Debentures may be issued at par, at a premium or at a discount.

When debentures are secured by a charge over assets it is usual to appoint trustees on behalf of the debenture holders to have custody of the documents of title and security, to ensure that the security is maintained, to check that covenants are complied with and to exercise any powers conferred by the trust instrument or by law.

Debentures are usually redeemed by way of setting up a sinking fund, out of profits or by the issuance of new debentures or shares. Debenture holders are not shareholders and have no voting rights.

Debentures provide lenders with certain advantages which may make them an attractive investment option and therefore a useful way of raising funds for a company. These advantages include:

- the possibility of a charge over company assets
- some measure of control for the lender through covenants
- less risk of fraudulent preference
- remedies in action for the holder, including the right to appoint a receiver, exercise power of sale and apply for a court order.

There are certain disadvantages and these include the ability of the company to deal in assets in a way that might erode the security value and the difficulty in placing a realistic valuation on a debenture. When exercising rights under a mortgage debenture the value of the assets can become depressed under a forced sale.

Debentures have also been used to raise funds for sports venues from time to time. These debentures may pay little or no interest but might entitle the holder to certain privileges such as the right to buy tickets for events at the venue.

Derivatives for hedging loan repayments

Derivatives are financial instruments whose values are derived from the value of some underlying asset, index or other item. The 'underlying' on which a derivative is based can be an asset such as a commodity, equity or loan or an index such as exchange rates, interest rates, stock market prices or a price index.

The main types of derivatives are forwards/futures, options and swaps. Derivatives are often used to hedge against a risk of loss arising from changes in the value of the underlying. They may also be used to speculate. In respect to loan repayments they may be used to hedge against future currency or interest rate movements.

Futures/forwards are contracts to buy or sell an asset on a future date at a price specified today. The term futures contract refers to a contract written by an exchange/clearing house where the contract can be traded. A forward contract is a contract written directly by the parties themselves.

Options contracts give the owner the right, but not the obligation, to buy (a call option) or sell (a put option) an asset. The price at which the trade takes place is called the strike price. The option contract will specify a maturity date. With a European option the owner has the right to require the sale to occur on (but not before) the maturity date; in the case of an American option the owner can require the sale to take place at any time up to the maturity date.

Swaps are contracts to exchange payments on or before a specified future date based on the underlying value of currencies/exchange rates/interest rates/commodities or other assets.

A derivative can also be a combination of two or three elements of the basic types described above. The term swaption refers to an instrument that gives the holder the right but not the obligation to enter into a swap on or before a future date.

Derivatives are discussed in later chapters on hedging and risk management. They are mentioned briefly here since they are relevant to currency and interest rate risk management related to loan repayment.

Bonds

Bonds are long-term debts issued by a company, such as debentures (mentioned above) or loan notes. Loan notes are long-term debt raised by a company. They may be either redeemable or irredeemable in the various forms of floating rate, zero coupon or convertible.

Deep discount bonds

Deep discount bonds are bonds issued at a large discount against the nominal value of the bond but which can be redeemed at maturity at a price that is above par. For this reason they will carry a low rate of interest.

Example

Loan notes with a face value of £30 issued in 2009 at £20 and redeemable in 2014 at par.

This would provide the holder with a £10 return over a 5-year period. The tradable value would generally get closer to the par value towards maturity. The holder would get taxed on the realised gain only at maturity. This has an advantage over the interest element which is taxed yearly.

The advantage to the issuing company is a low cost of issue and servicing and no repayment for 5 years. The issuing company may be able to deduct notional interest each year depending on the tax regime.

Zero coupon bonds

These carry zero interest but are issued at a discount to their redemption value. They carry the same tax advantage as deep discount bonds described above.

The advantages to the issuing company are immediate cash received with no repayment until the redemption date and the redemption cost is certain and can be planned for well ahead.

Convertible loan notes

These are bonds that carry the right to be converted to another form of security at a future date and price. The most common form of convertibles are bonds that can be converted to ordinary shares. Once a convertible has been converted into another form of security it cannot be converted back into the original form. The conversion premium is the difference between the issue value of the note and the conversion value. The calculation of conversion value and premium is shown in the following example.

Example

9% convertible loan notes quoted at £150 per £100 of nominal value. Conversion date is in 5 years' time. Conversion will be for 30 ordinary shares for every £100 of nominal loan note value. The current share price is £4.50. The bondholders want to obtain a return of 10% p.a. (compounded) over the 5-year period. What growth rate in the share price is required? What is the conversion premium as an amount per share and as a percentage of the conversion value?

Year	Quoted price (£)	Interest	10% discount factor	Present value (£)
0	(150)	0	1.000	(150.00)
1		9	0.909	8.18
2		9	0.826	7.43
3		9	0.751	6.76
4		9	0.683	6.15
5		9	0.621	<u>5.59</u>
				<u>(115.89)</u>

Therefore, to produce a minimum 9% return for investors the value of the 30 shares on conversion must be £115.89 or more. This means that the today money value at the end of year 5 has to be £186.62 (£115.89/0.621). Since the current market value of the shares is £135.00 (30 × £4.50), the required growth factor in the shares over the period is 1.382 (186.62/135.00).

Then:

(1 + growth) compounded for 5 years = 1.382

1 + growth = 1.067

growth = 0.067.

This means that the rate of growth in the share price needs to be 6.7% p.a. for each of the 5 years.

$$\text{The conversion premium will be: } \frac{£150 - (30 \times £4.50)}{30}$$

$$= £0.50 \text{ per share}$$

This can also be expressed as a percentage of the conversion value:

$$\frac{£0.50}{£4.50} \times \frac{100}{1} = 11\%$$

A company will want to ensure that it issues loan notes with as high as possible conversion premium because this will mean that on conversion it will have to issue a lower number of new shares. Investors will pay a premium that they feel reflects the future growth value of the company and the actual market price of convertibles will be influenced by the price of other debt, the time to conversion, current conversion values and other market factors concerning risk and expectations.

Unsecured notes and ETNs

These are simply notes that are not backed up by any form of collateral.

An exchange-traded note is an unsecured and unsubordinated debt security issued by an underwriting bank and backed only by the credit standing of the issuer. They carry additional risk compared with secured notes and enable investors to access the returns of market performance. The returns of ETNs are, therefore, linked to market benchmarks. The underwriting bank promises to pay on maturity the amount reflected in the index minus fees.

ETNs are linked to the performance of a market benchmark but they are not equities, although they are traded on exchanges. They do not own anything that they are tracking.

Subordinated debt/loan

Subordinated debt or subordinated loan ranks after other debts if a company should fall into receivership. It is subordinate in that the lenders have lower status in relationship to normal debt.

Subordinated debt holders will expect a higher return for the greater risk they have taken. This is because subordinated debt is repayable only after other debts have been paid and carry more risk.

Eurobonds – Eurodollars, Euroyens

Eurobonds are long-term loans that are normally raised by large international organisations with high credit ratings and sold to investors in a number of countries. They are often denominated in a currency other than that of the country that issued the bond. Eurobonds are usually for 5 to 20 years and can be traded by holders. Typically they are used to raise long-term finance for large capital-investment programmes. There may be a significant foreign currency exchange risk associated with a long-term currency loan such as a Eurobond which needs to be covered and added into the cost of borrowing if it cannot be 'matched'.

Eurobonds are denominated in various currencies and named accordingly (Eurodollars, Euroyens). They may be bearer bonds payable to the bearer. Eurobonds are commonly held and traded within the Euroclear or Clearstream clearing systems, with coupons being paid electronically.

GEARING AND CAPITAL STRUCTURE

We have previously discussed both equity and loan finance. We will now explain gearing, which is a term used to describe the ratio between equity and loan finance. Gearing is called leverage in the US.

- High gearing is when a company has a high proportion of loan to equity finance.

- Low gearing is when a company has a low amount of loan finance compared with its equity.

A basic definition of gearing

There are various definitions of gearing and of equity and loan capital. We will discuss these in due course. For now a simple definition of gearing will suffice.

$$\text{Gearing} = \frac{\text{Loan capital}}{\text{Equity}}$$

Thus if loan capital is £100K and equity is £200K gearing will be:

$$\frac{£100K}{£200K} = 0.5$$

The effects of gearing on shareholders and lenders

The effect of gearing on the return to shareholders is considerable. For example, when profits are high and interest rates are not too high the shareholders will benefit from high gearing. Consider the following example.

10% long-term loan	£700,000	
Equity (share capital and reserves)	£200,000	
Total capital employed	£900,000	
Gearing	3.5 (high)	

	2009 YR	2010 YR
Profit before interest and tax	90,000	180,000
Interest	70,000	70,000
Profit before tax	20,000	110,000
Tax @ say 35%	7,000	38,500
Profit after interest and tax	13,000	71,500

Although the profits before interest and tax in the year 2010 have doubled from 2009, the profits available to the shareholders after interest and taxation have actually increased by 5.5 times! So in this instance being highly geared has benefited the shareholders enormously. This is because net profits belong to shareholders and in a highly geared company there are fewer share-holders' interests to share the net profits. However, if interest rates had been very high and profits had been lower the position could be very different. Using a spreadsheet it is easy to prepare a sensitivity analysis on interest rates and on different profit levels. First substitute the 10% interest rate with various rates and see the effect on net profits available to shareholders. Then try substituting different profit levels. Substitute one variable at a time and see how sensitive changes to shareholders' final available profits will be to change.

Owners of a business might like their company to be highly geared. Interest costs are tax deductible whereas shareholder dividends are not. Ideally, shareholders would like to get rich on outside providers of low-cost loans. However, from a lender's perspective high gearing normally represents higher risk and they will want a greater return. High-interest gearing represents a higher danger of failure and insolvency.

In addition to the above method of calculating a gearing ratio there are a number of others in common use:

$$\text{Financial gearing} = \frac{\text{Prior charge capital}}{\text{Equity (total shareholders' funds)}}$$

or

$$\text{Financial gearing} = \frac{\text{Prior charge capital}}{\text{Total capital employed}}$$

The definition of total capital employed may either include or exclude certain items such as minority interests and deferred taxes and income. Using the first definition a company with a gearing ratio of less than 100% would be considered lowly geared. Using the second definition a company would be considered as lowly geared if the ratio was less than 50%. When comparing gearing ratios between companies or even in the same company over different periods of time it is important to ensure that a consistent method is being used.

Market-value gearing ratios

A gearing ratio may sometimes be based on the market values of debt and equity. This may be useful to potential investors when they are trying to determine the debt capacity of a company and its ability to borrow more. A disadvantage of this method is that it does not necessarily give such a good indication of assets for security as does gearing based on balance sheet values. The formula is:

$$\text{Market financial gearing} = \frac{\text{Market value of debt (including redeemable preference shares)}}{\text{Market value of debt plus market value of equity}}$$

Operational gearing

Operational gearing shows the risk involved in making low profits or losses. This measures the risk of having a high level of fixed costs. A company with high fixed costs will be at a greater risk if sales and profits slump because the contribution will also slump and there may not be an adequate margin between contribution and total fixed costs. Operational gearing gives a measure of this risk.

$$\text{Operational gearing} = \frac{\text{Contribution}}{\text{Profit before interest and tax}}$$

(contribution has been defined previously as sales less the variable cost of sales).

If operational gearing is low, the business risk will be low. This is because fixed costs will be low.

Interest cover

This measure shows how many times interest is covered by profits before interest and taxation. This is a most useful measure to lenders and to some extent demonstrates the company's capacity for more borrowing.

$$\text{Interest cover} = \frac{\text{Profit before interest and tax}}{\text{Interest}}$$

If the interest cover is low this may indicate that profits are too low for the level of financial gearing of the company.

Debt ratio

Debts may also be compared to total assets to give a measure of financial risk.

$$\text{Debt ratio} = \frac{\text{Total debts}}{\text{Total assets}}$$

The comparative costs of short-term and long-term debt, equity and issues of flexibility

It is most likely that, over time, the cost of debt will be lower than the cost of equity. This is because equity carries a greater risk and expects a greater return. Generally, long-term debt is higher than short-term debt because a long lender will feel that the risk is greater. But the arrangement fees of short-term debt may be the same as for long-term debt and, therefore, proportionately more over time.

Being locked into a long-term loan that has interest rates fixed for a long period may be beneficial if rates rise but not if they fall. There may be penalties for early repayments.

Interest has to be paid whatever the level of profit but dividends to shareholders do not.

Deciding on the optimal capital structure will be considered later in a separate chapter.

The effect of gearing on earnings per share and profits before interest and taxation

Another measure of financial gearing uses the earnings per share and the profits before interest and taxation.

$$\text{Financial gearing} = \frac{\%\ \text{change in EPS}}{\%\ \text{change in PBIT}}$$

This is a useful relationship to examine different financing plans.

Other key ratios to consider when determining gearing and capital structure

When considering a capital/gearing restructure also consider the effect on dividend cover, price earnings ratios and dividend yields.

$$\text{Dividend cover} = \frac{\text{Earnings per share}}{\text{Dividends per share}}$$

For example, if gearing is increased then interest will increase and earnings will decrease. This will reduce dividend cover.

$$\text{Price earnings ratio (PE)} = \frac{\text{Market share price}}{\text{Earnings per share}}$$

An increase in PE may demonstrate a market view of the projects that additional borrowing and an increased gearing fund.

$$\text{Dividend yield} = \frac{\text{Dividend per share}}{\text{Market share price}}$$

Increased borrowing and gearing affects dividends and dividend cover. The effect on market share prices will also be reflected in the dividend yield.

Summary of gearing and capital structure analysis

A company's capital structure and gearing are determined by the proportions of debt and equity capital. The optimal capital structure will maximise the value of the company.

Capital structure/gearing decisions are determined by:

- the tax deductibility of interest, which tends to increase the desirability of debts/loans and increase gearing

- the increased financial risk from increased use of debt, which tends to moderate the use of debt in the firm's capital structure.

This means that the optimal capital structure is a balance between these two factors.

Advantages from high gearing and using cheaper debt are offset or partially offset by increases in financial risk.

The reality is that it is difficult to precisely determine a company's optimal capital structure. Demand sustainability and volatility are considerations as well as cost stability when making gearing decisions. The decision maker is also on shifting ground and there are often a number of acceptable debt/asset ratios.

EXPORT FINANCE

Banks, specialist financial institutions and other organisations provide a range of services to help finance and insure export business. A few of the more commonly used services are bills of exchange, letters of credit and export guarantees/insurance. Details of these are given below.

Bill of exchange

The Bills of Exchange Act (1882) defines a bill of exchange as 'an unconditional order in writing, addressed by one person to another, signed by the person giving it, requiring the person to whom it is addressed to pay on demand, or at a fixed or determinable future time, a sum certain in money to or to the order of a specified person, or to bearer'.

Overseas trade finance may be provided by bills of exchange. When a banker discounts a bill he effectively buys the bill from the customer at a price that is normally the face value less the discount. This discount is the equivalent of interest.

Letters of credit

A letter of credit (LC) is a document addressed by a banker to a correspondent or agent requesting that an advance be made to the holder and to debit the sum paid to the banker. Letters of credit are used in export finance. An LC is not an unconditional order like a bill of exchange, it is not negotiable and requires no acceptance. There are various forms of LCs, including revocable, confirmed, unconfirmed, transferable, back to back and revolving. However, they are generally irrevocable or confirmed to a beneficiary against documents as defined in the LC.

Export credit guarantees

The Export Credits Guarantee Department (ECGD) is the UK's official export credit agency. It helps UK exporters of capital equipment and project-related goods and services win business and complete overseas contracts with confidence by providing insurance against non-payment by overseas buyers. It also provides guarantees for bank loans to facilitate the provision of finance to buyers of goods and services from UK companies. The department has many years' experience with new and developing markets.

BANK RELATIONSHIP STRATEGY

In Chapter 10 we discussed the importance of cash. In this chapter we have discussed short- and long-term finance, gearing and elements of capital structure. While working capital management and appropriate sources of business finance are essential, they do not amount to much if an inappropriate bank relationship strategy is in place. How many times have you heard businesses blame banks when they go under because of a lack of support? There is no doubt that many banks sometimes act too quickly to protect their own position at great cost to a business. There are many horror stories out there. However, it is likely that the majority of these situations could have been prevented if the company had had the correct bank relationship strategy in place from the outset and had not made itself quite so vulnerable. Consider the following sad case.

A long-standing family-run caravan park with no previous borrowing and plenty of spare freehold land wanted to expand by building log cabins. It went to its local bank and entered into a loan agreement to fund the construction. The company granted the bank a charge over all land, buildings and construction materials. The contract with the bank had many covenants, including turnover levels. As often happens with building contracts the work slipped and the project was not completed before the end of the holiday season. This meant no income in the year as forecast to the bank and no ability to repay the portion of the loan due for repayment. The company needed to reschedule by 9 to 12 months. Because the business was in default the bank loaded penalty fees and then 'pulled the rug'. The bank had protected its position, made a quick win for itself and put a sound proposition out of business. It is this sort of behaviour that has caused tension between banks and particularly small businesses. Clearly, one expects a professional banker to consider his customer's best interests alongside those of the bank. However, increasingly banks are employing transactional-level staff rather than relationship-experienced managers to front customer negotiations.

This case would seem to demonstrate the view that banks generally have become transaction rather than relationship driven – employing targeted front-office staff with narrow views and ability/authority. This is why it is important for a business to have a bank relationship strategy.

Key to a robust bank relationship strategy is the removal of the vulnerability that comes from having all your eggs in one basket. If a company relies on one bank to do everything then it may become vulnerable when that bank has a change in policy/attitude. However, having too many banking relationships can take up a massive amount of management time and the business might not enjoy the benefits that accrue from being a 'significant customer'. It is a question of striking the right balance. It is generally better to separate out key services and to introduce competition. To do this a company needs to identify its bank service requirements and their dependencies. Listed below are the services that most medium to large companies require:

- money transmission and banking
- current accounts
- long- and medium-term lending
- overdrafts
- working capital finance
- payment services
- international payments
- foreign exchange dealing
- money market dealing
- merchant and investment banking.

We will now discuss some of these services, their dependencies and strategies for robust banking relationships.

Money transmission and current account dependencies

Money transmission is principally concerned with getting a company's 'takings' into a bank. There is no reason why the bank that handles the transmission should be the bank where the funds end up being deposited into a current account and where overdraft and lending facilities are provided.

For many years in the UK many companies, both small and large, used A&L Girobank money transmission accounts to deposit the sales takings for forward transmission to their principal banker. Many did this simply to make savings in bank charges, but one significant other advantage was that they could instruct A&L Girobank to transfer the takings deposited into another bank should they choose to change bankers. This effectively meant that if a lending/current account bank increased charges the customer could negotiate with a new bank and have his takings transferred there.

This method puts the customer in control in addition to making savings in transmission charges. The potential for savings in transmission comes from the fact the Post Office (where A&L Girobank deposits are made) has a requirement for cash and that some of the benefit of this can be flowed back to the customer. Another operational advantage is that the Post Office still has many more branches than any one bank.

To make this work the customer simply opens a money transmission account with A&L Girobank and then makes deposits over various Post Office counters (the customer may or may not use a security service). The money deposited over the PO counters is collected into one transmission account and then each day the total value is transferred into the customer's principal bank account using either the BACS or the CHAPS system.

Apart from making savings in bank charges the customer can feel more confident in managing relationships with lending banks and providers of current accounts by being able to easily switch banks without changing transmission arrangements. This is particularly useful in the retail and wholesale sectors where deposits may need to be made at numerous locations. Some of the UK's largest retailers use the method.

Introducing more competition

Given that banks have become more transactional rather than relationship driven one can expect that each department/division of the bank a customer is dealing with will want to maximise its own profitability and not subsidise another department. They get little thanks within the bank for doing that. Therefore, it is essential to get competitive quotes for all foreign exchange transactions. To do this it will be necessary to have a number of dealing lines in place and the company will need to balance the facility costs against the potential savings that can be made. However, possibly more important than this is the potential to be not so constrained by one bank controlling its overall exposure to the company. For a company that has little foreign business this might not be important but for an importer/exporter adequate dealing line capacity and better rates are often obtained through having at least three dealing lines in place.

Working capital finance

We agreed in the previous chapter that cash is paramount to survival. Why then do many companies rely on just one institution to manage their cash? For example, many companies rely on the commercial banking arm of their current account provider to also provide invoice finance facilities. There are many independent invoice finance providers and it might be a more robust strategy to keep the current account provider separate from the invoice discounter. It will depend upon the rates charged and the devil in the detail of the contract. The invoice finance industry in the UK is not currently regulated and it is, therefore, even more important to understand what can go wrong and what will happen if things do go wrong. However, this aside, there is no real strategic advantage in having invoice finance provided by your current account provider if you do not believe a real relationship exists between you and the bank overall.

Overdrafts are repayable on demand and most working capital facilities are laden with covenants. A bank can change its attitude to lending, particularly when a recession looms. It might make arbitrary decisions across its entire lending portfolio that suddenly restrict a company's overdraft availability. A company might experience a fall-off in trade due to an overall economic decline and suddenly find that it is in breach of covenants. The effect of this on the availability of working capital can be devastating, especially when default penalty fees come rolling in, as we saw in our example of the caravan park. To shore up against this type of exposure is as much about strategic financial management as it is about bank relationship management. However, given that banks have become more transactional than relationship driven, some form of standby facility with another institution might be worth the cost in order to obtain the breathing space necessary in a recession.

General bank relationship strategy

From the above we might conclude that:

- banks have become more transactional than relationship driven
- a customer should separate out services with providers as far as it can and is efficient to do so
- transmission should be with a different provider than the current account provider
- standby and back-up facilities with an institution other than the principal bank might be appropriate
- the introduction of increased competition into banking relationships is generally a more robust banking strategy than relying on building a single relationship
- relationships can disappear.

The cost of capital

DEFINITION OF THE COST OF CAPITAL AND DISCUSSION

The cost of capital to an organisation is the return that it gives to its providers of funds. The cost of capital reflects the risk of providing funds to the organisation. The cost of capital can be used as a discount rate in the organisation's investment appraisal calculations.

Various methods can be used for calculating the cost of capital and these will be explained in this chapter. An organisation needs to know the cost of capital currently employed and the marginal cost of the next increment of capital employed so that it can measure current performance and valuation and whether proposed developments are likely to be profitable.

The cost of capital can also be thought of as the opportunity cost of finance since it is the minimum return that investors require. If they do not get this minimum they will invest elsewhere.

The cost of capital can be said to have three elements:

- the risk-free rate of return
- the premium for business risk
- the premium for financial risk.

Risk-free rate of return

The risk-free rate of return is the return that would be required if the investment was completely free of risk. Nothing, of course, is completely risk-free, as we learned in 2008. However, the yield on government securities is generally considered to be a risk-free yield because, to an extent, a government can always borrow or tax more!

Premium for business risk

This represents the increase in return required to compensate for the uncertainty of a business's future performance and existence.

Premium for financial risk

This is the premium required to cover high levels of gearing and debt. A highly geared company carries more risk.

The cost of capital = risk-free rate + premium for business risk + premium for financial risk

Cost will increase with risk. Different categories of lender will have a different level of risk and will require a different return. The cheapest source of finance will normally be secured debt and the most expensive will be equity (who can leave with nothing).

High cost of finance = High risk

Ordinary shares	Highest cost greatest risk
Preference shares	Have less risk than ordinary shareholders
Lenders with no security	Have priority over shareholders
Lenders with floating charges	Floating charge lowers risk
Lenders with fixed charges	Lowest cost – most secure having a certain fixed charge

Low cost of finance = Low risk

A company with a lower cost of capital than its competitors will be able to compete more effectively when investing in new projects. Companies may, therefore, benchmark themselves against their competitors in relation to their comparative costs of capital.

Marginal cost v average cost of capital

When evaluating investment opportunities it is the marginal cost of capital rather than the current average cost that should be used. This is because the project will have to be funded from new capital at the marginal/incremental cost and not from funds already used. This is best explained by a simple example.

Peter has financed his business as follows:

Commercial mortgage £10,000 @ 9% p.a.

Bank loan of £6,000 @ 14%

Other finance of £3,000 @ 18%

Peter's average cost of capital is:

$$\frac{(£10,000 \times 0.09)\ 1\ (6,000 \times 0.14) + (3,000 \times 0.18)}{£10,000 + £6,000 + £3,000}$$

Average cost of capital is 12%.

However, for future expansion of the business Peter can borrow from the market at only 25%. His marginal cost of capital is, therefore, 25% and this is the rate that should be used for investment appraisal.

Zero dividend policy and the cost of capital

If we assume that the most important objective of an organisation is to maximise shareholder wealth and that the lowest cost of capital is shareholder funds then is there an argument for simply using shareholder funds and having a zero or low-level dividend policy, ploughing everything back into the business and increasing shareholder value through an increase in market share prices? Microsoft had a zero dividend policy and by 2004 its cash balance had reached US$50 billion. It had paid its first dividend in 2003. Whether this is a sound policy that is acceptable to shareholders will depend upon the company's ability to obtain the best return that shareholders can get for their investment and on the market price of alternative sources of funds.

What do the theorists have to say about the effect of dividend policy on the cost of capital? Well, Modigliani and Miller argued that a company's dividend policy was irrelevant to the cost of capital and to the value of the firm in a world without taxes or transaction costs. Although such a world does not exist they demonstrated that when investors can create any income pattern by selling and buying shares on the market, the expected return required to induce them to hold firm shares will not be influenced by the way the company makes dividend payments and issues new shares. Since the company's cost of capital and assets are not affected by its dividend policy the company's market value is not affected by changes in the company's distributions. Therefore, it is argued that in certain circumstances a company's dividend policy is irrelevant to the cost of capital and valuations. Modigliani and Miller's (MM) theory suggests that dividends will vary with the company's investment and financing choices and will not show any systematic pattern over time.

The MM theory was developed in 1958 and is based on the behavioural proposition that investors would use arbitrage to keep the weighted average cost of capital constant when a change occurred in the company's gearing. They theorised that the weighted average cost of capital of a company and the market value of the company were not dependent on the level of gearing but on the discounted value of future expected earnings. They argued that with a rise in the level of gearing the cost of equity increases and exactly offsets the increased debt capital. Thus the weighted average cost of capital remains unchanged. Thus, the discount rate used to evaluate an investment project depends entirely upon the company's method of financing the investment.

We will now discuss different methods of calculating the cost of capital. Deciding which one to use is one of the most interesting and debated topics in financial management.

COST OF DEBT

The cost of debt is the cost of borrowing from lenders. For irredeemable debt this cost is the after-tax interest as a percentage of the ex interest value of the loan stock. For redeemable debt the cost is the internal rate of return of the cash flow. It is the cost of continuing to use rather than redeem the securities.

Irredeemable debt

The cost of irredeemable debt capital is:

$$K = \frac{i}{P}$$

where: K = cost of irredeemable debt capital
i = interest in perpetuity
P = current ex interest price.

Example   A company issues loan stock as follows:

Nominal value £100

Interest 8% p.a. on nominal value

Current market price of loan stock is £85.

The cost of the loan stock (K) is:

$$K = \frac{8}{85}$$

$$\boldsymbol{K = 9.4\%}$$

Redeemable debt

In the case of redeemable debt the holder will receive the redemption payment and the interest payment in the year of redemption.

Example   A company issues £100 debentures carrying an interest rate of 10%. If their market value is £95 ex interest, what would the cost of capital be if the debenture was irredeemable?

$$K = \frac{£10}{£95}$$

$$\boldsymbol{K = 10.5\%}$$

What would the cost of capital be if the debenture was redeemable at par after 10 years?

Between now and the redemption date the capital profit will be £100 less £95 = £5. Since this profit is earned over 10 years the annual profit will be

50p. This 50p is about 0.5% of the market value. Choosing discount factors around 10.6% which will give positive and negative net present values, prepare a discounted cash flow statement as follows:

Year		Cash flow	Discount factor 11%	PV £	Discount factor 10%	PV £
0	Market value	− 95	1.000	− 95.00	1.000	− 95.00
1–10	Interest (i)	+ 10	5.889	+ 58.89	6.144	+ 61.44
10	Capital repayment	+ 100	0.352	+ 35.20	0.386	+ 38.60
	NPV			− 0.91		+ 5.04

(note that the year 1–10 discount figures are the total from the tables for the 10 years divided by 10.)

The cost of the redeemable debt capital can now be found by simple interpolation:

$$10.5 + \frac{5.04}{(5.04 - 0.91)} \times 1$$

$$= 11.35\%$$

The above example has ignored taxation for simplicity. This is now considered below.

Taxation on debt capital

Under most taxation jurisdictions debt interest attracts tax relief. Dividends payments do not attract tax relief for the paying company. Therefore, it is not possible to directly compare the cost of debt to capital unless allowance is made for taxation. Tax relief on interest payments has to be recognised.

The after-tax cost of irredeemable debt capital is:

$$KD = \frac{i(1 - T)}{PO}$$

where:

KD = cost of debt capital

i = annual interest payment

T = the rate of taxation

PO = market price of the debt capital ex interest.

Example A company pays out £90,000 p.a. in interest on irredeemable loan stock that has a nominal value of £90,000. The market price is £75,000. The rate of tax is 35%. What is the cost of the debt?

$$KD = \frac{£9,000(1 - 0.35)}{£75,000}$$

$$KD = 7.8\%$$

Note that the tax benefits of debt finance compared with equity will increase as the rate of taxation increases. Therefore, theoretically, if a government increases the rate of taxation it will encourage companies to borrow more by using debt rather than equity.

Convertible debt

Where the conversion of debt is expected to occur the normal IRR method of calculating the cost of redeemable debt is used with some modification. Replace the number of years to redemption with the number of years to conversion and replace the market value with the conversion value.

$$CV = PO_{ex} (1 + G)^n SR$$

where:

PO_{ex} = current ex dividend ordinary share price

G = expected annual growth in the ordinary share price

n = number of years to conversion

SR = number of shares received on conversion.

Preference shares

The cost of preference shares is:

$$KP = \frac{DR}{PP_{ex}}$$

where:

KP = cost of preference shares

DR = dividend received

PP_{ex} = market price of preference share dividend after current dividend payment.

WEIGHTED AVERAGE COST OF CAPITAL (WACC)

The weighted average cost of capital is the average cost of a company's finance from all sources weighted according to the proportion of each source to the total capital. It is calculated taking into account the relative weights of each component of the capital structure. For example:

Source	Amount	Cost	Cost × Proportion
Equity	£200K	10%	6.7%
Debt	£100K	7%	2.3%
Total	£300K		WACC 9.0%

Taking into consideration taxation the formula for the WACC will be:

$$\text{WACC} = w_d (1 - T) \, r_d + w_e \, r_e$$

where:
w_d = debt portion of capital
T = tax rate
r_d = debt rate
w_e = equity portion of capital
r_e = equity rate.

Using the above example with a zero rate of tax WACC is:

$$\text{WACC} = 33.33\%(1 + 0) \, 7\% + (66.67\% \times 10\%)$$

$$\text{WACC} = 2.33\% + 6.67\%$$

$$\text{WACC} = 9\% \text{ (as above)}.$$

If the rate of tax was 30% then substitute 30% for T in the above formula.

DIVIDEND GROWTH MODEL

The dividend growth model calculates the cost of equity on the assumption that share values are directly correlated to the expected future dividends from the shares. It is a valuation model that considers dividends and their growth, discounted to current values. This model works from the basis that the valuation of shares is based on:

- current dividend
- future growth in dividend
- the required rate of return.

Example:

Assume that shares pay £3.00 per year in dividends, growing at 2.5% per year. The investor's required rate of return 11%.

The formula for the dividend growth model is:

$$\text{Value} = \frac{\text{Current dividend } (1 + \text{dividend growth})}{(\text{Required return} - \text{Dividend growth})}$$

$$\text{Value} = \frac{£3(1 + 0.025)}{(0.11 - 0.025)}$$

$$\text{Value} = \frac{£3.075}{0.085}$$

$$\text{Value} = £36.18$$

This means that the shares should yield an 11% average annual return at a price of £36.18.

This standard dividend growth model has certain weaknesses in its assumptions. The major weaknesses include:

■ it assumes that there are no issue costs for new shares

■ no allowance has been made for the effects of taxation

■ risk has not been incorporated

■ the growth assumption is probably too simplistic in that dividends may not often grow smoothly at a constant rate.

CAPITAL ASSET PRICING MODEL (CAPM)

The capital asset pricing model (CAPM) is used to determine the theoretical price of a security. Investors would expect to receive:

$$E_s = R_f + \beta_s (R_m - R_f)$$

where:

E_s = the expected return for a security

R_f = the expected risk-free return in the market (government bonds)

β_s = the sensitivity to market risk for the security

R_m = the historical return of the stock market

$(R_m - R_f)$ = the risk premium of market assets over risk-free assets.

In simple English this means that:

the expected return % = the risk-free return % + the sensitivity to market risk × (the historical return % − the risk-free return %).

The model assumes investors will expect a return that is the risk-free return plus the security's sensitivity to the market risk multiplied by the market risk premium. The risk-free rate is normally taken as being the yield on government bonds.

The sensitivity to market risk (β_s) depends upon many factors and is unique to each company. This can be estimated only from past experience and with similar companies in the same business sector.

The cost of retained earnings is equal to the cost of equity. Dividends are part of the return on capital to equity holders and form part of the cost of capital.

Example:

The risk-free rate of return is 8%. The average market return is 10%. The beta factor (sensitivity to market risk) is 0.9. What will be the expected return from a share?

$$\text{Expected return} = 8\% + 0.9(10\% - 8\%)$$

$$\text{Expected return} = 9.8\%$$

You will see from the above simple example of the basic CAPM that it is based upon a comparison of the risk of individual investments with the risk of the total market. A main benefit over the dividend growth model is that it incorporates risk.

The risks involved in holding shares can be split into:

■ unsystematic risk which is specific to the company and can be diversified away

■ systematic risk which relates to the whole market and cannot be diversified away.

An investor in a single company will have a high level of unsystematic risk compared with systematic risk. The more companies invested in, the more diverse a portfolio becomes and the unsystematic risk will be 'diversified away'. The lower the level of risk, the lower the level of return. A totally diverse portfolio may provide a safer return that is close to the overall market performance. A portfolio manager will have risk and return objectives that guide strategy.

The beta factor is a measure of the systematic risk of a security relative to the market. If a particular share price were to rise or fall at 1.5 times the rate of the market it would have a beta factor of 1.5. In the above example the company had a share price that was not as volatile as the market and was 0.9. If the share price exactly mirrored the market it would have been 1.0.

The CAPM theory assumes that:

■ investors require a return in excess of the risk-free rate. This is to compensate them for the systematic risk

- investors do not require a premium for unsystematic risk. They can after all, diversify away unsystematic risk by widening their portfolio of investments

- investors require a higher return from companies with a higher level of systematic risk.

The market risk premium is the difference between the expected rate of return on a market portfolio and the risk-free rate of investing in government bonds. A CAPM principle is that market returns on shares are expected to be higher than returns on risk-free government bonds. The difference between government stock and market returns is called the 'excess'. Therefore the difference in return from a specific security and the risk-free return can be calculated as the 'excess' return multiplied by the security's beta factor.

When using CAPM it is obviously important to ensure that the assumptions used are realistic.

SUMMARY

The cost of capital can be considered as the opportunity cost of investment capital or the marginal rate of return required by investors. It is the rate of return that a company pays to obtain funds and reflects the risk to investors.

The capital asset pricing model when used to calculate the cost of equity incorporates risk through a comparison between the risk of individual investments and the risks of the total market. The risk of holding shares can be divided into unsystematic risk (specific to the company) and systematic risk (relating to the whole market). Unsystematic risk can be diversified away. The beta factor is a measure of a share's volatility in terms of market risk.

The cost of debt is the return to lenders. In the case of irredeemable debt this is interest after tax as a percentage of the ex interest market value of the preference shares or loan stock. In the case of redeemable debt the cost is the internal rate of return of the cash flows.

The dividend growth model calculates the cost of equity on the assumption that the market value of a share is directly related to the expected future dividends from the share.

The weighted average cost of capital is the weighted cost of all sources of finance used by the company.

Potential investments should be evaluated using discounted cash flow and discounting using the marginal cost of capital. As can be seen from the methods in this chapter there are arguments for and against each method of calculating the cost of capital. The weighted average cost of capital is widely used. Some large organisations even use an average of methods. The most important thing is to understand the shortfalls of each method and be able to determine how these apply given any set of variables.

Capital structure

BACKGROUND

We have discussed gearing and outlined the basics of capital structure. In this chapter we will examine the question of whether there really is an optimal mix of capital that a company should achieve.

The traditional view is that the optimal mix of capital is achieved when the weighted average cost of capital is minimised. Modigliani and Miller took a different view and show how a company's weighted average cost of capital is not influenced by any changes in its capital structure. Capital structure refers to the way a company finances its assets through a combination of debt and equity. A company's capital structure is the composition of its sources of funds.

The Modigliani–Miller work gives a theoretical basis for understanding capital structure. Their theory is that, in a perfect market, the value of a company is irrelevant to how it is financed. The traditional and real-world view is that capital structure is relevant and that a company's value is affected by its capital structure. This discussion considers whether there is an optimal capital structure which will maximise the value of a company.

THE MM VIEW

The MM view assumes a perfect capital market with no transaction or liquidation costs and one where there is perfect information, a market where companies can borrow at the same interest rate, where there are no taxes and investment decisions are separate from financing decisions. MM made two significant findings under these perfect conditions. The first was that the value of a company is independent of its capital structure. The second was that the cost of equity for a highly geared company is equal to the cost of equity for a lowly geared company plus an added premium for financial risk. That is, as gearing increases, while the burden of individual risks is shifted between different lending groups, the total risk is constant and hence no extra value created. This observation makes perfect sense within the limits of the perfect market it belongs to.

MM analysis was then extended to include the effect of taxes and debt risk. The tax deductibility of interest makes debt financing valuable because of the value of the tax benefit. The cost of capital decreases as the proportion of debt in the overall capital structure increases. The optimal structure would seem to have virtually no equity at all.

In summary, the MM view is that, with the absence of taxation, the total market value of the company would be determined by two factors:

- the total earnings of the company
- the operating risk associated with those earnings.

To calculate the market value of a company, simply discount the total earnings using a discount rate that reflects the operating risk.

The MM theory suggests that:

- the cost of debt does not change with the level of gearing
- the cost of equity rises to a level that keeps the weighted average cost of capital constant.

This is represented in Figure 13.1:

Ke = cost of equity

Ko = weighted average cost of capital

Kd = cost of debt

Figure 13.1

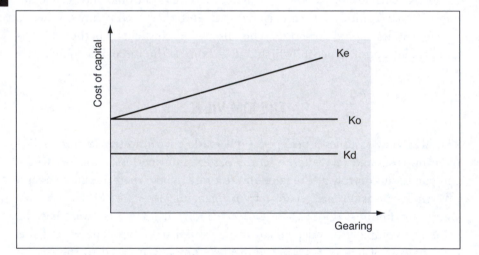

It is, however, unlikely that the cost of debt will remain constant whatever the level of gearing. This is because a lending bank will generally consider that as gearing increases so does the level of risk and as risk increases so does the return expected by the market. A lending bank view may be that there is indeed a positive correlation between an increase in gearing and an increase in the cost of debt.

MM modified their theory to allow for the fact that tax benefits on interest payments reduce the weighted average cost of capital. This is demonstrated in Figure 13.2:

Figure 13.2

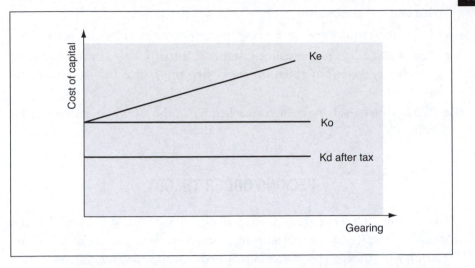

TRADITIONAL VIEW OF THE COST OF CAPITAL

The traditional view is that the cost of capital declines initially and then rises as gearing increases. This implies that the optimal capital structure will be reached when the weighted average cost of capital is at its lowest point (point P in Figure 13.3).

The traditional view is that there is an optimal capital structure which if achieved will increase the total value of the company.

■ As gearing increases, the cost of debt remains the same but only up to a point, after which it increases. This would follow the premise that as

Figure 13.3

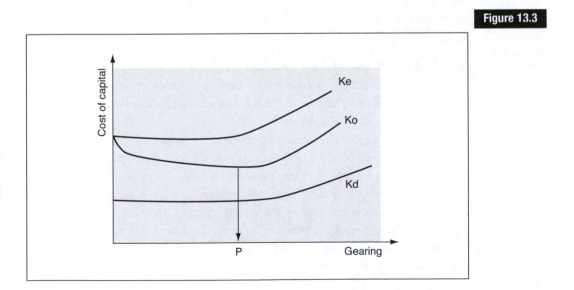

gearing increases lenders would see the company as more risky and would demand a higher return.

■ The cost of equity rises as gearing increases and financial risk increases.

■ The WACC does not remain constant. It initially falls as the proportion of debt increases but then increases with the rising cost of equity and debt.

■ The optimal level of gearing is reached when the WACC is minimised (at point P).

PECKING ORDER THEORY

The Pecking Order theory, developed by Stewart C. Myers and Nicolas Mailuf in 1984, states that companies prioritise their sources of financing, starting with the internal source of retained earnings then moving on to debt and lastly equity on the basis of doing what involves the least effort. Internal funds are easy and will be used first; when these are used up debt is the next easiest source; finally when it is not easy or sensible to issue more debt, equity is issued. Pecking Order theory maintains that businesses adhere to a hierarchy of financing sources. This simple truth probably applies up to a certain level of incremental funding but probably not for a major capital restructure.

The 'pecking order' starting with the preferred option is:

1. Retained earnings or other internal sources.

2. Debt.

3. Convertible debt.

4. Preference shares.

5. Equity (ordinary) shares.

The Pecking Order theory introduces a human element that may help explain why companies actually take certain courses of actions in capital structure decisions. Perhaps it explains what they actually do rather than what they necessarily should do.

Pecking order exists because it is easier to use retained earnings than it is to raise new funds and have to comply with all of the performance and reporting demands of the new providers. Also, there are no issue costs involved when using retained earnings. There are issue costs associated with debt and they are even higher for equity. Equity may be a less preferred source of capital because when a company issues new equity investors may believe that the company thinks it is overvalued and possibly taking advantage of this overvaluation. This may result in investors placing a lower value to the new equity issue. An issue of debt might imply that there is a lack of confidence in issuing equity!

CAPITAL STRUCTURE, COST OF CAPITAL AND INVESTMENTS

Capital structure affects the cost of capital and the cost of capital affects the market value of the company. The lower the weighted average cost of capital, the higher the net present value of cash flows and the higher the company's market value. When appraising new investments, which cost of capital should be used? This is a matter of judgement taking into account all of the factors we have so far discussed. However, as a rule of thumb:

Use the WACC in investment appraisal when the project is small in relation to the company's overall activities, it is expected that the existing capital structure will be maintained and the project has the same business risk as the company's overall business risk.

Use CAPM in investment appraisal when it is necessary to compare projects with different risk. It uses a discount rate that is based upon the systematic risk of the individual investment.

When an investment has different business and finance risks from the rest of the existing business in a company it is possible to allow for this by using a 'geared beta'. Geared betas are found by using a two-step process:

1. Ungear the industry betas.

2. Convert the ungeared betas back into a geared beta that reflects the organisation's own gearing.

   a) To convert the industry beta values into ungeared betas use this formula:

   $$\beta_a = \beta_e \times \frac{V_e}{V_e + V_d + (1 - T)}$$

   b) To convert the ungeared beta β_a back into a geared beta β_e reflecting the company's own gearing use the following formula:

   $$\beta_e = \beta_a \times \frac{V_e + V_d (1 - T)}{V_e}$$

where:

β_a = ungeared beta

β_e = geared beta

V_e = market value of equity capital in geared company

V_d = market value of debt capital in geared company

T = rate of taxation.

Apply the CAPM process using the project-specific geared beta to calculate the project-specific cost of equity and the project-specific cost of capital based on weighting this cost of equity and the cost of debt capital.

PRAGMATIC SUMMARY

There may be an optimal mix of finance that minimises a company's cost of capital. However, not everyone believes this to be the case and in this chapter we have discussed the better-known theories regarding capital structures and the cost of capital. The traditional view is that the cost of capital initially declines and then rises again as gearing increases and that the optimal capital structure is at the point where the weighted average cost of capital is at its lowest. Modigliani and Miller theorised that without taxation, capital structure would have no impact on the weighted average cost of capital. However, the lower the weighted average cost of capital, the higher the net present value of cash flows and the higher the market value. Geared betas can be used to allow for differing risks between investments and existing business.

Target capital structures will vary enormously from company to company and between industries. Each company will have a different way of finding an appropriate and optimal capital structure. It is a potentially complex area covering many facets of finance, valuation, strategy and taxation. In considering capital structure a company will seek to:

- determine a target for the optimal capital structure
- determine the cost of capital.
- identify and analyse all strategic options.
- appraise projects with an appropriate cost of capital.
- assess dividend policy and the impact of this on capital structure, tax efficiency, the cost of capital and the market.

THE THEORETICAL VIEW – THE PERFECT MARKET VERSUS THE REAL WORLD

In a perfect capital market with perfect information and no transaction cost, etc. organisations can borrow at the same interest rate. Investment decisions may not be affected by finance decisions. In this perfect market Modigliani and Miller made two findings. First, that the value of a company is independent of its capital structure. Second, that the cost of equity for a high-geared firm is equal to the cost of equity for a low-geared firm, plus an added premium for financial risk. This would imply that as gearing increases, while the burden of individual risks is shifted between different investor classes, the total risk remains the same and accordingly no additional value is created.

The analysis was further developed to include the effect of taxes and higher-risk debt. Under a normal taxation regime (the UK, for example) interest is tax deductible and this makes debt financing valuable in that the cost of capital decreases as the proportion of debt in the capital structure increases. It might be assumed, therefore, that the optimal structure would be to have as little equity as possible!

If, in the perfect market, capital structure is irrelevant, then imperfections of the real world can be considered as the cause of its relevance.

The trade-off theory of capital structure assumes that liquidation costs exist. This theory assumes that there is a tax advantage of financing with debt and that there is a cost of financing with debt (liquidation costs). The trade-off is that the marginal benefit of increases in debt will decline as debt increases, while the marginal cost increases. An organisation that hopes to optimise its overall value will be aware of this trade-off when deciding on the split between debt and equity. It is thought that this trade-off theory may explain the differences in debt/equity ratios between industries but it does not explain the differences that might exist within an industry sector.

Pecking Order theory states that companies prioritise their sources of financing according to a law of least effort. The basic assumption is that raising equity is a lot of effort and is, therefore, used only as a last resort. The theory assumes that internal debt is used up first and when it has gone debt is issued. Then, when it is no longer practical to borrow any more externally, new equity is issued. In practice this is what happens much of the time. The Pecking Order theory assumes that organisations have a hierarchy of financing sources preferring internal financing when available, and debt is preferred over equity if external financing is required.

Agency costs may help explain the relevance of capital structure.

■ Asset substitution effect: as the debt/equity ratio (gearing) increases, the incentive to undertake more risky projects increases. This occurs in a highly geared company because shareholders get all the upside and debt providers get the downside. Wealth may be transferred from debt holders to equity share holders.

■ Underinvestment problem: when debt is risky as in a start-up company, the gains from a new project may accrue to debt holders rather than the equity shareholders. Directors may then have an incentive to reject positive projects that might have added to the organisation's value.

■ Free cash flow: increasing gearing imposes financial disciplines on an organisation's executives who might otherwise not give free/surplus cash back to investors and fritter it away destroying the organisation's value.

Other theories include the neutral mutation hypothesis, where companies fall into various habits, and the market timing hypothesis.

Since we operate in the real world and not the theoretical perfect market it might be observed that companies develop their capital structure in an unpredictable manner. However, a knowledge of the theories is useful to a finance manager when making capital structure decisions.

14

Business valuations

BACKGROUND

Business valuations are estimates of the economic value of a business or an interest in a business. A valuation is used by buyers and sellers to establish the price they are prepared to pay or receive for a business. Business valuations are also used for estate, taxation and a wide variety of other legal purposes where parties may need to value an interest.

At the commencement of a valuation it is necessary for the instruction document to explain the reasons and circumstances surrounding the valuation. This is because the outcome of a valuation can vary enormously depending on the premise for the valuation. For example, a going concern valuation will probably be very different to a realisable assets valuation.

The fair market value (FMV) concept is central to a business valuation. There are various definitions for FMV. It is essentially the price at which property would change hands between a willing buyer and a willing seller when neither party was under any compulsion or duress. Of course, the actual conditions under which buyers, sellers and the market operate may be far from the perfect conditions required for an FMV. However, knowing the FMV sets a uniform standard.

Business valuations start with an analysis of the general economic and industry conditions surrounding the business. This will be followed by an analysis of the business's financial statements and comparison of these to the rest of the industry. The analysis should position the business within the market and compare it with its competitors.

A number of different approaches can be used in business valuations. The most common are the income/earnings approach, the net assets approach and the market approach. It is normal for a business to be valued using several methods and then for the differences in result to be compared and explained. It is also possible to combine approaches. Each technique has its advantages and drawbacks in relation to a particular business valuation.

The reasons why valuations are required include the following:

- There is a takeover bid for a quoted company. The offer price may reflect a fair market value which is in excess of the current share market price.
- A holder of shares wishes to dispose of a significant holding of shares, especially to a purchaser who will, as a result of the acquisition, gain a controlling interest.
- A company goes into liquidation.
- A company wants to obtain additional finance.
- An unquoted company wants to go public and needs to determine an issue price for its shares.

- A merger is being negotiated.
- The taxation department needs a valuation.
- As a basis for loan collateral valuation.
- As a basis for the valuation required in a management buy-out.

For small business valuations the principal methods are as follows.

The book value: this is a valuation based on the value of a business recorded in its accounts. The owner's equity (assets less external liabilities) is the book value. However, accounting records may not accurately reflect the true value of the assets and liabilities.

The adjusted book value: there are two types of adjusted book value for business valuations, the tangible book value and the economic book value. The tangible book value method deducts from book asset values intangible assets such as goodwill.

The economic book value method adjusts the book assets to their market value. This valuation method takes assets including goodwill at their market value.

Discounted cash flow of earnings: this determines the value of a business based on the present value of future earnings.

The income capitalisation valuation method: this establishes a capitalisation rate. This is the rate of return required for the risk of operating the business. Then divide earnings by the capitalisation rate. The capitalisation should be comparable with the rates of similar investments.

The price earnings multiple: this is the price of a company's share in the market divided by its earnings per share multiplied by the net income to give a value for the business.

Sales and profit multipliers: sales and profit multiples using industry benchmarks may be used in valuing a business.

Dividend capitalisation: a dividend paying capacity based on net income and cash flow is estimated. The income and cash flow that can be used for the payment of dividends is estimated.

Replacement values: these estimate the replacement value of the business assets to give a valuation.

Liquidation valuations: this method uses the non going concern realisable value of assets including scrap values.

BUSINESS VALUERS AND THE INFORMATION THEY REQUIRE

It is most likely that a business or share valuer will be a qualified accountant, lawyer or banker. This is because they require a working knowledge of the law surrounding valuations for commercial and taxation purposes and need to understand the appropriateness and application of a number of valuation methods. They also need a consummate understanding of business and finance and in particular specialist knowledge of the industry sector of the business they are valuing.

The information that is required for a valuation will include:

- audited financial statements including balance sheets, profit and loss accounts and statements of changes in financial position/sources and applications of funds statements. These will be required for recent and past years
- current management accounts and projections
- cash flow statements
- aged debtors listings showing the split between current, 30 day, 60 day, 90 day and over
- aged creditor listings
- prepayments and accruals
- stock valuations for raw materials, work in progress and finished stocks on the basis of the lower of cost or net realisable value. Stock turnover and obsolescence
- details of contracts and agreements with suppliers and customers
- lease and rental agreements
- freehold titles
- schedule of securities
- list of customers
- industry and competitive information
- list of shareholders and their holdings
- schedule of charges
- organisation chart
- employment contracts.

This required information is not exhaustive. The relative importance of each item will depend upon the business. For example, an aged debtors listing may not be so important in a fast-moving retail business.

ASSET-BASED VALUATIONS

An asset-based valuation is equal to the value of the sum of the component parts of the business including fixed and current assets less external liabilities. This approach to business valuation is based on the principle that an investor will not pay more for the business assets than the cost of acquiring similar assets.

Accounting conventions require that assets are recorded at cost less depreciation. Under the asset-based approach the valuer will list net assets at cost less depreciation and will make comparisons to the fair market value. Intangible assets such as goodwill are difficult to verify and the asset-based approach does not value the company accurately as a going concern.

The company owns the assets. The shareholder owns shares in the company and may not have the authority to access the assets directly. A shareholder with a controlling interest may be able to direct the company to sell assets. Therefore, the value of a company's assets is not usually the best of value to a shareholder. Having said this, the asset-based valuation is a useful fundamental check against other valuation methods such as the earnings approach. It may be used to provide the lower limit to valuations.

The net assets method for share valuation

The net assets method of share valuation simply takes the net tangible assets attributable to the shares and divides them by the number of shares. Assets which have a market value will be included, for example patents that can be sold will be included. Items that are hard to value such as goodwill are not included in this type of valuation.

Example		
Total assets less current liabilities		£500,000
Less: goodwill and other intangible assets		− £50,000
Total tangible assets less current liabilities		£450,000
Less: preference share capital and loans		− £90,000
Net assets value		£360,000
Number of ordinary shares		60,000
Net asset value per share		£6

The problems with asset valuations lie in the assumptions and methods used in valuing. For example, is the firm a going concern or is it to be broken up and sold off? What methods are appropriate for valuing? Historic cost, replacement cost or realisable value? This is why the reasons for the valuation and the economic environment need to be established at the outset.

The net assets basis will be used to provide a bottom-level valuation or 'floor value'.

INCOME/EARNINGS-BASED VALUATIONS

The income/earnings approach establishes a value by considering the company's going concern future earnings.

The price earnings ratio method of valuation

This method calculates the market value per share based on the P/E ratio.

$$\text{The P/E ratio} = \frac{\text{Market value}}{\text{Earnings per share}}$$

Therefore:

Market value = Earnings per share × P/E ratio

$$\text{Note: EPS} = \frac{\text{Profit attributable to ordinary shareholders}}{\text{Weighted average number of ordinary shares}}$$

The earnings yield method of valuation

Earnings yield is the percentage of earnings per share to the market price per share. It is the quotient of earnings per share divided by the share price and is the reciprocal of the price earnings ratio.

$$\text{Earnings yield} = \frac{\text{Earnings per share}}{\text{Market price per share}} \times 100\%$$

$$\text{Market value} = \frac{\text{Earnings}}{\text{Earnings yield}}$$

CASH FLOW VALUATIONS

Cash flow-based models include:

- the dividend valuation model
- the dividend growth model
- the discounted cash flow method.

The dividend valuation model

This model assumes that an equilibrium price for a share on the market is the discounted expected future income stream discounted. The expected annual income stream for a share is the expected future dividend earned in perpetuity and the equilibrium price is, therefore, the present value of the future income stream.

The formula for market valuation based on the dividend valuation is therefore:

$$\text{Market value (ex div)} = \frac{\text{Annual dividend expected in perpetuity}}{\text{Shareholders' required rate of return}}$$

The dividend growth model

Allowing for dividend growth the market valuation would be:

$$\frac{\text{Expected dividend in one year's time}}{\text{Shareholders' required rate} - \text{growth rate}}$$

Example PB paid a dividend of £300,000 this year and it is expected to grow each year at a rate of 5% p.a. Shareholders expect a return of 12% p.a. What is the valuation of PB using the dividend growth model?

$$MV = \frac{£300,000 \, (1.05)}{0.12}$$

$$MV = £2,625,000$$

Dividend models assume that investors will act rationally and in a similar way. This, of course, is not always the case.

Discounted cash flow basis for valuations

This method discounts the future cash flow of the target company to arrive at a market valuation or purchase price. It is often used by an acquiring company to value the benefits of purchasing a target company.

For example, company A wishes to acquire company B. After spending money on process improvements A believes that in the first 5 years the acquisition of B would produce the following after tax cash flow (not including the purchase price paid). The cost of capital (after tax) for this diversification is 9%. What is the maximum purchase price that A should pay for B?

Year	After tax cash flow £
0	(75,000)
1	(65,000)
2	100,000
3	110,000
4	140,000
5	<u>170,000</u>
	380,000

Year	After tax cash flow of acquisition through process improvement £	9% discount factor	Present value £
0	(75,000)	1.000	(75,000)
1	(65,000)	0.917	(59,605)
2	100,000	0.842	84,200
3	110,000	0.772	84,920
4	140,000	0.708	99,120
5	170,000	0.650	110,500
	380,000		244,135

The maximum price that A should offer for the acquisition of B is £244,135.

What this means is that the value to A is £244,135 based on the post-acquisition cash flow of B using A's own cost of capital. The value to another acquiring company could be different depending on the acquiring company's cost of capital and how it would expect the cash flow of the acquisition to materialise. The maximum purchase price to A of £244,135 might not represent a fair market value. This depends upon the value to other investors, whether they can improve the performance of B and many other market factors. This is why the parameters of the valuation need to be clearly understood. The valuer needs to explain the extent to which a valuation has covered the market.

DEBT VALUATION

A company's equity value is simply the total value of the company less the value of debt. The value of debt is, therefore, an important component of a valuation of the firm's equity.

The value of a company's debt is the amount that the holders of the debt expect to receive less any defaults. Default risk is calculated from the probability of default and the amount that could be recovered. For cash flow modelling it is assumed that the cash from the recovered amount is received at the end of the year of the default.

To value debt either:

■ discount the expected cash flow at the expected debt return or

■ discount the scheduled debt payments at the rating-adjusted yield to maturity.

Irredeemable debt

Irredeemable debt is where a company will continue to pay interest in perpetuity without any loan redemption. To calculate the ex interest value of irredeemable debt use the following formula:

$$\text{Market price of debt ex interest} = \frac{\text{Interest } (1 - \text{Rate of taxation})}{\text{Cost of debt capital}}$$

Redeemable debt

Value = (Interest earnings × Annuity factor)+ (Redemption value × DCF factor)

Example

9% debentures with a par value £120,000. Redeemable on 31 May 2013 for £100,000.

Interest payable quarterly. Redemption yield is 4% p.a. (1% each quarter). What is the market value of the debentures on 30 November 2009?

Solution:

The period between 30 November 2009 and 31 May 2013 is 42 months. This is equal to 14 quarters. Using the 1% quarterly discount factor (add the discount factors in the 1% column for period 1–14 to give 13.002), calculate the net present value:

Period	Payments	Cash flow £	Discount factor 1%	Present value £
1–14	Interest payments £120,000 @ 9%/4	2,700	13.002	31,205
14	Redemption payment	100,000	0.870	87,000
				118,205

The market value of the debentures on 30 November 2009 is £118,205.

Convertible debt

To calculate the conversion value of convertible loan debt use this formula:

$$Value = Pord(1 + g)^n R$$

where:

$Pord$	=	current ex dividend ordinary share price
g	=	annual growth rate of ordinary share price
n	=	number of years until conversion
R	=	number of shares received on conversion.

SUMMARY

When valuing a business it is, first of all, important to understand the reasons for the valuation, the different values to potential buyers and the economic conditions surrounding the sale. Then it is necessary to collect and analyse information about the business for sale and its industry sector. It is normal practice to value the business using a number of appropriate methods and understand the reasons for their different values. Finally it is a question of selecting a value from the different methods and rationalising the reasons for adopting this value. The final price that the buyer and seller agree will, perhaps, indicate how accurate a valuation was.

Business valuations – market sentiment and fundamental analysis

Most business valuations relate to smaller, often unlisted companies where market information is not available. In the case of larger companies there is the additional benefit of market information to assist in the valuation. However, markets are often influenced more by sentiments than by fundamentals and in times of recession market prices can quickly move back to more fundamental values.

In this chapter we have considered certain aspects of valuation and in particular the reasons for buying. A business may have more value to one buyer than it does to another for strategic and synergistic reasons.

Business valuation, therefore, is a complex process and there is often much dispute regarding a valuation. It includes a number of procedures to estimate the economic value of an owner's interest in his business and the value to a buyer.

The owner's valuation is used by potential buyers to help them determine the price they are willing to pay in accordance with the owner's expectations. Valuations may also be used to resolve disputes, calculate taxation, decide on partnership allocations, assess buy-in agreements and assist in many other business areas.

Two concepts central to business valuations are standard/premise of value and fair market value. We have discussed how the standard and premise of value needs to be ascertained and the reasons surrounding the business valuation determined. The standards of value are the conditions under which the business will be valued and the premises of value are the assumptions taken regarding things like going concern, etc. Business valuations will vary depending upon the standard and premise of value. Buyers and sellers each want to achieve the best result from their own perspective and given a reasonable spread of buyers this will reflect a fair market value. The term fair market value is used by many organisations but it can have many meanings. It may be described as the price at which property would change hands between a willing buyer and a willing seller who are both well informed and are not under any compulsion to sell.

The principal elements of any business valuation will include an analysis of the prevailing and future economic conditions and a financial analysis. The approach used in the valuation will commonly include valuations based on:

- income
- assets
- markets.

The techniques used will include net present value and discounted cash flow.

There are several methods of determining an appropriate discount rate. The discount rate is made up of the risk-free rate and the risk premium.

The capital asset pricing model is a method for determining the appropriate discount rate in business valuations. It derives the discount rate by adding a risk premium to the risk-free rate. The risk premium is arrived at by multiplying the equity risk premium times 'beta'. Beta is a measure of share price volatility and is published by various sources for industry sectors. Beta is associated with the systematic risks of an investment. The weighted average cost of capital is another approach to determining a discount rate. The WACC approach determines the company's actual cost of capital by calculating the weighted average of the company's costs of debt and equity. Matching of an appropriate discount rate to the selected measure of economic income is key to meaningful business valuations.

The build-up method is another method of determining an after-tax net cash flow discount rate, which yields a capitalisation rate. This method uses the sum of risks associated with various classes of assets. The total of the risk-free rate and the equity risk premium gives the long-term average market rate of return. The method also recognises that investors in smaller company shares require a greater return because they are more risky than blue-chip company investments. These elements of the build-up discount rate can be taken to reflect systematic risks. However, the discount rate must also include the unsystematic risks of the industry premium and the specific company risk.

The asset-based approach to valuations works on the basis of substitution in that no rational buyer would pay more for business assets than the cost of obtaining those assets directly. This method is a simple estimate of asset acquisition values. The value of intangible assets is generally difficult to estimate and this is why the asset-based approach is not necessarily the best way to determine an organisation's true value as a going concern.

The market approach to business valuation is based upon principles such as an efficient market and free competition. However, market sentiment may at times move valuations far from the fundamentals. Other approaches include methods of simple comparisons with other companies, public data and recent transactions.

The methods of valuation described in this chapter attempt to calculate a value that would otherwise be decided in the marketplace. Even with its imperfections and sentiment the market is perhaps the only place to confirm/determine a fair value.

Foreign currency and exchange risk management

THE NATURE OF FOREIGN CURRENCY RISK

An organisation that has income in one currency and expenditure in another is exposed to the risk of changes in rates of exchange between currencies. An organisation that holds foreign assets is exposed to currency risk and all organisations are exposed to foreign competitors gaining advantage through movements in exchange rates. These currency risks can take the form of an exposure to a particular transaction, to translation on the consolidation of foreign branches, subsidiaries and assets or to general economic conditions that affect the rates of exchange and the competitiveness of an organisation. The management of foreign currency risk is, therefore, crucial to most organisations. Some examples of foreign currency risk are given below.

Transactional risk example

A company based in New Zealand imports computer equipment from the US. It has an approved budget of NZ$20,000,000 for the year 2010. This is based on a rate of exchange of NZ$1 = US$0.53, the US$ cost of the equipment at the time of the budget being US$10,600,000.

When the company orders the equipment in June 2010 the rate of exchange has shifted to NZ$1 = US$0.51.

	NZ$	Rate of exchange	US$
Budget	20,000,000	0.53	10,600,000
Actual order value	20,784,314	0.51	10,600,000
Loss on exchange	**784,314**		

Because the rate of exchange between the NZ$ and the US$ has moved adversely for the NZ-based company it will require an additional NZ$784,314 in order to complete the transaction and acquire the equipment from the US. It may not have budgeted funds to do this. There are various hedging strategies that the NZ company could have adopted to manage this exposure and these will be discussed later.

Translation risk example

A UK-based company has assets in New Zealand. In 2010 these are valued at NZ$15,000,000 using a rate of exchange of NZ$2.40 = £1, giving a UK accounting value of £6,250,000. At the end of the financial year in 2011 the rate of exchange had moved to NZ$2.55 = £1.

Value at year end 2011 NZ$15,000,000/2.55   =   £5,882,353

Value at year end 2010 NZ$15,000,000/2.40   =   <u>£6,250,000</u>

Loss on translation   <u>£367,647</u>

By translating the NZ$ asset value at the rate on the 2011 balance date the company would have to record a loss of £367,647 in its sterling accounts. But what if the day after the balance date the asset was sold at a more favourable rate? We will discuss this and aspects of currency management later in this chapter.

Economic risks example

A UK-based farmer grows tomatoes to supply a superstore chain. The pound sterling has just strengthened against the euro, enabling the UK superstore to purchase tomatoes from a French supplier for fewer pounds. Movements in exchange rate that affect long-term competitiveness are referred to as economic risk factors.

REASONS FOR EXCHANGE RATE MOVEMENTS

The interaction between supply and demand for a currency in the foreign exchange market affects a currency's exchange rate relative to other currencies. The principal factors are the comparative rates of interest and inflation in different countries and the underlying economic health of countries. Other factors include market sentiment, government policy and general speculation.

Interest rate parity

To a certain extent it is believed that foreign exchange markets are linked to the international money markets. This concept of interest rate parity assumes that the difference between spot rates and forward rates reflects the differences in interest rates.

- Spot rate: the current rate. A currency spot rate is the rate for immediate delivery.
- Forward rate: an exchange rate set now for delivery at a future date.

This link between the currency and money markets is not perfect but does, however, provide some understanding of the differences and causes of exchange rate fluctuations.

Example

To help understand interest rate parity and the effects of interest rates on spot and forward rates it is helpful to work through an example.

A manufacturing company domiciled in New Zealand wishes to secure equipment from the UK for £5,000,000. Payment is due on despatch in 90 days' time. The current spot rate of exchange is NZ$2.40 = £1. Money market interest rates in NZ are 8% p.a. and in the UK are 6% p.a. The company has no idea what the rate of exchange will be in 90 days and wants to firm up on the price today since the current rate is affordable. Assuming the company buys today, what is the NZ$ cost of the equipment? The spot rate in 90 days' time turns out to also be NZ$2.40/£1.

£5,000,000 @ 2.40	NZ$12,000,000
NZ interest paid (£5,000,000 @ 8% × 90/360)× 2.4	NZ$240,000
UK interest received (£5,000,000 @ 6%× 90/360)× 2.4	(NZ$300,000)
Net NZ$ cost if currency is bought today	NZ$11,940,000

This NZ cost comprises the cost of buying the sterling at spot rate plus the cost of borrowing (or interest foregone) partially offset by the interest received on the sterling balance held for 90 days converted into NZ$.

If the currency markets were perfect and there were no other factors the forward rate to buy the sterling may have been:

$$\frac{NZ\$11,940,000}{£5,000,000} = NZ\$2.388 = £1$$

Forward rate	2.388
Spot rate	2.400

In this example the difference between the spot rate and the forward rate reflects the difference between the UK and NZ interest rates.

Forward rate	2.388	
Spot rate	2.400	
Difference	0.012	
Percentage difference	0.5%	(0.5% being 0.012/2.400)
NZ$ interest rate	2%	(8%× 90/360)
UK interest rate	1.5%	(6% × 90/360)
Difference		0.5%

The 0.5% difference in 90-day money market rates reflects the difference in exchange rate. A useful exercise at this point would be to examine the financial pages and see whether the differences between spot and forward rates are close to the differences between money market rates.

Example Rates of exchange between NZ$ and the UK £ sterling are listed today as:

$$
\begin{array}{ll}
\text{Spot rates} & \text{NZ\$2.400} = \text{£1} \\
& \text{£1} = \text{NZ\$0.417} \\
\text{90-day fwd rate} & \text{NZ\$2.45} = \text{£1} \\
& \text{£1} = 0.408
\end{array}
$$

The NZ annualised interest rate for a 90-day deposit is 8%. Assuming a 360-day year, what is the assumed interest rate in the UK?

Using the spot rate, we could buy NZ$2.400 today for £1. These NZ$ could be invested for 90 days to provide interest of NZ$2.400 × (8% × 90/360). This is equal to NZ$0.048. With interest the NZ dollars would grow to NZ$2.448 in the 90 days.

Now, using the 90-day exchange rate the equivalent £ sterling is £0.999 (NZ$2.448/2.45).

The annualised expected rate of UK interest is 4.0% (0.00999 × 360/90).

Proof:

NZ interest on 90 day deposit is 8% × 90/360 = 2%

UK interest = uki

90 forward rate = 0.413

Spot rate = 0.408

Then:

uki = 1+ NZi × spot/fwd

uki = 1.02× 0.413/0.408

uki = 1.007 per qtr

uki = 4.0% p.a.

Purchasing power parity

The purchasing power parity assumes that the rate of exchange between two currencies will depend upon the relative purchasing powers of each currency in its own country. Spot rates will change according to changes in prices. Purchasing power parity is reflected in the following formula:

$$
\text{Expected spot rate} = \text{Current spot rate} \times \frac{(1 \times \text{Expected rate of inflation country B)}}{(1 \times \text{Expected rate of inflation country A)}}
$$

Purchasing power parity (PPP) generally affects exchange rates over the long term and is useful in long-term investment appraisal. PPP theory uses the long-term equilibrium exchange rate of two currencies to equalise their purchasing power. It was developed by Gustav Cassel and is based on a law of one price for identical goods. In a totally efficient market, identical goods are assumed to have only one price. The theory is that, for a basket of goods, the purchasing power exchange rate will equalise the purchasing power of different currencies in their home countries.

Fisher

There is a general view that when a country increases its interest rate people will deposit money in that country and that through this buying the currency will strengthen. The Fisher hypothesis shows how this is not necessarily so.

The Fisher hypothesis incorporates a theory that the real interest rate in an economy is independent of monetary variables. If we also assume that real interest rates equalise between countries then the country with the lower nominal interest rate should also have a lower rate of inflation. This would eventually raise the real value of its currency.

This theory is the opposite of what we generally think and what we actually see in the market. Investors generally move money from countries with low nominal interest rates to those with high nominal interest rates. They do this to get the highest possible rate of return on deposits. Similarly, a borrower will want to borrow from a country with a low rate. These international money movement practices cause an increase in the value of the currency of the country with the higher nominal interest rate, contrary to the international Fisher effect.

The international effect of the Fisher theory is that the differentials between interest rates of countries may provide a useful prediction for future changes in currency exchange rates. It is assumed that the currency of countries with high interest rates will depreciate. Higher interest rates simply compensate for currency depreciation. In a free market the rates of return in different countries will equalise over time in line with movements in currency exchange rates. Although this may in theory be true, it is of more use to long-term planning than in hedging strategies for short- to medium-term transactions.

Equilibrium

Having an understanding of the causes of exchange rate movements will enable better risk management. We have discussed some of the reasons for exchange rate movements and some of the theories behind equilibrium. A four-way equivalence model suggests that when in perfect equilibrium the differences between forward and spot rates, interest and inflation rates are equal. While this may be of interest to government, treasury and long-term corporate planners, it might not be useful in shorter and medium-term financial management. The most important thing to remember in currency management is the nature and objectives of your business and not to speculate if this is not your business. Exchange rate management in this text is concerned with how to manage currency risks associated with normal business activities, not including currency trading or speculation.

CURRENCY RISK MANAGEMENT

A business needs to identify and manage its foreign currency risks. This is because an overexposure to fluctuations in currency markets can ruin a company. All aspects of running a business involve risk, but currency risk may not be one of the risks that a company is qualified or has been established to take on. The principal methods of hedging risk and managing exposure are described in this section.

Matching

If, for example, a company has a foreign asset it can match this with a foreign liability of similar value in the same currency to eliminate or reduce the exposure to a similar level. An example of this might be a UK company that has a debtor in the US. If the US$ weakens or the pound strengthens, the US$ debt will be worth fewer pounds when it is realised and converted into sterling. To hedge against this the company can take out a US$ loan and then, when the US debt is realised, use the proceeds to pay back the loan, thereby eliminating the currency exposure.

A company might also reduce its foreign exchange exposure by matching its receipts and payments that occur in the same foreign currency. This is simply done through the operation of a foreign currency bank account.

Invoicing

An easy and obvious way for an exporter to eliminate currency risk would be for exporters to invoice foreign customers in the exporter's domestic currency. This simply passes the problem over to the foreign customer who takes the risk. This may not be acceptable to the customer but it removes the risk to the exporter if it is.

Advance payments

In order to secure an acceptable rate of exchange a purchaser of foreign goods may arrange to pay for them in advance.

Intra-group trading and netting off balances

It might be possible, subject to the laws and regulations in various countries, to net off debit and credit balances on intra-company trading so that only the net balance is paid. Not only will this reduce the foreign exchange exposure, it will also reduce payment and transaction costs.

Forward exchange contracts

We have discussed how the differences in forward and spot rates arise. The forward-rate market exists to provide forward contracts that give in advance a rate at which currency will be sold.

A forward exchange contract is an agreement between two parties to exchange one currency for another at a forward or future date at a certain rate of exchange. A forward contract enables a buyer to arrange for delivery of an amount of currency on a future date, at a current forward market price. Forward contracts protect buyers against the risk of variable currency rates when buying foreign currency to meet their future liabilities.

Future exchange rates are very difficult to predict because they depend on so many variables. Even if, for example, a currency is described as soft and likely to depreciate in the longer term against certain hard currencies, this type of prediction may not be helpful in the shorter term of a business transaction. The prediction may even be inaccurate in the longer term. A forward exchange rate may help market prediction of possible future rates, but not necessarily.

The principal features of a forward contract are:

- it is for purchase or sale of a specific currency
- it is at an exchange rate fixed at the date of the contract
- it requires performance in that the currency must be delivered and paid for at the future time specified in the contract
- it is binding on the parties.

Example

A UK-based business wishes to import goods from New Zealand valued at NZ$20,000. This sum is payable in 30 days' time. The business takes out a forward-rate contract with the bank for NZ$20,000 for delivery in 30 days at a rate of NZ$2.34/£1.

The UK business can be sure now that the cost to it will be £8,547:

$$\frac{NNZ\$20,000}{2.34} = £8,547$$

This provides the certainty that the UK business needs and removes the risk.

If the spot rate on the delivery date of the forward contract was lower at, for example, 2.31, the spot price would have been £8,658 and the UK business would feel he had done well. If the spot rate on delivery had been higher than the forward rate, at say 2.42, the cost would have been only £8,264 and the UK business might feel it had lost. However, this is absolutely not the way to view the forward decision. The forward contract was taken out to firm up on a position and to eliminate risk. It was not to gamble.

In the event that a customer fails to meet his obligations under a forward contract the bank will normally close out the contract and arrange for the customer to foot the bill between spot and forward rates on the failed delivery date. It depends on the detail in the contract.

Hedging on the money market

Rather than take out a forward contract, a business with a future currency exposure might decide to borrow in home currency, convert the borrowed money into the required foreign currency and keep it on an interest-bearing deposit account until it is required. For example, a UK meat importer has a NZ$10,100,000 liability in 60 days. The spot rate on day 1 is NZ$2.5/£1. UK money market short-term loan rates are 4% and NZ money market deposit rates are 6%.

Day	Transaction	Principal £	Principal $	Interest £	Interest $
1	Borrow	4,000,000			
1	Buy and deposit		10,000,000		
1–60	Interest cost			−26,667	
1–60	Interest income				+100,000

In 60 days' time the UK company will have NZ$10,100,000 in its NZ$ account. The cost to the company in sterling would be £4,026,667.

This is another way of creating certainty in a foreign transaction and eliminating exchange risk. The cost should be very similar to using a forward contract. Money market hedging and forward exchange contracts should produce a similar result. The above example relates to a foreign payment. A similar process can be set up to manage a receipt.

When contemplating whether to hedge using the money market or a forward contract it is simply a matter of comparing the relative costs of both methods, making sure to allow for all fees.

In the above example the sterling cost of acquiring the NZ$10,000,000 was £4,026,667. If on day 1 the 60-day forward rate had been NZ$2.48/£, the UK cost would have been £4,032,258 and the company would have chosen the money market hedge option.

It is normal to obtain three forward options and three money market options simultaneously in order to obtain the best price. To do this the business will need dealing lines set up and staffed. This is normal for a large company but may not be so easy for a smaller or medium-sized operation.

CURRENCY DERIVATIVES

Under this section we will describe futures, options and swaps and how these derivatives can be used to hedge foreign currency risk. Derivatives are used by many organisations to manage their currency risks. They are a valuable tool because of their direct relationship to an underlying asset or index.

Forms of derivative have been around for many years. They have been used in the agricultural sector as a defence against falling product prices. A producer would enter into a contract to sell product at a specified price at a future date and time. This would secure revenues before a harvest. This basic idea led the way to the creation of instruments for managing other market risks.

Futures, options and swaps are the foundation of financial derivatives. Forwards and swaps are privately negotiated, options and futures are traded on open markets. There are also different combinations of basic derivatives such as options on futures.

Currency futures

Currency futures were created on the Chicago Mercantile Exchange in 1972. They are contracts where the underlying is a currency exchange rate and they are traded in the same way as other futures. This is different to the forward contracts we have discussed, which are not traded on a futures market. Currency futures are traded on futures exchanges and are based on the exchange rates of two currencies and settled in the underlying currency of the futures market. The EUR futures market is based upon the euro to US dollar exchange rate and has the euro as its underlying currency, which means that settlement will be in euros. Day traders in this type of market will not normally hold a contract until expiry and will not, therefore, take delivery. A currency future is then a futures contract to exchange one currency for another at a specified date in the future at a price that is fixed on the purchase date.

Currency futures are used to:

■ hedge against foreign exchange risk

■ speculate where there is authority to do this.

For the purpose of this text we will only discuss the use of currency futures in relation to hedging as a means of managing an underlying trading activity risk.

The advantages of currency futures include the following:

■ They are fully tradable and can be bought and sold on the market at market prices, unlike forward contracts.

■ The transaction costs are generally lower than other contractual methods of hedging.

The disadvantages of currency futures include the following:

■ Only a limited number of currencies are available on the futures exchanges.

■ They do not allow a company to take advantage of subsequent favourable rates of exchange as do options (options are discussed later).

■ The futures price may move differently from the underlying.

Example A futures contract

A US-based manufacturing company buys parts from a French company for €800,000, payable in 30 days' time. The US company wants to hedge against its foreign currency exposure by using the currency futures market.

Rates now are:

Spot	US$0.9300/€
Futures rate	US$0.9400/€

In 30 days' time the spot rate is:

Spot	US$0.9500/€

The closing futures price is: US$0.9550/€

Future contract size is: €160,000

Then, assuming 3-month contracts are available, we will need to buy € or sell US$. The number of contracts we need to buy is:

$$\frac{800K}{160K} = 5 \text{ contracts exactly (if not exact then round off to whole number)}$$

The tick size (the smallest unit of movement in the contract price) is 16.00 (160,000 × 0.0001).

Then:

Opening futures price	buy	0.9400
Closing futures price	sell	0.9550
'Tick' movement (buy − sell)		150

Futures profit is 150 ticks @ US$16.00 per tick × 5 contracts = US$12,000

Therefore the net payment in 30 days' time will be:

30 days spot (800,000 × 0.9500)	$760,000
Futures profit	$(12,000)
Net	$748,000

Since it is exceedingly easy to make a mistake in this type of calculation and in interpretation of the contract, this type of facility requires staff skilled and trained in futures dealings. The wording in contracts can be confusing. Plot out your understanding in your own way and get the bank to confirm that your understanding is correct before entering into this type of agreement.

Currency options

A currency or foreign exchange option is a derivative financial instrument that gives the owner the right but not the obligation to exchange one currency for another on a specified date at a pre-agreed rate of exchange. In a sense a currency option enables a company to limit downside exposure without limiting upside gains. This is because the user of an option is not obligated to buy or sell. The most that an option holder can lose is the premium paid (limited downside), but the gains are unlimited.

Currency options are commonly traded OTC (over the counter between two parties) and a number are traded on exchanges.

Some of the common terminology used by options users is listed below:

■ Underlying – the underlying asset, future, interest rate, index or in this instance foreign exchange rate upon which the derivative is based.

■ Call option – the right but not the obligation to buy the underlying.

■ Put option – the right but not the obligation to sell the underlying.

■ Strike price – a guaranteed price chosen by the user/client. Since options are not like forwards or futures, where the current rate in the market is predetermined, the client chooses the rate that may be better or worse than the current market rate. The guaranteed price chosen by the client can be:
 – ATM – at the money
 – ITM – in the money
 – OTM – out of the money.

ATM is the same rate as the market, ITM is a better rate than the market and OTM is a worse rate than the market.

- Exercise – the conversion/take-up of the option into the underlying transaction.

- Expiry – the date when the option expires.

- Value date – the date when the underlying is delivered.

- American – an option that can be exercised on any day of business up to and including the expiry date.

- European – an option that can be exercised only on the expiry date.

- Bermudan – an option that can be exercised on certain selected dates.

- Asian – a 'smoothed' option which is linked to the average rate over a period.

- Intrinsic – the difference between the strike price and the current market value.

- Premium – the price paid by the client for the option. The premium is comprised of two components, the intrinsic value and the time value. The relationship between the premium and the time to expiry is non-linear, although the further out the expiry date, the greater the premium.

- Time value – the difference between the premium and the intrinsic value.

- Fair value – a value calculated by the option price model which is a combination of the intrinsic value and the time value.

- Volatility – a measure of the range of possible outcomes for the underlying. It is one of the key assumptions in options pricing models. A trader of options may wish to speculate on the level of volatility. It is a normalised/annualised standard deviation of the underlying reference rate.

- Pricing model – a price model used by institutions to determine the premium. Inputs to the price model include the reference rate/benchmark, strike, volatility and interest rate.

- Collar – a collar option gives the holder the right but not the obligation to sell or buy currency at a specified rate of exchange on or before a specified date. If the client is able to transact at a rate that is better than a second predetermined level, the client agrees to give up any further profit. A collar option involves a combination of a call and a put, with both transactions being simultaneous. A collar reduces the risk of adverse currency movements and retains the client's ability to benefit from part of a favourable movement. It is, therefore, less expensive than a standard option. The client selects the degree of risk that is acceptable.

- Greeks – the term given to the sensitivity factors of certain variable factors used in the pricing model that can change with the market. They include delta, gamma, theta and vega.

A GB£/US$ foreign exchange option contract allows the owner to sell £2,000,000 and buy $3,000,000 on 31 December 2010. The pre-agreed strike price is 1.5000 and the notionals are £2,000,000 and $3,000,000. This contract is both a call on US$ and a put on £ sterling.

If the rate is 1.4000 on 31 December 2010 (the dollar is stronger and the pound is weaker) then the option will be exercised. The owner will then sell £2,000,000 at 1.5000 and immediately buy it back in the spot market at 1.4000, making a profit of £142,857 equivalent as below:

£2,000,000 @ 1.5 = $3,000,000.

$3,000,000 @ 1.4 = £2,142,857

£2,142,857 − £2,000,000 = £142,857

A company might use an option to hedge an uncertain cash flow in a foreign currency. If the cash flow was certain, a forward contract might be more appropriate. They must be paid for when they are bought and if they are tailor made they will not be negotiable. They are available only in major currencies.

Since the option gives a profit on 31 December 2010, the holder will exercise the option. The net cost will be the cost of the underlying plus the premium less the profit.

Currency swaps

Currency swaps are contracts where two or more parties agree to exchange interest obligations/receipts for a period between two currencies and at the end of the period to re-exchange the principal amounts at a rate that was agreed at the start of the agreement. Currency swaps require an exchange of interest in two currencies and also an exchange of principals. They are generally used to hedge a risk.

There are three types of currency swap:

- fixed/fixed
- floating/floating
- fixed/floating.

The main features of a currency swap are:

- interest rates agreed in advance
- exchange rates agreed in advance
- at maturity the two parties exchange the principal sums.

Figure 15.1 **Currency swap flow**

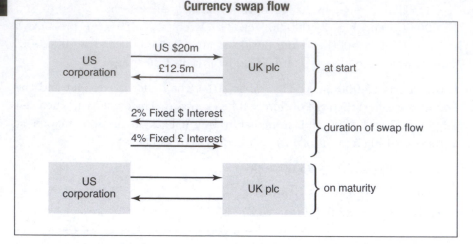

In a currency swap the parties contract to swap equivalent amounts of currency for a period of time – exchanging debt from one currency to another. This is best explained by means of an example.

Example A UK company needs to invest in France and borrows £15 million from its UK bank at 4% p.a. The £15 million will be converted into euros at a spot rate of €1.10 = £1. The income from the French investment is in euros. The UK company agrees to swap the £15 million for €16.5 million with a French company which becomes the counterparty to the transaction. Interest at 5% is payable on the €16.5 million. The UK company will invest the €16.5 million in France.

For the duration of the swap:

- the UK company receives interest of €0.825m (€16.5m @ 5% p.a.)

- the UK company gives this 0.825m to the French company so that the French company can pay its interest liability

- the French company passes its interest of £0.6m (£15m @ 4%) to the UK company

- the UK company pays the £0.6m over to its lender.

At the end of the swap period:

- the UK company pays back the €16.5m

- the UK company receives back the £15m

- the UK company pays back the £15m to its lender.

Most currency swaps are between banks and their customers. They are relatively easy to arrange, with low transaction costs. In addition to exchanging currency the company may swap fixed-rate into floating-rate debt or floating to fixed rates. They are used as a hedge against currency movements for longer periods of time than would normally be possible in the forward market. In the strictest sense they are not really a derivative since they always involve an exchange of principal. However, they are treated as a derivative in the market. They are available in most major currencies, usually in minimum amounts of £5 million or US$5 million, with most deals being for 7 years or less. Longer periods are possible. An important consideration is the accounting treatment required in the jurisdiction of the parties to the swap. Is it required to be treated like a back-to-back loan and carried in full on the balance sheet, thus affecting key ratios and performance indicators? This varies from one country to another and the possible implications for the balance sheet need to be understood before a decision is made.

16

Interest rate risk

INTRODUCTION

At the time of writing interest rates are at a 50-year low and some financial managers might be feeling that interest rate management is not their top priority. However, as Figure 16.1 shows, they are volatile and from both a borrower's and an investor's view always need careful management.

US interest rates

Figure 16.1

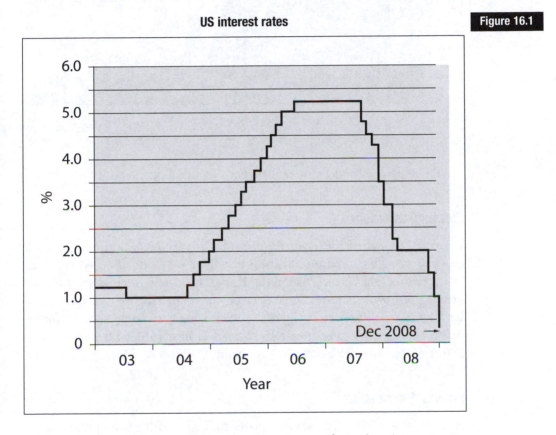

There has hardly been a period that I can remember when interest rates did not change by at least 50 basis points in any 6-month period.

Figure 16.2, which has been derived from Bank of England statistics, shows UK bank rates between 1975 and 2009.

Interest rate risk relates to the sensitivity of a company's profits to changes in interest rates. Some companies are more vulnerable than others. A highly geared company with a large amount of external borrowing might be more vulnerable than a lower-geared company with a smaller amount of external borrowing. A company will need to know how vulnerable it is to rate changes and how its competitors are geared before deciding on how to manage the risk of interest rate changes.

Figure 16.2

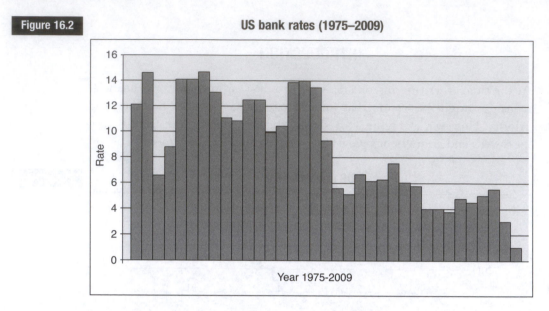

US bank rates (1975–2009)

Year 1975-2009

Different types of debt carry different types of risk.

Floating-rate debt

Floating-rate debt is debt where the rate will vary according to changes in the base rate. For example, floating-rate debt may be expressed as a percentage over the bank base rate. If the base rate increases, the total floating-rate will increase. Some floating-rate debt risks in a company may be all or partially offset by increases in floating-rate assets such as money market deposits. A company needs to be clear how vulnerable its profits are before taking any risk-management action.

Fixed interest rates

At first glance one might assume that a company with a high proportion of fixed interest rates is less vulnerable than an organisation with a high proportion of floating rates. To an extent this is the case. However, if general interest rates fall sharply its competitors on floating rates will obtain a cheaper source of funds and this might erode some competitive advantage. Understanding a company's vulnerability to interest rate changes includes knowing what the competitors are doing.

Unmatched basis risks

A company may have liabilities and assets that are matched in amount but not matched in terms of the 'basis' rate in the contract. Different 'basis' may not change at the same time and in perfect correlation, giving rise to what is termed 'basis risk'.

Gap exposure

Gap-analysis techniques can be used to determine the degree of exposure to interest rate changes. There are two types of gap:

- negative gap – where interest-sensitive liabilities exceed interest-sensitive assets maturing at the same time
- positive gap – where interest-sensitive assets exceed interest-sensitive liabilities maturing at the same time.

THE CAUSES OF INTEREST RATE FLUCTUATIONS

It is helpful to understand some of the principal causes of interest rate fluctuations since this may help with longer-term planning and choice of hedging strategy.

There are many reasons why interest rates vary between markets and sectors. These include:

- deposit size – a larger deposit may attract a higher rate from a bank because of an economy of scale in bank aggregation

Yield curves

Figure 16.3

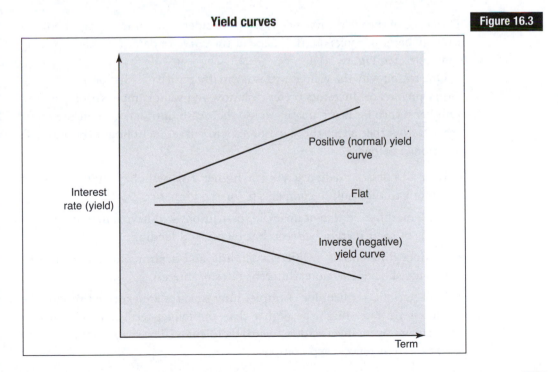

Figure 16.4

Positive and negative yield curves

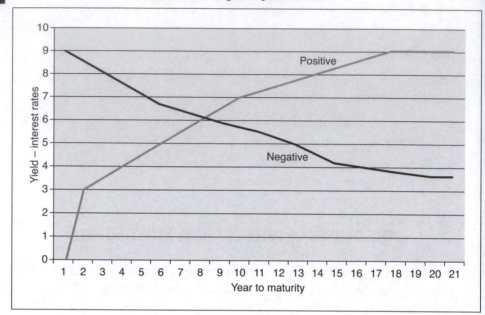

■ term of deposit – rates will vary according to the term of the deposit. Normally, the longer the term, the higher the rate, as shown by the positive yield curve in Figure 16.3. However, sometimes the yield curve is negative.

The shape of the yield curve needs to be considered when selecting a hedging strategy because banks use the shape of the curve to determine their pricing strategies. See Figure 16.4.

One reason why the yield curve is normally positive is that of investor liquidity preference. Investors prefer cash now and want compensation through a higher return for being unable to use their cash until later. There are many other factors that affect the slope of a yield curve, including 'expectations', mentioned below.

■ Risk – a lesser credit carrying a higher risk will pay higher rates of interest to the bank to compensate for the higher risk.

■ Bank margins – different financial institutions will have different needs in terms of their margin between borrowing and lending.

■ Product differentials – different lending and deposit products carry different risk and, therefore, different rates of interest.

■ Expectations – when, for example, interest rates are expected to fall, the short-term rates might be higher than the longer-term rate. This would be shown by an inverse (downward) yield curve. The shape of the curve to some extent reflects expectations.

- Governments – government policy can have a significant effect on expectations.

- Sectors – different market sectors carry different risks and interest rates. The risks within one sector can change at a different rate or in a different direction to another sector. For example, during a recession the demand for luxury products may decline while the demand for essentials remains constant.

- Investors' need for real returns and inflation – investors want to earn a 'real rate' of return (above the rate of inflation) on their investments. Uncertainty regarding inflation will perhaps encourage the demand for higher yields on investments.

- National deficit and controls – a country that has a balance-of-payments deficit might not allow its currency exchange rate to depreciate within the market by increasing interest rates to attract foreign investment to finance the deficit.

- A global market – the interest rates and expectations in one country will be influenced by the rates and expectations in another country. Governments may wish to avoid capital transfers and changes in exchange rates.

Understanding the shape and reasons for a yield curve and how each of the above factors affects a company will help it determine how sensitive its borrowing and investment interest rates will be to changes. For example, in December 2008 the Monetary Policy Committee (MPC) of the Bank of England set UK interest rates at an all-time low. This might have been partially or largely responsible for a fall in the value of sterling against the euro. This reduction in interest rates and the effect on exchange rates might be good news for companies with large external debt and for those which export and are helped by the weaker pound. It might, however, be bad for importers which have to pay more pounds for their imports. Knowing how sensitive your company is to changes in interest rates and understanding the causes will enable better overall financial planning and management.

In January 2009 the MPC set the UK bank rate at 1%, an all-time low. Now that interest rates are set by the MPC it may be assumed that politics has been taken out of the equation of UK interest setting. If we plot bank rates over the last 35 years against the political party in government we get the picture shown in Figure 16.5.

While the MPC now sets rates independently from government, it might be assumed that government policy has an effect on the economic and financial environment that the MPC considers when setting rates. Trying to forecast interest rates is rather like trying to forecast the weather but without the help of the seasons. We might guess that when rates are at an all-time low eventually they are likely to increase. However, this is only a 'likely'.

Figure 16.5

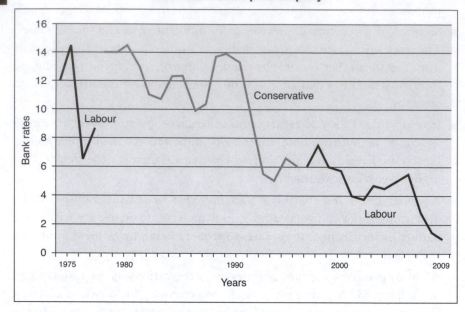

Bank rates versus political party

The all-important questions of by how much and when are unanswered. As a colleague recently said to me, 'These things are normally left to the masters of the universe who operate in the City gambling with other people's money.'

TYPES OF INTEREST RATE

- Variable rate – a variable rate changes when the lender alters its lending rate and depending on the rate of the central bank. Variable rates vary between lenders depending upon their own cost of capital and new business strategy.

- Discounted rate – discounted rate may be available for a period when a discount off the variable rate is given. The rate will vary whenever the lender changes its variable rate and the discount will be taken off the new variable rate.

- Fixed rate – fixed rates have the interest rate fixed for a period. They provide a guarantee to borrowers that their payments will not change for the specified period. A fixed-rate contract may include penalties for early redemption.

- Capped rate – a capped-rate loan includes a guarantee that the interest rate will not exceed a certain specified level. They are usually like variable-rate loans but with a maximum 'capped' rate limit.

- Capped and collared rate – a capped and collared loan is where the rate will not exceed a certain level (the cap) or fall below a certain level (the collar).

The rate of interest charged by a bank in the UK may be a specified amount or a margin (%) above a specified rate such as the Bank Base rate or LIBOR (London Inter Bank Offered Rate).

For example, a bank loan may be offered at 2% above LIBOR. Some of the more common specified rates are as follows:

- The base rate is the official Bank of England base rate (BOEBR). BOEBR is the rate that the Bank of England pays banks for money deposited with it. Changes in the base rate are considered and recommended by the MPC and implemented by the Govenor of the Bank of England. The base rate is the government's key tool for enacting monetary policy.

- LIBOR is a daily rate based on the interest rates at which banks borrow unsecured funds from banks in the London wholesale money market or interbank market.

- EURIBOR (Euro Inter Bank Offered Rate) is a daily reference rate based on the average rates at which banks offer to lend unsecured funds to other banks in the euro wholesale money market or interbank market.

- The prime lending rate is a term used in many countries to refer to a reference rate used by banks.

- The US prime rate is approximately 300 basis points above the federal funds rate. The best-known US prime rate is the Wall Street Journal Prime Rate.

- The US federal funds rate is the rate at which private depository institutions and banks lend balances at the Federal Reserve to other depository institutions.

INTEREST RATE RISK MANAGEMENT

Interest rate risk is the risk to a borrower of increased funding costs or to an investor of reduced yields on investments.

A borrower or investor has two principal choices when considering interest rate risk:

1. Do nothing and go with the market.

2. Fix a rate.

If a decision is made to manage interest rate risks then there are several techniques available. Choosing a technique will, to a large extent, depend upon the term of the exposure. The following table is a guide to risk-management techniques appropriate to different exposure terms:

Term of exposure	Risk-management technique
0–3 years	Forward-rate agreements (FRAs), financial futures, interest rate options, caps, collars, floors, swaps, swaptions
3–5 years	Swaps, swaptions, caps, collars, floors
5–10 years	Swaps, caps
10 years or more	Swaps

In addition to using external hedging techniques a company can use the internal hedging of asset liability management, matching and smoothing.

We will discuss some of the more common interest rate-management techniques below.

Matching

This is the method whereby a company matches its assets and liabilities with similar interest rate bases. For example, a company may have both borrowings and investments. To reduce interest rate exposure in both directions it might ensure that both its borrowings and investments are based upon a common rate such as LIBOR. This means that an increase in LIBOR-based borrowing expense will be offset or partially offset by a similar increase in LIBOR-based lending yields.

Smoothing

Smoothing is the technique of keeping a balance between fixed- and floating-rate borrowing so that a rise in interest rates that will make floating-rate borrowing more expensive will be compensated for by no increase in the fixed-rate borrowing. This is more a case of 'not having all your eggs in one basket'.

FRAs (FORWARD-RATE AGREEMENTS)

An FRA fixes a rate on future borrowing. FRAs are normally available for loans of £1 million upwards and for a period of up to 1 year. The bank fixes the rate for future borrowing. If the actual rate turns out to be higher than the agreed forward rate the bank will pay the company the difference between the two rates on the principal sum. If the actual interest rate is lower then the company pays the bank the difference.

Key features of an FRA include the following:

- Guarantee – the bank guarantees a rate of interest for a transaction that commences on a future date.

- Settlement – the principal amount is not exchanged; only the difference between the FRA rate and the market rate on the agreed future date is exchanged by the parties.

- Profit – there is no profit potential for the hedging party. The trader can make a profit.

- Costs – there are no significant costs to the hedger just as there are no profits. What the hedger gets is a guaranteed rate of interest.

- Set up – there is a risk to the bank that the company may not settle any difference due. Therefore, the company will need a credit line set up with its bank. To obtain competitive quotations it will need to set up lines with a number of banks.

Example

A UK plc needs a £20 million five-month fixed-interest-rate loan in 3 months' time and wants to use an FRA to hedge its interest rate exposure. The current FRA rate is 4%. In 3 months' time the FRA rate for a similar 5-month loan has increased to 5%.

1. The FRA required is a '3–8', that is an FRA that starts in 3 months' time and then lasts for 5 months.

2. Because the interest rate has increased (from 4% to 5%) the bank will pay the UK plc.

FRA receipt £20m × (5%–4%) × 5/12	£83,333
Payment on underlying loan (£20m × 5% × 5/12)	£416,667
Net payment	£333,334

$$\text{The effective rate is } \frac{£333,334}{£20,000,000} \times \frac{12}{5} = 4\%$$

INTEREST RATE DERIVATIVES

Interest rate derivatives can be used to manage interest rate risks or to speculate. Although speculation enables the market to operate, our interest is in the hedgers who use derivatives for risk management. We will discuss futures, options, caps, collars, floors and swaps.

Financial futures

The London International Financial Futures and Options Exchange (LIFFE) and similar exchanges around the globe trade interest rate futures contracts that can be used as a means of hedging against the risks of movements in interest rates. In the market, traders operate on behalf of the speculators, arbitrageurs and hedgers who make the market. A financial futures contract is an agreement to make or take delivery of a standard quantity of a financial instrument at a certain date and price through open trading on the exchange floor.

Example

A company contracts to buy £100,000 of a notional 20-year bond bearing a 7% coupon in 6 months' time at a price agreed in the market. It has done this because it feels that the futures price is going to vary with changes in interest rates and this action will, therefore, be a hedge against possible future adverse interest rate movements. The outlay to buy the future is less than that for buying the actual financial instrument, enabling the company to hedge with a small initial outlay.

Example

Hedging with short-term interest rate futures

A UK plc has decided to hedge the following position using futures.

It is 15 February and a UK plc has a requirement to borrow £20 million on 25 June. The company has taken the view that UK interest rates will increase. The 3-month LIBOR market on 15 February is 3.0%. The market is reflecting a future 3-month LIBOR rate of 3.3% since the current future is trading at 96.70.

On 15 February the UK plc sells 25 June short sterling futures for 96.70. Until 25 June the UK plc will receive and pay the daily market-variation margin (£20m/£500K = 40 contracts).

On 25 June the UK plc borrows from the inter-bank market at 3-month LIBOR rate of 4.0%.

On 25 June the UK plc buys back the futures contract at 96.0 (100 − 4).

On 25 June the UK plc receives back initial margin plus interest.

The profit on the futures trade is 96.70 − 96.0 = 70 ticks.

Futures profit value is 40 contract × 70 ticks × £12.50 tick value × £35,000 [(£20m/40) × (3/12) × £12.50].

The UK plc would have paid on £20 million @ 3.3% LIBOR × 90/360	= £165,000
The UK plc actually paid the final rate of 4% on £20 million × 90/360	= £200,000
Extra paid was	£35,000

The £35,000 extra paid was offset by the profit on the futures trade which means that the hedge achieved its result.

Warning. It is exceedingly easy to make a mistake in calculations of this type!

Because interest rate futures are standardised, corporate finance managers and treasurers might find their use as a hedging tool somewhat limiting. This is because they cannot always be matched precisely with a particular interest rate exposure.

What we are actually buying with an interest rate future is the entitlement to interest receipts. What we are selling is the promise to make future interest rate payments. A borrower will hedge against a possible interest rate rise by selling futures now. A lender will wish to hedge against the risk of interest rates falling by buying futures now and selling futures on the date the lending starts.

LIFFE futures contracts have maturity dates at the month ends of March, June, September and December.

Futures contracts and taxation

HMRC gives examples on its web site of how to calculate chargeable gains and losses on futures contracts. One example of this is given below and has been extracted from the HMRC site (www.hmrc.gov.uk/manuals/CG3 manual/CG56101.htm).

CG56101 – Futures: financial futures: contracts for differences: example

In both examples below, the shares in ABC Plc stand at £5 per share at commencement.

1. An investor expects the shares to rise, and enters into a long position over 20,000 shares. He puts up a deposit of £20,000 (20% of the full value of £100,000). The broker who is counter-party to the deal debits the investor's account with "interest" on the unpaid balance of £80,000 at 0.75% per calendar month (£600 per month). After two months, the company pays a dividend of 2p per share, and the broker credits the account with £400 (equivalent to the dividend on 20,000 shares).

   After three months the shares stand at £6.50 per share, and the investor closes out the contract. The increase in value of 20,000 shares over the life of the contract is £30,000, and this is credited to the investor's account. The broker also charges commission of £500.

   In summary, the account is as follows:

Deposit	£20,000
Less "interest" – 3 months @ £600 pm	£ 1,800
	£18,200
Plus "dividend"	£ 400
	£18,600
Plus increase in value of shares	£30,000
	£48,600
Less commission	£ 500
Final balance	£48,100

The chargeable gain is £28,100, the difference between the amount deposited and the closing balance. This can be expressed as:

Increase in value of 20,000 shares		£30,000
Plus "dividend" equivalent		£ 400
		£30,400
Less "interest" charges	£1,800	
Commission	£ 500	£ 2,300
Net gain		£28,100

If the shares had decreased in value to £4.50, the decrease in value of 20,000 shares (£10,000) would be debited from the account.

At close, the account would then be:

Opening deposit	£20,000
Less "interest" as above	£ 1,800
	£18,200
Plus "dividend"	£ 400
	£18,600
Less decrease in share price	£10,000
	£ 8,600
Less commission	£ 500
Closing balance	£ 8,100

The allowable loss is £11,900, the difference between the amount deposited and the closing balance. This is made up of:

Decrease in price of 20,000 shares	£10,000
Plus "interest" charges	£ 1,800
Commission	£ 500
	£12,300
Less "dividend"	£ 400
Net loss	£11,900

2. The investor expects the shares to fall. He enters into a short position over 20,000 shares. Once again, he deposits £20,000, 20% of the value of 20,000 shares. The broker credits "interest" of £450 per month (based on an interest rate of 0.5625% per calendar month), and debits an amount equivalent to a dividend of 2p per shares paid on 20,000 shares.

After three months, the investor closes out the contract when the share price is £3.75 per share. His account is credited with the reduction in price of 20,000 shares (£25,000).

The summarised account is:

Opening balance	£20,000
Plus "interest" for three months	£ 1,350
	£21,350
Less "dividend"	£ 400
	£20,950
Less commission	£ 500
	£20,450
Plus reduction in share price	£25,000
Closing balance	£45,450

The investor has a chargeable gain of £25,450, the difference between the amount deposited and the closing balance. This is made up of:

Decrease in share price		£25,000
Plus "interest" credits		£ 1,350
Net gain		£26,350
Less "dividend"	£400	
Commission	£500	£ 900
		£25,450

If the investor was wrong, and the shares in fact increased in value to £5.75 per shares between the opening and closing of the contract, the account would be:

Opening balance		£20,000
Plus "interest" credits		£ 1,350
		£21,350
Less "dividend" charge	£ 400	
Commission	£ 500	
Increase in value of 20,000 shares	£15,000	£15,900
Closing balance		£ 5,450

The investor has an allowable loss of £14,550, the difference between the amount deposited and the closing balance. This can be reconciled as:

Increase in value of the shares	£15,000
Less "interest" credits	£ 1,350
	£13,650
Plus "dividend" charge	£ 400
Commission	£ 500
	£14,550

Interest rate options

An interest rate option is the right but not the obligation to fix a rate of interest on a notional loan or deposit for a specified amount for a period or on a future date. A premium is paid for the option.

Interest rate options are derivatives used to hedge interest rate exposure. They have the following features and advantages:

- Limited downside for the client. The client pays a premium to insure against adverse movements. In this respect they are a type of insurance.

- Unlimited upside for the client. The option can be allowed to lapse since there is no obligation on the client. The client can, therefore, benefit from favourable movements in rates.

- Sell back to the bank. While options are not transferable they can still be sold back to the bank for a fair value if they are no longer required.

- Cash settlement by the bank on exercise.

The terminology used in interest rate options includes the following:

- Strike price – the interest rate where the client can exercise the right to cash settlement.

- Borrower's option – an option to hedge or speculate against an interest rate increase.

- Lender's option – an option to hedge or speculate against a fall in rates.

- Exercise – to take up the option on expiry.

- Expiry – the date when the option can be exercised.

- Premium – the price paid for the option.

- Intrinsic value – the difference between the strike price and the current market rate.

- Value date – the settlement date.

- Time value – the option premium less the intrinsic value.

- OTC – over-the-counter interest rate options are those that are tailor made for a client by a bank for specific maturity dates, values, currencies and agreed rates.

A hedging with a sterling interest rate option: **Example**

A UK plc has a £10 million loan with a rollover in 6 months' time on 1 December. On the rollover date the LIBOR will be re-fixed for another 6 months. The current 6-month LIBOR is 4.25%. The company thinks that rates may increase and arranges a borrower's option to protect the current level of 4.25%. The bank rate for the option is 16 basis points per annum.

The premium for the option is £10m × 0.16% × 182/365 = £7,978.08.

On 1 December the 6-month LIBOR is 5.25% and the company will, there-fore, exercise its option. This will give it a borrowing cost of 4.41% (being 4.25% + 0.16%). By taking out the borrower's option the company has hedged its rate successfully and achieved a net borrowing cost of 4.41% against the rate on expiry of 5.25%.

Had the LIBOR fallen to say 3.25%, on 1 December the company would allow the option to lapse. This would give an effective borrowing rate of 3.41% inclusive of the option premium (3.25% + 0.16%).

By taking out the option the company had limited its downside to 4.41% at a time when the current LIBOR was 4.25%. However, it had unlimited upside.

Interest rate caps, floors and collars

Caps

An interest rate cap is an option which includes an interest rate ceiling. It is a derivative product that protects the holder from rises in short-term interest rates by making a payment to the holder when the underlying interest rate, the "index" or "reference" interest rate, exceeds a specified strike rate known as the cap rate. Caps are purchased for a premium and can be OTC. Payments are made to the holder monthly, quarterly or semi-annually.

Floors

A floor is an option that has a lower limit to interest rates. Floors are derivatives that protect the holder from declines in short-term interest rates by making a payment to the holder when the underlying interest rate, the "index" or "reference" interest rate, falls below a specified strike rate or "floor rate". Floors are purchased for a premium. Payments are made to the holder monthly, quarterly or semi-annually.

Collars

An interest rate collar is a contract whereby if the client's funding cost is more than an agreed level it will be reimbursed down to that agreed level. If the funding cost falls below a second agreed level the client will repay the bank any extra benefit. A collar combines the purchase of a cap and the sale of a floor to specify a range within which an interest rate exposure can fluctuate. Collars insulate the buyer against the risk of a rise in a floating rate but limit the benefits to the buyer from a drop in the rate.

Interest rate swaps

An interest rate swap is where two parties agree to exchange interest rate payments. They can be used to switch from one type of interest to another, for example from fixed to floating rate (known as a plain vanilla swap). They can be used by one party to obtain lower rates on borrowing and by another to secure better rates on deposits. There are combinations of currency and interest rate swaps, such as a fixed- to floating-rate currency swap.

The features of an interest rate swap include:

- no premium is required
- tailored to exact underlying requirements
- a guaranteed rate of interest
- only the interest payments are swapped, not the principal amounts
- the credit risk of the counterparty needs to be evaluated. It might be guaranteed by an intermediary bank
- a credit line will be required.

In a fixed- to floating-rate swap each party agrees to pay to the other either a fixed or floating rate denominated in a particular currency. The rate (fixed or floating) is applied to the notional amount (the principal). The notional amount is used only for calculating the sums to be exchanged between the parties and is not itself exchanged.

An interest rate swap (fixed for floating, same currencies)

Example

A pays a fixed rate (the swap rate) to B and receives a floating rate (based on LIBOR) from B. A agrees to pay B fixed interest rate payments of 2.00% in exchange for receiving variable interest rate payments from B of LIBOR + 50 basis points (0.5000%). There is no exchange of a principal. Interest rates are based on a notional principal amount of £5 million.

Interest payments are settled net according to schedule. If LIBOR was 1.2% then party A pays 0.3% and party B receives 0.3% of the principal amount (2.00% − LIBOR + 50bps).

A pays to B 0.3% being 2% − (1.2% + 0.50%)

B pays to A 0.3% being 2% − (1.2% + 0.50%)

In this example the swap rate was 2.00% and the notional amount was £5 million. The interest rate of 0.3% would be applied to the principal amount for the duration (period) of the swap.

The swap would have been priced from the start at a rate that gives an NPV of zero so that if party A wants to pay 50 bps above the swap rate then party B would have to pay approximately 50 bps over LIBOR.

The most common types of interest rate swaps are fixed-for-fixed, fixed-for-floating or floating-for-floating. Swaps can be in the same currency or different currencies. There must, of course, be something to swap.

Fixed-for-floating rate swap, different currencies

A fixed-for-floating swap in different currencies is used to convert a fixed-rate asset/liability in one currency to a floating-rate asset/liability in another currency, or vice versa.

For example, a New Zealand company borrows NZ$10 million for 5 years at 6% p.a. payable annually. A UK company borrows the sterling equivalent of NZ$10 million (£3.8 million) for 5 years at LIBOR plus a margin of 0.5% payable semi-annually. Under a swap agreement the NZ company would pay the UK company sterling interest in return for the UK company paying the NZ company NZ$ interest. See Figure 16.6.

Figure 16.6   **Fixed-for-floating rate swap in different currencies interest payments.**

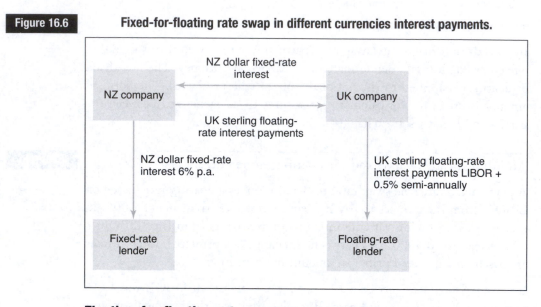

Floating-for-floating rate swap, same currency

For example, a company pays Japanese yen LIBOR monthly to receive Japanese yen TIBOR monthly on a notional (principal) of Japanese yen for 5 years. Floating-for-floating rate swaps may be used to hedge or speculate on the spread between the two indexes widening or narrowing. They are also useful where both parties reference the same index on different payment dates.

Floating-for-floating rate swap, different currencies

For example, one party pays or receives floating-rate interest in yen to receive/pay floating-rate interest in US$ on a notional value at an initial rate of exchange for a specified period.

This type of swap might be useful to fund overseas growth where the borrower is not well known in the overseas country. This problem might be partially overcome by issuing local currency debt and then converting to the overseas currency. However, this introduces the risk of currency exposures which will need to be hedged.

Fixed-for-fixed rate swap in different currencies

As an example, one party pays/receives fixed interest in sterling to receive/pay fixed-rate interest in US$ for 5 years.

An interest rate swap – floating to fixed rate

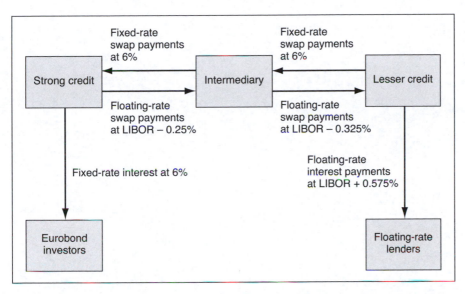

The interest payable by the 'strong credit' in the capital markets is lower than the rate payable in the bank credit market. It is advantageous, therefore, for the 'strong credit' who is wishing to borrow on a floating-rate basis to issue fixed-rate bonds on a capital market and then swap into a floating-rate loan since it can obtain a floating-rate borrowing at a relatively lower rate.

In this example, the 'strong credit' borrows effectively on a floating rate at 0.25% below LIBOR when the rate of interest if it had borrowed directly from the bank market would have been over LIBOR. The 'lesser credit' will also benefit.

Interest rate swap summary

There are many types and variations of swap structures. With all swap transactions the detail can be confusing and to help understand them it is best to always draw a simple chart of the cash flows generated by the agreement for both parties.

Swaps are a flexible risk-management device that can cover interest rate exposures of between 1 month and more than 50 years. They are a means whereby one party exchanges a benefit it has in its own market with another party for a benefit in their market. The market for swaps is enormous. In June 2008 the Bank for International Settlements reported the notional amount of swaps to be US$356,772 billion.

Investment decisions

INVESTMENT AND THE CAPITAL BUDGETING PROCESS

Investment is expenditure made with the expectation of future income. Investment can be made into capital expenditure (property, plant, equipment, etc.) and into revenue expenditure (materials, wages, selling costs, etc.). This chapter looks at the techniques for investment appraisal and in particular how they are applied to capital expenditure.

A capital budgeting process was defined by Paul King in his 1975 paper entitled 'Strategic Control of Capital Expenditure'. He identified six stages for capital investment decisions and concluded that decisions emerged as a result of a complex social process of which formal consideration by management formed only a small part. The six stages were:

1 triggering   4 evaluation

2 screening   5 transmission

3 definition   6 decision.

Figure 17.1 shows how the stages normally flow and what they mean.

Figure 17.1

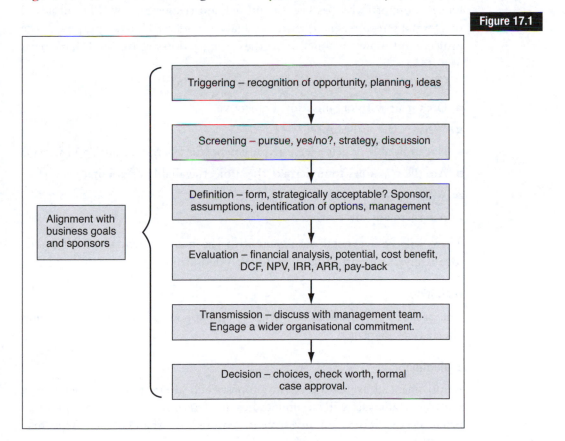

It is likely that an organisation will merge several of the six capital budgeting stages.

Some companies might put more effort into the evaluation and analysis stage before the budget is approved. Another company might give budget approval without so much detailed analysis.

However, before an actual commitment is made the six stages will normally have been completed.

Triggering and origination of proposal

An investment opportunity will be recognised from both internal and external 'environmental' scans. These scans look for market openings, competitor activity, customer needs, production improvements and any other ideas which will lead to an increase in shareholder value. A company should have a formal mechanism set up that carries out investment opportunity reviews as a part of its planning and budgeting process. The review should look for opportunities that are consistent with the organisation's overall objectives and strategy.

Screening

Once an opportunity has been identified and triggered it will be subjected to a formal screening and qualitative analysis to determine the purpose of the project and how this fits into the organisation's goals and long-term objectives.

Questions that will need to be answered include:

- Does it fit with organisational objectives?
- What is the real purpose?
- Is it avoidable or is it a legal requirement (for example, health and safety)?
- Are the resources to undertake the project available or obtainable?
- What are the risks?
- Are there any alternatives?

There will be a general discussion with the management team before the idea is given support for a more detailed definition.

Definition

The proposal sponsor will be identified and appointed, assumptions set and alternatives identified.

Evaluation

A full financial evaluation of the proposal and alternatives together with a sensitivity analysis will be undertaken to determine whether the proposal produces the return on investment required by shareholders. This may include DCF, NPV, IRR, ARR and pay-back analysis. The evaluation will also consider the socio-economic implications and environmental considerations.

Transmission

This stage is all about getting acceptance from a wider group within the organisation. The cooperation of other managers and functions will be required for both approval of the proposal and its ongoing success. This will require transmission of the proposal to obtain wider organisational commitment. This transmission may be through both a formal and an informal process.

Decision

This will require a formal case together with choices to be considered for approval by the executive committee who will accept responsibility for their go or no-go decision. Once the project has been approved in the capital budget it may require a final approval in the budget year before a commitment is actually made and contracts are signed.

Project monitoring and critical path analysis

Once the decision is made to commence with the project a project manager and team will be established to ensure that the project is completed on time, within budget, to the standards expected and to ensure that the benefits of the project are obtained. The project manager will normally prepare a critical path analysis (CPA) to control the project completion. This technique will show the network of activities and events within the total project and in particular will identify which activities are on the 'critical path'. Any delay on the critical path will cause an overall delay in the total project. There may be slack in parts of the project where a delay will not affect the overall project completion date.

The accounting system will need to record expenditure against the project and also against activities. It is possible that there will be multiple contracts and sources of expenditure relating to any one activity on the project. The project's CPA will need to reconcile to the accounting records, a task normally carried out by the project accountant, cost engineer or quantity surveyor.

RELEVANT CASH FLOW

Certain costs are not totally relevant in investment appraisal. For example, past cost or costs already committed are not totally relevant to decision making because the decision affecting their existence has already been made.

Costs that are really relevant to investment appraisal are those new costs associated with the decision and opportunity costs (the costs of forgoing one opportunity for another). What really interests us in investment appraisal are costs that arise as a consequence of the decision we are evaluating.

Benefits that are relevant include increased cash flows from a project, cost savings from efficiencies, improved customer relationships (business retention/extension) and better staff retention.

Relevant costs and benefits include:

- incremental costs associated with the proposed new investment
- opportunity costs
- additional taxation arising from the investment
- residual values
- working capital
- selling, distribution and marketing costs
- infrastructure costs
- human asset costs
- savings in staff and operating costs
- additional sales revenue
- income from the sale of existing assets that the proposed investment might release
- better customer retention
- customer business extensions
- better staff retention.

Example A manufacturer is considering purchasing a new machine for US$300,000. It will replace an old machine which cost US$190,000 and is nearing the end of its working life. The old machine has a scrap value of £5,000. Annual production and sales from the new machine would be 10,000 units selling at US$40 per unit. The unit product costings are:

Direct material	US$10
Direct labour	US$5
Fixed costs	US$10

The unit contribution is $40 − ($10+$5)= $25.

The new machine would have a life of 5 years with a residual value of US$10,000. To install and operate the new machine would require a diversion of 1,000 hours p.a. of scarce supervision resource which currently makes a contribution of US$10 per hour.

The relevant costs are:

		US$
Year 0	Purchase price	−300,000
Years 1–5	Contribution 10,000 units × $40 – $15)	+250,000 p.a.
	Opportunity cost 1,000 × $10	−10,000 p.a.
Year 5	Residual value	+10,000

The above costs and benefits are relevant to the decision and will be used in the pay-back and/or discounted cash flow calculations. The pay-back analysis will simply demonstrate the length of time it will take for the project benefits to pay for the investment. The discounted cash flow will evaluate the relevant costs, taking into account the time value of money by considering the timing of the cash flow of the relevant costs.

The other costs shown in the example are not really relevant to the decision. The cost of the old machine is a past decision. The scrap value of the old machine would have been relevant if the old machine's replacement was optional. However, it had reached the end of its life and would have been scrapped whether a new machine was purchased or not.

PAY-BACK PERIOD METHOD OF EVALUATION

This is the time that it takes for the cash inflows from an investment project to cover or equal the cash outflows. Although, as we shall see, this method has certain inadequacies, it is used as a quick and simple measure of a project's viability. The pay-back period is measured in years or months and obviously the shorter the period, the more attractive the project will be in pay-back terms.

For an example of a pay-back analysis consider two projects:

	Project A	Project B
	£	£
Initial investment	90,000	90,000
Profits		
Year 1	30,000	22,250
Year 2	30,000	22,250
Year 3	30,000	22,250
Year 4	10,000	22,250
Year 5	0	22,250

Project A has a payback period of 3 years. Project B has a payback period of 4 years. Therefore, on the basis of pay-back alone, project A wins.

However, as you would have observed, there is a weakness in this argument because project B earns income for a longer period and overall is more profitable. Neither of these observations has taken into account the time value of money, which in a period of high interest rates could be very significant.

The pay-back method is very useful as a first measure but even then it should not be used in isolation and the full cash flow and timings should also be taken into account. It is useful during first-stage screening particularly in a situation where capital is rationed and quick additional cash is a key selection criterion. Most finance managers use a pay-back analysis alongside other methods of appraisal such as ROCE, DCF and IRR.

RETURN ON CAPITAL EMPLOYED (ROCE)

ROCE can be useful in investment appraisal. This measure of return shows the percentage that profits earned on an investment compared with the cost of the investment. There are several different definitions of ROCE, profits and investment. Some of these that are relevant to investment appraisal are given below.

$$\text{ROCE} = \frac{\text{Average profits}}{\text{Average investment}} \times 100\%$$

$$\text{ROCE} = \frac{\text{Total profits}}{\text{Initial investment}} \times 100\%$$

$$\text{ROCE} = \frac{\text{Average profits}}{\text{Initial investment}} \times 100\%$$

The first method is commonly used. Whichever method is chosen it should be used consistently and explained. When comparing with ROCE figures produced by another party, ensure that you are comparing like with like.

A company requires a return on capital employed of 11% p.a. It has the opportunity to invest in a 5-year project costing $100,000 with a nil scrap value. Income after depreciation from the investment is estimated to be $12,500 p.a. during years 1 to 3 and $6,000 p.a. in years 4 and 5. Should it undertake the project?

$$\text{Average earnings} = \frac{(3 \times \$12,500) + (2 \times \$6,000)}{5 \text{ years}}$$

Average earnings = $9,900 p.a.

$$\text{ROCE} = \frac{\$9,900}{\$100,000} \times 100\%$$

ROCE = 9.9% p.a.

Since this is less than the company's required return of 11%, on the basis of ROCE the project would not be undertaken.

ROCE can be useful when comparing mutually exclusive projects or in the case of capital rationing. However, it does have its drawbacks. It does not take account of the timing of investments and cash flows. This is a serious drawback, especially when interest rates are high. It is also a relative measure and does not take into account the absolute size of an investment and returns. However, it is a simple and familiar method which can be used alongside other methods.

ACCOUNTING RATE OF RETURN (ARR)

This method of investment appraisal compares profits with the original cost of investment or average net book values. There are several formulae:

$$\frac{\text{Average annual profit after depreciation}}{\text{Original cost of investment}} \times 100\%$$

$$\frac{\text{Average annual profit after depreciation}}{\text{Average net book value}} \times 100\%$$

$$\frac{\text{Total profit over } n \text{ years after depreciation}}{\text{Original cost of investment}} \times 100\%$$

The main disadvantage of the ARR is that it does not take into account the timing of cash flows.

DISCOUNTED CASH FLOW, NET PRESENT VALUE AND INTERNAL RATE OF RETURN

This chapter explains the discounted cash flow and net present value techniques for investment appraisal which take into account changes in the value of money over time. The techniques previously discussed in this chapter have important weaknesses in that they do not allow for time value changes. Discounted cash flow methods overcome this problem.

The two methods that use discounted cash flow are net present value and internal rate of return. The discounted cash flow method considers the cash flow of a project for both costs and benefits and their timing. It does not consider non-cash items.

Compounding

The future value of a project with interest is:

$$FV = PV (1 + r)^n$$

where:

FV = the future value of an investment together with interest
PV = the present value of the initial investment
r = the compound rate of interest/return during the period
n = the period.

For example, the future value of £100 invested at a rate of 5% for 3 years is:

$$FV = £100 (1 + 0.05)^3$$

$$FV = £115.76.$$

Present value and discounting

If the future value is: $FV = PV (1 + r)^n$

then present value must be $PV = FV \dfrac{1}{(1 + r)^n}$

For example, if a company normally earned 5% p.a. on its investments, how much should it invest today to have £115.76 in 3 years' time?

$$PV = £115.76 \times \frac{1}{(1 + 0.05)^3}$$

$$PV = £115.76 \times 0.8638$$

$$PV = £100.$$

Note the 5% discount factor for year 3 calculated using the formula was 0.8638. This can be obtained from the discount tables given in Appendix 1. For the rest of this chapter we will use discount tables.

Present value and net present value

Discounting can be used to bring a future cash flow stream back to present values. The sum of the present values is the NPV. This is best explained by means of an example:

A company is considering a capital investment with the following cash flow:

	£
Year 0 Investment	−300,000
Year 1 Income	+110,000
Year 2 Income	+115,000
Year 3 Income	+120,000

The company has a cost of capital of 5%. Should it undertake the project?

Year	Cash flow £	5% discount factor	Present value £
0	−300,000	1.000	−300,000
1	+110,000	0.952	+104,720
2	+115,000	0.907	+104,305
3	+120,000	0.864	+103,680
		NPV	+12,705

The NPV is the total of all the present values. It is a positive figure at +£12,405. Since it is positive it means that the DCF yield is greater than the company's cost of capital which was used to discount the cash flow. Since the yield is greater than the cost of capital, the project should be undertaken.

Present value of a cash flow an annuity in perpetuity

To calculate the present value of an annuity (PVA) use the following formula:

$$\text{Present value of annuity} = P\left(\frac{1 - \frac{1}{(1 + i)^n}}{i}\right)$$

where:

P = principal amount

i = interest rate

n = number of years or period.

Alternatively simply divide the principal sum by the discount rate (return rate). The present value of £1 invested annually for ever (in perpetuity) using a discount rate of 10% is £1/0.10 = £10.

What this means is that £10 today is equal to £1 in perpetuity when the discount rate is 10%. You can check this out by using the above full formula. Using $n = 70$ (say), $PVA = £1(0.9987/0.1)$
$PVA = £10$.

Example

A company has a £100,000 investment opportunity that will yield cash inflows of £20,000 in perpetuity. It has a cost of capital of 12%. Should it undertake the project?

Present value of cash inflow in perpetuity is £20,000/0.12 = £166,667.

Since this exceeds the initial investment of £100,000, the project should be undertaken.

The NPV of the project will be $-$ £100,000 + £166,667 = £66,667.

The internal rate of return (IRR)

The IRR is the rate at which the NPV of a cash flow is zero. The easiest way to calculate the IRR is by interpolation. If the expected IRR exceeds the target rate of return then the project would be worth undertaking (ignoring other factors). The IRR is an easily understood measure and can be compared to the targeted yield. However, it does not demonstrate the relative size of projects.

Example

A company has a cost of capital of 9%. It has a project opportunity with the following cash flow:

Year	Cash flow £000s
0	$-1,000$
1	$+600$
2	$+600$

Using the IRR as a criterion, should the company undertake the project?

Solution

The IRR is the discount rate that will produce an NPV of zero. By trial and error, select a rate that will produce a small positive NPV and then a rate that will produce a small negative NPV. In this case it is 12% and 14%. The IRR will lie between these two rates and can be found by interpolation.

Year	Cash flow £000s	Discount factor 12%	PV £000	Discount factor 14%	PV £000
0	−1,000	1	−1,000	1	−1,000
1	+600	0.893	+536	0.877	+526
2	+600	0.797	+478	0.769	+461
		NPV	+14	NPV	−13

A discount rate of 12% gives an NPV of +£14K and a discount rate of 14% gives an NPV of −£13K. Therefore, the IRR lies between 12% and 14%.

Using interpolation we can see that a 2% move (from 12% to 14%) has resulted in a −£27K change (from +14 to −13) in the NPV. Therefore, to move from =14 to zero we would need the following discount rate:

$$12\% + (14\% - 12\%) \times 14/(14 + 13)$$

$$= 12\% + 1.04\%$$

IRR = 13.04%.

Since the IRR of 13.04% is greater than the company's cost of capital of 9%, the project should be undertaken on this criterion.

The IRR can also be determined by using a quadratic equation or from a programmable computer.

Proof of IRR calculation:

Year	Cash flow £000	Discount rate 13.04%	PV £000
0	−1,000	1	−1,000
1	+600	0.8846	+531
2	+600	0.7826	+469
		NPV	Zero

Using the discount rate of 13.04% has produced a zero NPV.

The discount rates were determined from the following formula:

$$DR = 1/(1 + i)^n$$

$$DR\ Year\ 2 = 1/(1.1304)^2$$

DR Year 2 = 0.7826.

Figure 17.2 shows a project's NPV curve at different costs of capital and the point of the IRR being where the NPV curve crosses the cost of capital line.

The IRR example we have used is a conventional cash flow in that there is an initial investment followed by cash inflows. Had the cash flow been non-conventional (outflows at various stages) then there could have been a

Figure 17.2

IRR = ZERO NPV

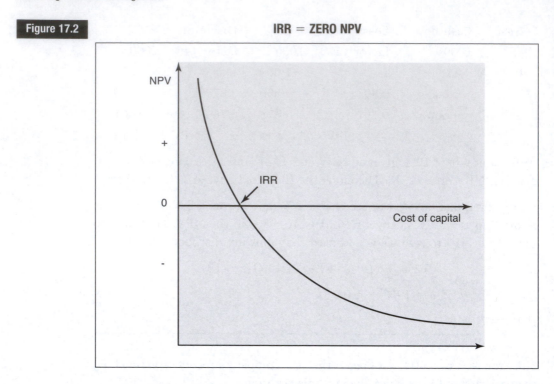

number of IRRs. Most analysts would not normally use IRR when there is a non-conventional cash flow. Multiple IRRs if not noticed during the calculations can lead to incorrect decisions.

CAPITAL RATIONING

Capital availability has its limits and a company may have to choose between projects it is able to undertake within the constraints of available capital. When doing this it will seek to maximise the return from projects undertaken subject to the constraint of capital available.

There are two principal capital-rationing situations:

1. Where projects are divisible.
2. Where projects are not divisible.

Example

Capital rationing where projects are divisible:

A company has £2,500,000 of funds available for investment in new projects. The following is a summary of the project costs and their NPVs shown in £000s. The projects are divisible and can be partly undertaken. The company requires a minimum return on investment of 30%.

	Project A	Project B	Project C
Cost in year 0	1,000	300	1,500
NPV	500	240	900
% NPV to cost	50%	80%	60%

How should the company prioritise its investment across the three possible projects?

Solution:

B produces the highest return on investment and will, therefore, be subject to maximisation. Then C and any residue capital available will be spent on A.

Project	Investment	NPV
	(£000)	(£000)
B	300	240
C	1,500	900
A	700	350 being 500 × (700/1000)
	2,500	1,490

By spreading the £2,500,000 investment across the projects in the priority of their return on investment (highest first) the company will maximise the total of NPVs to £1,490,000.

Not all projects are, however, divisible. If the above projects were not divisible and had to be undertaken in their totality or not at all then the situation would be as shown below.

Capital rationing where projects are not divisible:

Example

Where projects are not divisible a company may choose to select the projects that produce the highest NPVs within the constraint of capital available. In the above example the selection could be:

Project	Investment	NPV
	(£000)	(£000)
A	1,000	500
C	1,500	900
	2,500	1,400

This selection has used up all of the capital available and produced the highest total NPV in a situation where the projects were not divisible.

THE EFFECT OF TAXATION ON INVESTMENT APPRAISAL AND DCF

The effect of undertaking a project will be to increase or decrease tax liabilities and payments in any year. The effect that undertaking a project has on taxation payments should be included in the project cash flows, DCF and NPV.

One major effect of taxation on project DCFs in the UK is caused by the system of capital allowances which encourage companies to make more investments by acelerating the tax benefits of capital expenditure. When taxation is included in the cash flow and DCF calculations a post-tax required rate of return should be used. For the purpose of DCF calculations the two major UK taxation considerations are:

- corporation tax
- capital allowances.

Corporation tax is payable on a company's profits nine months after the company's year end. This cash outflow at the prevailing rate of tax should be allowed for in the cash flow and DCF calculations.

Capital allowances are used to reduce tax payments. The timing of these tax savings should be determined and their value built into the cash flow and DCF.

Mergers and acquisitions (M&A)

BACKGROUND AND DEFINITIONS

A merger is where two separate companies amalgamate to form one company. An acquisition is where one company gains a controlling interest in another through external investment.

An acquisition is sometimes referred to as a takeover. It is where one company buys another company referred to as the target company. In a friendly acquisition the two companies cooperate with each other in their negotiations. In a hostile acquisition or hostile takeover the target company is unwilling to be purchased and the target's board will put the case that the acquisition is not in the shareholder's best interest. An acquisition may be the purchase of a smaller firm by a larger one. In the case of a reverse takeover a smaller firm may acquire management control of a larger company.

An acquisition might be the takeover of a public company by another public company, the takeover of an unquoted private company by a public company or the takeover of one unquoted private company by another. Where the target company is an unquoted private company, the valuation will not have the benefit of a share market valuation guide as would be the case of a plc target.

Where the acquisition involves public companies with shares quoted on the stock market or Unlisted Securities Market (USM), the companies must adhere to the City Code on Takeovers and Mergers.

There are certain types of acquisition. These include:

- a share purchase where the purchaser acquires a majority of shares and control of the target company. Ownership and control of the target company give control over the assets and liabilities of the company.

- an asset purchase where the buyer acquires certain or all of the assets of the target company.

When companies join together through acquisition or merger there must be combined overall benefits and synergy whereby the combined value is greater than the sum of the constituent parts. Some of the main reasons behind a business acquisition or merger are to:

- improve liquidity
- grow faster
- improve risk profile and credit rating
- diversify
- obtain economies of scale
- combine competitors and increase market share

- acquire a management team
- improve quality of earnings
- enter a new market
- acquire new products, technologies and patents
- improve customer base and spread
- improve geographical diversification
- consider tax advantages but bearing in mind anti-avoidance provisions
- share services
- obtain lower-cost labour or other resources
- gain cross-selling opportunities
- obtain the benefits of a vertical integration (supplier and customer, for example)
- share information.

The shareholders of an acquiring company may experience either negative or insignificant returns following a merger/acquisition announcement. However, the shareholders of target firms may benefit from significantly positive gains. Overall, the combined companies' value may increase and this might be due to the effect of synergy between the two companies where the value of the whole is considered by the market to be worth more than the value of the sum of the parts.

A merger is a combination of two companies into one larger company. This can be voluntary through a share swap and/or cash payment. A share swap enables the shareholders of the two companies to share the risk involved in the combination. Mergers may be:

- horizontal where the two companies' products and industry sector are the same
- vertical where the two companies work at different stages in the production of the same finished product
- conglomerate where the two firms work in different industries
- combinations of the above and situations where two companies are in the same industry but do not have a buyer-to-customer relationship.

CONSIDERATIONS ON ACQUISITION

When making an acquisition decision the directors of the bidding company will need to consider the effects of the proposed acquisition or merger on the following:

1. The earnings per share attributable to the existing organisations and the

proposed combined organisation. It is undesirable that there should be a drop in the EPS. Existing shareholders will not want to see a dilution of earnings.

2. Gearing. For example, an acquiring company may need to borrow in order to raise the purchase consideration and this may create an undesirable level of gearing. However, the use of borrowing may be less expensive to the acquiring company than equity since the interest on borrowing is allowable as a tax-deductible expense.

3. Whether any consideration in the form of shares or whether funds raised through new shares can be accommodated within existing authorised capital constraints.

4. Changes in control of the companies.

5. Constraints on borrowing limits.

6. Whether the shareholders of the target company have a preference for shares in the bidding company as consideration rather than cash.

7. Liabilities to tax arising from cash considerations.

8. The ability to maintain income post merger or acquisition.

Factors which will influence a proposed takeover decision include the following:

1. The price and valuation.

2. Valuation method – earnings, assets, value of synergy, growth prospects.

3. Existing shareholder reactions.

4. Market response.

5. Form of purchase consideration – shares or cash?

6. Funding of consideration – raise equity, dilution, loan?

7. Effect on financial reporting.

8. Dividend policy.

9. Staff and management contracts.

10. Bidding company's shareholder reaction to proposal.

11. Compliance with stock exchange rules.

12. Target company resistance and reasons for this.

13. Target company defensive tactics.

14. Damage and costs of a failed acquisition attempt.

DEFENSIVE TACTICS

The directors of a company receiving a bid must always act in the best interests of their company, shareholders, creditors and employees. If they feel that the offer is not in the best interests of the company then they may decide to contest the offer. Some of the grounds for rejection of an offer are listed below.

Grounds for rejection

1. Initial rejection may lead to an improved offer. The existing offer is simply not good enough.

2. The target company employees are opposed to the bid.

3. The proposed merger or takeover shows no advantages or synergy.

4. The directors feel that the proposals will fail for any number of reasons (monopolies, existing shareholder reactions, etc.) and that the failure will take up valuable management time and perhaps damage their company's value or share price.

Defensive moves

To fight off an unwelcome bid the directors can:

1. Issue statements to existing shareholders and the market showing expected future profits and dividends and demonstrate that the price offered is too low. This has to be an accurate and honest forecast. Such a statement together with the bidder's offer might have the effect of increasing the market value of the shares. This will either deter the bidder or at least obtain a better price from them. At the same time and as part of this release of information to shareholders and the market, ensure that all assets are re-valued if this is possible within the time constraints of an early response.

2. If appropriate bring to the attention of the Competition Commission through the Office of Fair Trading. If the proposed merger is not in the public interest the Competition Commission has powers to make recommendations to the Department for Business Innovation and Skills (BIS, formerly the BERR/DTI) and the companies involved.

3. In the press releases attack (if true) the accounts and performance of the bidding company. Try to prove that an offer of equity in the bidding company is not as good as it has been held out to be.

4. Find a 'white knight'. This is a company that will make a welcome takeover bid.

5. Arrange a management buyout.

6. Make a counter bid for the predator company if it is of a similar size.

Which tactic to use and when to use it will depend upon the ultimate objectives of the target company. For example, the target company board might only want to push up the offer price and will hold off on some of the other tactics initially. Tactics will be selected and used as events unfold. They can be expensive in terms of professional fees and other defensive costs. However, all tactics must be fair, ethical and honest and must comply with the City Code (in the UK) or equivalent codes and regulations in other countries.

The bidding company will seek to persuade shareholders of the target company that its offer is a good price and provides the opportunity for a capital gain. The bidder will succeed only if it can convince enough shareholders of the target company that this is the case.

COMPETITION COMMISSION

In most countries there are regulations to ensure that large mergers and takeovers are in the public interest. In the UK the Office of Fair Trading (OFT) might scrutinise significant mergers and takeovers. If the OFT thinks that a merger or takeover is not in the public interest it may refer the case to the Competition Commission (CC). If the CC thinks the merger or takeover is not in the public interest it will make recommendations to the BIS and to the companies involved.

The CC is the independent body responsible for investigating mergers and takeovers under UK competition law. The Competition Commission was created by the Competition Act of 1998 and replaced the Monopolies and Mergers Commission on 1 April 1999. The Act created a competition law structure for the UK that is similar to competition law in the European Treaty.

The CC or the OFT will look to see that the merger or takeover is not:

1. anti-competitive within any market

2. creating a cartel

3. abusing a dominant position

4. reducing competition

5. restricting the number of outlets.

On the positive side the Commission will look to see whether the merger or takeover:

1. improves overall efficiency

2. reduces prices

3. improves exports and international competitiveness.

An example of a CC finding extracted from the CC press release on its web site is given below:

> The Competition Commission (CC) has blocked the proposed acquisition by BOC Limited (BOC) of the packaged chlorine business and assets of Ineos Chlor Limited (Ineos Chlor). The principal use of packaged chlorine is by the UK water industry for water disinfection.
>
> In its final report published today, the CC has concluded that the merger would result in a substantial lessening of competition in the markets for the distribution of packaged chlorine in cylinders and in drums in the UK. This confirms the conclusion of the provisional findings report which was published on 16 September 2008.
>
> After carefully considering alternative remedies, including those proposed by BOC and Ineos Chlor, the CC has concluded that prohibition of the merger is an effective and proportionate remedy, and that it is a lower-cost remedy than the alternatives considered.
>
> *Diana Guy, Inquiry Group Chairman, commented:*
>
> We found that the proposed merger would reduce the number of competing distributors and would end the rivalry between BOC and Ineos Chlor, which are currently each other's closest competitors in these markets.
>
> Our conclusion is that the merger would be anti-competitive and would lead to customers paying higher prices and having less choice than would otherwise be the case. We fully considered alternative remedies which were advanced by the parties, including one which held out the possibility of lower prices for customers than if we simply prohibited the merger. However, we were not convinced that these alternatives would be effective nor that prices would indeed be lower. These alternatives also involved risks and costs that would not arise if the merger were prohibited.
>
> *The CC's reasoning can be found in its report which is published.*

What the Competition Commission investigates

The following table from the Commission's web site (www.competition -commission.org.uk/our_role/what_investigate/) explains what the Commission investigates and where the referral comes from. Note that the CC investigates referrals from referring organisations and that an enquiry must go through a referring organisation.

Type of inquiry	Enactment	Referring organisation
Completed merger	Enterprise Act 2002 s22	Office of Fair Trading
Anticipated merger	Enterprise Act 2002 s33	Office of Fair Trading
Article 21(4) – protection of legitimate interests	Enterprise Act 2002 (Protection of Legitimate Interests) Order 2003	Secretary of State
Merger raising public interest issues, including some newspaper and other media mergers	Enterprise Act 2002 s45	Secretary of State
Merger raising special public interest issues	Enterprise Act 2002 s62	Secretary of State
Market	Enterprise Act 2002 s131, 132	Office of Fair Trading, sectoral regulators with concurrent powers (the Office of Communications (Ofcom), the Gas and Electricity Markets Authority (GEMA), the Director General of Water Services, the Northern Ireland Authority for Energy Regulation (NIAER), the Office of Rail Regulation and the Civil Aviation Authority or Minister)
Water merger	Water Industry Act 1991 s32	The Office of Fair Trading
Water and sewerage, determination under conditions of appointment	Water Industry Act 1991 s12	Director General of Water Services
Water and sewerage appointment modification	Water Industry Act 1991 s14	Director General of Water Services
Water supply licence modification	Water Industry Act 1991 s17K	Director General of Water Services
Airport price regulation (quinquennial reviews)	Airports Act 1986 s43 or Airports (Northern Ireland) Order 1994 art 34	Civil Aviation Authority
Gas licence modification	Gas Act 1986 s24, or Gas (Northern Ireland) Order 1996 art 15	GEMA, NIAER

Type of inquiry	Enactment	Referring organisation
Gas non-licensable activities	Gas Act 1986 s41E	GEMA
Electricity licence modification	Electricity Act 1989 s12, or Electricity (Northern Ireland) Order 1992 art 15	GEMA, NIAER
Electricity non-licensable activities	Electricity Act 1989 s56C	GEMA
Railways licence modification	Railways Act 1993, s13	Office of Rail Regulation
Railways access charges	Railways Act 1993 Schedule 4A	Office of Rail Regulation
National Air Traffic System	Transport Act 2000 s12	Civil Aviation Authority
Price control telecommunications references	Communications Act 2003 s193	Competition Appeal Tribunal
Postal services licence modification	Postal Services Act 2000 s15	Postal Services Commission
Regulatory provisions or practices	Financial Services and Markets Act 2000 s162 or s306	Office of Fair Trading
Public bodies – efficiency and costs	Competition Act 1980 s11	Secretary of State
Scottish water price control and licence modification references	The Water Services etc. (Scotland) Act 2005 (Consequential Provisions and Modifications) Order 2005	Water Industry Commission for Scotland

The Competition Commission has no authority to commence an investigation on its own initiative. All enquiries follow from a referral, most often by the Office of Fair Trading or the Secretary of State and Industry. In the case of mergers the Commission will be asked to investigate if the takeover target has a turnover above a certain threshold or if the resulting company would have 25% or more of a market.

ACQUISITION CONSIDERATION

A company might acquire another company by issuing more of its own shares to pay for the acquisition. This can be done in several ways:

1. By issuing shares on the stock market to raise cash to be used in buying the target company's shares as in a cash bid.

2. By issuing new shares to be made available to the target company's shareholders in exchange for their shares. This is called a paper offer.

The acquisition consideration can be a mix of a cash bid and a paper offer. The choice between paper and cash will depend on how the offer is viewed by the bidding company shareholders and the target company shareholders. They will need to understand how their share values might be diluted and how this might be offset by increased shareholdings and additional value created through the merger/takeover synergy.

THE MARKET VALUE OF SHARES DURING A TAKEOVER

When a company makes a paper offer bid the market value of its own shares and those of its target are vital. For example:

Company A's shares are currently quoted on the exchange at £5 per share. It makes a paper offer to take over company B for one company A share for every two company B shares. Before the offer company B had 100,000 shares in issue and the market price was £2 per share. A is, therefore, putting a value of £2.50 per share in B (£5/2) and an offer price of £250,000. This is, however, only a paper offer valuation and if during the course of the offer and before acceptance the market value of A's shares falls below £5 then the offer will become less attractive. If the market value of B's shares increases above £2 then the offer will also become less attractive. When a paper offer is made the bidder will need to consider what effect the offer will have on the share prices of both the bidding and the target company.

THE EFFECT OF TAKEOVERS ON PE RATIOS, EPS AND CREATING PAPER VALUE

When a company acquires another through issuing shares its own earnings per share will change according to the price earnings ratio of the target company acquired.

Example

A takes over B by offering 2 × A shares for every 1 B share. The takeover has no recognised synergy and is not expected to produce earnings growth. Company details are:

	Company A	Company B
Number of shares	2,000,000	100,000
Market value of shares	£5	
Earnings p.a.	£400,000	£60,000
EPS	20p	60p
P/E	25	

The offer by A has placed a valuation on B's shares of £10 per share. Therefore, the implied P/E ratio of B on acquisition is 16.7 (£10/60p). This is lower than A's P/E ratio.

After acquisition the combined company results would be:

	A & B Group
Number of shares (2,000,000 + 200,000)	2,200,000
Earnings (£400,000 + £60,000)	£460,000
EPS	20.9p

A, by acquiring B, a company with a lower P/E ratio, has benefited from a rise in EPS.

The important point to remember here is that in an acquisition strategy a buying company needs to recognise that if it is buying a company on a higher P/E ratio it is necessary that the acquired company offers strong growth and synergy to ensure that the buying company can maintain its EPS.

A dilution of earnings on merger or takeover, whilst not desirable, might be accepted if there are other good strategic reasons. For example, a bidding company might acquire valuable assets or customers that it is able to utilise more profitably than its target company was able to do. For example, a large information technology company might acquire a small niche solution provider because it can unleash the value of software with the assistance of its large product development and marketing strength.

When estimating pre- and post-acquisition positions, use a spreadsheet showing the two companies' and the new consolidated company's balance sheets and profit statements with full ratio analysis. Then it will be possible to prepare a full sensitivity analysis of each item to changes in variables.

EFFECT OF MERGERS AND TAKEOVERS ON DIVIDEND COVER

Some companies have a policy of paying lower dividends and funding more growth through shareholders' funds. Others may have a policy of paying out the maximum possible dividends each year. It all depends upon a company's business sector, risk perceptions, cost of funds and shareholder expectations. When two companies come together through a merger or takeover, consideration has to be given to what the future dividend policy of the new combined group will be. The acquisition consideration to the shareholders of a target company will need to compensate for any fall in post-acquisition dividends.

Example

The balance sheets of Bidder plc and Target plc in pounds sterling are as follows:

	Bidder plc	Target plc
Net assets	4,000,000	500,000
Financed by:		
Ordinary shares	2,000,000 (£1)	300,000 (50p)
Reserves	1,000,000	200,000
Loan stock	1,000,000	0
	4,000,000	500,000

Earnings and dividends are:

Profits	300,000	40,000
Dividends	100,000	30,000
Dividend cover	3 times	1.3 times

Bidder plc and Target plc are to merge. The shareholders of Target are concerned about the conservative dividend policy of Bidder and how this will affect their future dividend payouts. The merger agreement will value Bidder plc shares on a P/E multiple of 10 and Target plc shares on a P/E multiple of 5. The new merged company will be named Big plc and will issue £1 ordinary shares (at par) in exchange for the shares in Bidder plc and Target plc.

The merger will have the following effect on the EPS for the current shareholders in Bidder plc and Target plc:

	Bidder plc	Target plc
Profits	300,000	40,000
Shares	2,000,000	600,000
EPS	15p	6.7p
P/E	10	5
Value	£1.5	£0.335

Value of Bidder plc shares	(£1.5 × 2,000,000)	£3,000,000
Value of Target plc shares	(£0.335 × 600,000)	£201,000
Value of £1 shares issued in Big plc		£3,201,000

Ignoring the effects of synergy the EPS of Big plc would be:

$$\frac{£300,000 + £40,000}{3,201,000 \text{ (shares)}} = 10.62\text{p}$$

Bidder will receive 1.5 shares in Big plc and Target will receive 2 shares in Big plc for every 10 currently held.

EPS of 1 share in Bidder is	15p
EPS of 1.5 shares in Big plc is (1.5 × 10.62p)	16p
Gain in EPS to Bidder shareholders is	1p
EPS of 10 shares in Target plc is (10 × 6.7P)	67p
EPS of 2 shares in Big is (2 × 10.62p)	21p
Loss in EPS to Target shareholder	46p

Target will suffer a loss in earnings after the merger.

Clearly this loss is going to be unacceptable to the Target plc shareholders and the new combined company (Big plc) will need to amend its dividend policy or ensure the purchase consideration compensates Target shareholders for this.

The bidding company will need to complete these calculations so as to make an attractive offer and the target company will need to work through the same calculations so as to be in a position to advise its shareholders and to decide upon the correct defensive strategy if appropriate.

REVERSE TAKEOVERS

This is where a small company takes over a larger one. It can be a way of going public whereby a private company acquires the shares of a public company and then merges. A reverse takeover is less affected by market conditions than IPOs. An IPO can be risky to undertake because the deal depends on market conditions and the process extends over a long period of time. A reverse takeover can be a useful means for a private company to go public in just a month without the risks or cost of an IPO. The downside, however, is that a reverse takeover comes with potentially unknown or underestimated liabilities.

DEMERGERS

A demerger is where a company is split up into separate independent companies. This may be done to sell off unprofitable subsidiaries or business that is no longer a core business. A demerger may also be used to change the risk profile of the company or to make a profit on sale that can be better utilised with another or a core business activity. A demerger may result in a loss of economy of scale, profits or status affecting credit ratings.

THE CITY CODE ON TAKEOVERS AND MERGERS

The Panel on Takeovers and Mergers, which was established in the UK in 1968, is an independent body whose main purpose is to issue and administer the City Code on Takeovers and Mergers and to regulate and supervise takeovers and other matters to which the City Code applies in accordance with the rules set out in the Code. It is a supervisory authority to carry out certain regulatory functions in relation to takeovers pursuant to the Directive on Takeover Bids (2004/25/EC). Its statutory functions are set out in the Companies Act 2006 and specific rules are set out in the actual Code. The rules may be changed from time to time and rules may also be set out in other documents as specified by the Panel. Information relating to the Panel and the Code can be found on the Panel's website at www.thetakeover panel.org.uk.

The Code is designed to ensure that shareholders are treated fairly and equally. They are not to be denied any opportunity to decide on the merits of a takeover. The Code also provides an orderly framework within which takeovers are conducted and it is wise for a bidding company to consult the Code before putting together an offer. It is designed to promote integrity.

The Code is not concerned with the commercial or financial advantages or disadvantages of a takeover since these are matters for the companies and their shareholders to consider. It is not concerned with competition issues since these are the concern and responsibility of the other government departments previously mentioned in this chapter under the section on Competition Commission.

Some of the general principles of the City Code include the following:

- Equality between all shareholders of the same class. The bidding company cannot offer one group of shareholders in a class different terms than it offers to another group in that class.

- Shareholders must be given sufficient information to reach a decision.

- Information cannot be made available to some shareholders and not others.

- Once an offer has been received it should be communicated to all shareholders by their board and the board cannot take any action to frustrate the offer without the shareholders' approval. This is to ensure that shareholders of the target company have full opportunity to consider the offer and response.

- Rights of control must be exercised in good faith and minorities must not be oppressed.

- Where control (more than 30%) of a target is acquired, a general offer to all shareholders is normally required.

The City Code also contains rules relating to the conduct of the parties in a takeover. These include matters such as:

- the announcement of a takeover bid
- how a predator should approach a target
- the obligation of the target board to seek independent professional advice
- the general conduct of the offer.

DOCUMENTS IN A TAKEOVER BID

The following is a general guide to the documents that must be issued in a takeover.

The offer document

An offer document must be issued by the offeror normally at least 28 days before the announcement. This document will contain:

- a declaration of intention – this will include what the offeror intends to do with the target company in terms of continuity of business, employees, assets and a justification for the proposed takeover
- audited financial information about the two companies, including the last five years' financial accounts, dividends, earnings and dividends per share
- details of any changes since the last set of audited accounts

- a statement of the offeror's shareholdings and dealings with the target company
- independent confirmation, normally from a banker, that the offeror has the financial resources to complete the offer.

Target board circular

The board of the target company must issue a circular which gives its opinion on the offer, including alternatives and the findings of the independent professional advice (normally a merchant bank) it has received. This should normally be sent within 14 days of the publication of the offer document.

SUMMARY OF ORDER OF EVENTS IN A TAKEOVER

The following list, whilst not comprehensive, provides a guide to the main points that need to be attended to in the event of a takeover.

1. The bidder, who will normally be advised by a merchant bank, must announce its intentions to the target.

2. The target must appoint a professional independent adviser. This is usually a merchant bank. The target must, with the professional advice, check out the ability of the bidder to make this bid.

3. Insider dealing of the shares of the bidder and the target companies is of course illegal. Both the bidder and the target company executives involved in the takeover discussions have inside information which they should not use to personal advantage.

4. If other companies are intending to launch bids for the target then the information about the bidders' offers should be made available to all.

5. The bidder's offer should be kept open for at least 21 days and any revisions to the offer for a further minimum of 14 days.

6. Once in receipt of an offer the target company must notify all of its shareholders of the complete details of the offer and issue a press release. An offer document is issued to the shareholders of the target company.

7. If the bidding company has acquired a stake of 30% or more of the target company's equity then it should make a bid to the remaining shareholders at the highest price paid for shares it acquired during the past 12 months.

8. The bidder must not offer any preferential terms to some of the target's shareholders.

9. Once the offer has been received the directors of the target company cannot make substantial changes to their balance sheet so as to thwart the bidding company's offer. For example, they cannot issue more shares, sell off substantial assets or take on large liabilities.

10. It is illegal for a company to try to influence the market price of its shares during a takeover by providing finance for the purchase of its own shares.

11. True arm's length dealing in shares is permitted but this will require daily reporting to the stock exchange, the Takeover Panel and the press.

CROSS-BORDER M&A

We have discussed M&A mainly from a UK perspective. The above summary of events is applicable to the UK. However, different countries have different rules. This makes cross-border M&A very challenging. There has been a steady increase in cross-border activity in recent years, but due to the complicated nature of cross border M&A many have been unsuccessful. Cross border intermediation has many more levels of complexity, including regulations, politics, culture, exchange rates, employee protection to name a few. A large cross border deal may affect the relative currencies of the two companies. Most cross-border deals run into difficulties with the integration process. Achieving synergies through acquisition is all about integration and realising the strategic benefits of a merger. It requires full interaction and co-ordination of the two companies in every area to gain the strategic potential of the deal. For a cross border deal to succeed very special attention must be given to the integration plan.

Two major considerations in cross border M&A are:

1. The value creation from a merger comes through the realisation of synergy, the ability to cut costs or enjoy some economies of scale and increase revenue through cross selling and growth.

2. The above benefits cannot be realised without effective integration.

The following is a checklist of the type of issues that need to be given particular attention on a cross border merger or takeover. They are relevant to all mergers and acquisitions, but when you consider each item on the list you will recognise the issues that need to be overcome and planned for.

1. Time differences – this may seem trivial but it can make it difficult to talk if a subsidiary has a 12-hour time difference.

2. Language differences.

3. Differences in business culture.

4. Differences in national laws and regulatory environments.

5. The need for a sound integration plan and map to determine the extent of what will be changed and what will be kept and the implications of these changes across all areas of the business.

6. Organisational structures.

7. Organisational processes.

8. Governance.

9. Decision making.

10. HR processes and employment laws.

11. Leadership and management capability.

12. Differences in national culture and working habits.

None of these issues should stand in the way of a well-thought-out merger or takeover, but without careful planning and anticipation they can lead to failure, poor results and lack of benefit realisation.

These issues should be considered over each of the main stages of a merger or takeover, including the following:

- transaction – initial evaluation, offer, acceptance and deal closure
- integration – including people culture and communications
- ongoing evaluation and adjustment – seeing how it is really working on the ground and ensuring the benefits are achieved.

The world is moving towards a truly global marketplace and concerns over the political and wider implications will increase from time to time. Cross-border deals should be made with full political, socio-economic, national security implications in mind and should not come into conflict with governmental regulations. In the past companies in developing countries have often been targets for takeover bids from more wealthy countries. This is now changing and deals are coming in the opposite direction. It is widely believed that emerging market companies buying into the developed world will be a growing feature in cross-border mergers and takeovers.

HOW WILL THE 2009 RECESSION AFFECT THE M&A MARKET?

Towards the end of 2008 M&A activity was reported to have fallen. This would seem to be in line with our experience during previous recessions. The same reasons as before (fear, uncertainty, falling markets, etc.) contributed to the decline and added to this was a general lack of funds.

Predicting M&A activity in the short term is, of course, extremely difficult and trying to predict the longer term from previous trends and cycles is also difficult because the 2008–2009 recession is different from previous recessions. In fact, large-scale M&A activity is lumpy and difficult to predict from trends and projections. A far more precise and specific approach is needed.

In the new post-recession global world order we can expect that M&A activities will be more global. We can also expect a continued increase in cross border and emerging market deals.

The main difference in the current (2009) downturn is access to funds. M&A in an environment with easy access to capital is not the same as acquisitions in a downturn with restricted funds. When an opportunity does arise and funds are available, a decision will need to be fast. The time between announcements and deal closures may be shorter than under normal conditions. The proportion of equity-funded to externally funded acquisitions will increase. Faster due diligence and board/shareholder support will be required to win opportunities arising from distress situations.

19

Outsourcing and shared services

BACKGROUND

Outsourcing, both local and cross border, has been going for a very long time. In the early 20th century the British Merchant Navy sourced its very competent crews from overseas countries with a low labour cost and willing market of 'able' seamen. This was more than just employing low-cost human assets but involved an overseas management team to handle management issues including employee retention and training. Companies have always sought to exploit their competitive advantage to increase markets, share and profits. In the 1950s and 1960s, diversification to broaden market bases and take advantage of economies of scale was high on the strategic agenda. Many large organisations developed strategies to focus on their core business by identifying processes that could be outsourced.

For some reason it was not widely identified as a business strategy until the late 1980s and 1990s. However, it should be recognised that all organisations outsource to some extent by putting out resource requirements that they have no internal competence to supply. Later, organisations focused on cost reduction and outsourced necessary functions that were not directly related to the core business, such as accountancy and security. The emphasis was on cost reduction whilst maintaining the same quality level of service, although many consumers have become cynical of the latter. However, there are those companies which outsource customer service because they recognise the importance of it and also recognise that it is not one of their core competences.

WHAT IS OUTSOURCING?

There are many definitions, including the following:

- Outsourcing is the strategic use of outside resources to perform activities previously performed by internal resources.

Outsourcing is a business strategy whereby organisations contract out major functions to specialised service providers. The difference between subcontracting and outsourcing is that outsourcing involves the restructuring of a business activity. This may include the transfer of staff.

Companies outsource in order to:

- reduce costs
- focus more on their core competence
- enable internal charging

- increase the transparency of costs
- access next-generation technology
- improve their overall quality of service
- obtain world-class services
- make internal resources available for other activities
- offload a troublesome activity
- obtain scarce resources
- spread risks.

Critical success factors for outsourcing include:

- clear corporate goals, objectives, strategy and planning
- executive team and corporate buy-in
- identification of career benefits to staff. for example, accounting staff that are outsourced to a major accounting firm might feel that they have better career prospects than they had previously
- choice of outsourcing partner
- relationship management
- a clear contract with performance measures
- open communication with affected individual/groups
- senior executive support and involvement
- careful attention to personnel issues
- short-term financial justification.

An outsourcing programme can be considered under a number of stages:

- programme concept and outline
- detailed programme definition and plan
- contract
- implementation
- ongoing relationship management.

Programme concept and outline

This stage is concerned with documenting the intentions, ideas and performance measures into an outline contract.

Detailed programme definition and plan

This stage covers the activities required to take the programme concept and outline to a planned outsourcing transition programme. This includes:

- outsourcing programme transition project definition

- employee issues such as contracts and transfer options
- determination of service levels required; outline service level agreement (SLA)
- integration of SLA reporting with existing management reporting processes
- plan for outsourcing implementation
- service handover plan
- service continuity and management plan.

Contract

This is the preparation of final contract incorporating the agreed changes identified during the above two stages.

Implementation

This is all about moving forward, accepting the new arrangements and getting on with things to ensure success. The contract has been signed and there is no advantage in harking back to how things used to be. Both sides need to ensure that the arrangements are a success and that the benefits to both organisations and staff are realised. It is often said that there are winners and losers in these deals and the implementation plan needs to ensure that any staff that might feel worse off are recognised and compensated as far as is possible. The handover and implementation plan needs to be well considered and should anticipate problem areas. For example, it is no use just having an executive team with an eye on cost savings and offloading an unpopular activity but who have failed to consider all of the detailed consequences for staff and service quality.

Ongoing relationship management

The outsourcing relationship is one of strategic partners and warrants ongoing relationship management. This is more than just paying attention to SLAs and performance measures but should seek to find additional opportunities to add value in the relationship.

THE OUTSOURCING DECISION

Outsourcing might enable an organisation to reduce costs and become more efficient. To understand potential cost saving it is necessary to know how costs will be affected and this requires a thorough knowledge of variable and fixed costs and long-term contractual commitments. For example, an organisation wishing to outsource part of its call centre services might have a high level of fixed costs relating to premises used by the existing call centre which

Outsourcing process

Figure 19.1

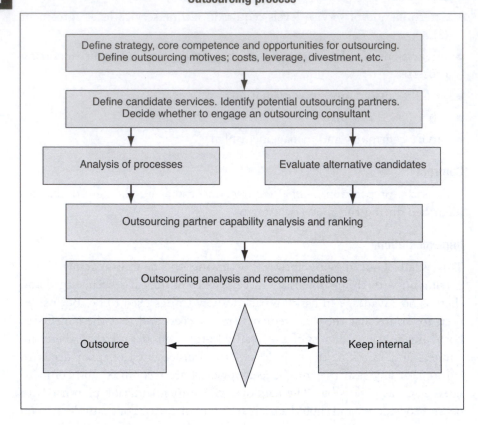

are on a long-term lease and cannot be easily sublet or used in another business activity. Outsourcing is generally more of a strategic than a tactical decision and requires the buy-in of the executive team and board approval. This is because it involves divesting a business function and the transfer of staff and other assets. The process is shown in Figure 19.1.

A financial analysis will be required throughout each step of the process. Because of the complexity of outsourcing definitions, scoping, pricing and legal considerations, often cross border, many companies will engage the services of outsourcing consultants to help.

If one of the main considerations in outsourcing is cost reduction then the client company will need to know precisely which costs can potentially be saved. For example, a company considering outsourcing its accounting function will need to know the following:

- Which accounting services can be outsourced from financial accounting, management accounting, taxation, payroll services, banking, treasury, etc?
- Which services will be kept and what will their dependencies be on the

services outsourced. For example, if it is decided to keep management accounting (budgeting) and treasury in house, how will they be supported by the outsourced services?

- A complete analysis of personnel costs and identification of which staff and costs will be taken by the outsource provider.
- An analysis of variable and fixed costs associated with the services to be outsourced.
- An understanding of which costs can be saved and those that will remain.
- Identification of opportunities for alternative uses of fixed costs that will remain after the outsourcing is complete.
- Knowledge of all potential rationalisation cost savings since these need to be part of the deal.

Once it is understood which costs can really be saved then negotiations can commence with an outsourced service provider. It is at this stage where the services of a consultant can be valuable in identifying suitable providers and helping with negotiations. Handling responses from providers can be very time consuming and confusing and clear criteria need to be set in an invitation-to-tender document.

To make a good, informed decision about using an outside manufacturing or processing supplier a business might undertake an activity-based cost study. This will require the identification of:

- fixed costs
- variable costs
- engineering processes, quality assurance and their costs
- training and implementation costs for the supplier's staff
- supply chain and resource management
- ongoing costs involved with managing the strategic supplier relationship
- cash flow implications
- guarantees and other service-related costs
- the full costs of stock shortages
- an understanding of how the market will view the deal
- a sensitivity analysis of the outsourcing business case to changes in variables and volumes
- a full understanding of the impact on customers
- an understanding of further opportunities created by the outsource deal
- risk analysis.

Make good decisions about which processes to keep in house and do whatever is needed to ensure success once a decision has been made.

- Keep operations that are critical and are core competencies in house. These may be what define your competitive differentiators.
- If services or products have a large impact on end quality and customer satisfaction, consider carefully the competence of the outsource provider to improve them. Otherwise keep them in house.
- Is the business you intend outsourcing important to the supplier? How hard will he try to ensure delivery and the meeting of SLAs?
- Be honest with yourself and the supplier about problems. Exporting a secret problem is not a solution.
- Only put services and products outside which are a core competence of the supplier.
- Fix quality and technical problems before outsourcing. A hidden problem not in the outsourcing contract can have enormous consequences. An outsourcing contract needs to be 'in utmost good faith'.
- Document service and product design parameters.
- Train the supplier's team in all matters essential for a smooth transition. Ensure the support of staff being transferred.
- Install product-performance assurance measures.
- Agree quality-assurance systems with the supplier.
- Establish auditing processes.
- Develop relationship-management processes and appoint an executive responsible for managing the relationship.
- Develop joint cost-reduction and improvement processes and review.
- Find ways to improve the supplier's performance.
- In case it all goes wrong have a contingency plan ready. This may take the form of alternative suppliers or in-house resources.

Benefits that need to be factored into the outsourcing decision

These include:

- access to world-class services
- ability to concentrate on own core competence
- better qualified and more experienced staff.
- better development for existing staff transferred
- ability to divest and offload unnecessary resources and assets
- knowledge-transfer capability
- cost savings
- better customer service

- more sustainable services
- flexibility – lower fixed-cost base.

A company that has fewer fixed costs is more agile and this is generally considered to be a desirable competitive advantage.

These benefits need to be weighed against the risks and disadvantages.

Risks

A full risk analysis will need to be completed and understood before any contingency plans can be made. Business continuity is one of the major concerns. What happens if the outsourced services fail? What factors could make them fail? Are they more or less likely to fail if overseas? It is commonly felt that offshore outsourcing has greater risk just because it is offshore, but some companies choose offshore outsourcing to reduce risk or to spread risks. Therefore, a risk analysis needs to understand the risks of both internal and outsourced services and the company's attitude to risk. Political and cultural issues are often raised. Politics matters and culture counts too. Is an offshore political landscape more dangerous to plans than the existing political environment? Are cultural differences properly understood and will communications between the two companies and between the offshore company and local customers be easy?

OUTSOURCING GROUPS, ASSOCIATIONS AND INFORMATION SOURCES

In the UK the National Outsourcing Association (NOA) exists as an outsourcing trade association. The NOA promotes best practice and represents outsourcing end users, vendors and other parties involved in outsourcing. Its other activities include research, events and education. NOA has collected a body of information on the subject known as the BOOK (Body Of Outsourcing Knowledge). Contact and research through www.noa.co.uk.

The UK Business to Business Directory (www.b2bindex.co.uk) provides an online directory of outsourcing companies, consultancies and general information.

The major accounting and management/strategic consulting firms and many other specialist outsourcing consultancies provide initial online discussion and help pages.

SHARED SERVICES

Shared services and outsourcing are different concepts. Shared services are a fundamental change to an organisation's service delivery model. Shared services generally will drive, or be a part of, an organisational and functional transformation that leads to lower cost and better quality services. Shared services can make use of external or internal resources or a combination to deliver the transformation. Transformation will not necessarily be the reason why an organisation adopts outsourcing.

The finance sector is an industry that has widely adopted shared services and we can use this sector as an example of how an industry seeking to improve customer service and profitability has increasingly turned to shared services.

A shared service is simply an efficient business architecture that creates substantial business advantage through the sharing of pooled resources. This architecture does not necessarily require the usage of common business processes. The main drivers of shared services are cost reduction and performance improvement, although there can be other benefits, including the ability to leverage investments in new technology.

In the banking sector shared services range from the consolidation of back-office processing (sometimes on a chargeable basis) through to full business process outsourcing. The areas most frequently associated with shared services are IT, payments, finance, HR, payroll, accounts payable and certain back-office treasury functions.

Possibly the best track record of shared services within the banking sector has been in the provision of services on a joint-venture basis to multiple customers. A good example is the UK BACS system, which was set up and jointly owned by a number of banks to provide payment services to the owning and other banks. Another early example was the establishment of DataBank Systems in New Zealand to provide IT services on a shared basis, initially to four owning banks and eventually to other institutions.

Shared services should not be confused with outsourcing. The decision to outsource, often considered at the same time, requires a very different investment evaluation.

Many institutions consolidate services first and manage them as an internal service before considering any form of outsourcing. As their maturity develops they typically progress along a journey of shared services and outsourcing initiatives such as:

- initial outsourced joint-venture activities such as BACS (payments) and DataBank (It services)
- sharing of resources through the consolidation of group back-office services

- sharing common processes through the creation of internal service centres for consolidated services, including internal charging for HR, finance, payroll, management services, etc
- full outsourcing, for example insurance claims
- client consortiums such as credit card call centres.

Usually, banks have preferred to take a high level of control of outside suppliers of shared services.

The benefits that shared services have offered the finance sector

These have included:

- improvement in customer service
- cost reduction
- improved efficiency
- standardisation and harmonisation of business processes
- refocusing of back-office staff
- increasing the transparency of costs and enabling effective benchmarking
- improved quality
- access to next-generation technology
- internal charging
- expansion to other geographical sites
- flexibility and a lower fixed-cost base
- general centralisation.

Shared services options

One common mistake is to overlook the wide variety of shared services options available. In the finance sector, for example, these include the following:

- *Outsourced joint venture*: a JV supplier is set up with one or more third-party suppliers to provide shared services. Early examples were BACS in the United Kingdom and DataBank in New Zealand.
- *Internal delivery:* an internal shared service centre such as the bank's central IT services.
- *In sourcing:* an internal supplier is established to manage a third-party supplier. Some banks have internal HR services which control contracts with recruiters and then charge internally within the bank for recruitment.
- *Full outsourcing:* shared services are fully outsourced to a third-party sup-

plier. In the early 1990s many banks outsourced their catering functions to an outside catering supplier.

- *Client consortium:* a JV supplier is set up by two or more companies with similar needs to share common services. For example, some credit card companies.

- *Best-of-breed consortium:* shared services are fully outsourced to a third-party supplier which subcontracts to other third-party suppliers.

- *Multi in sourcing:* an internal supplier is the primary supplier which manages the service delivery of a range of other internal suppliers.

- *Multi sourcing:* shared services are fully outsourced to a number of third-party suppliers.

- *Prime contractor:* a prime contractor vehicle is set up by a number of third-party suppliers in order to supply a range of shared services to customers.

- *Captive contractor:* a provider of outsourced services is contracted to provide those services to only one bank.

There are also many variations and combinations on the above theme. The banking sector is a good example to use to obtain an understanding of the possibilities.

There has been widespread recognition for many years that certain services within an organisation do not directly generate revenue and are, therefore, non-core functions that can be readily outsourced. Also, an outside supplier of these services should be more efficient. This may or may not be the case, but the rule of thumb tends to be that services should be considered for outsourcing where this results in lower costs and no increase in risk.

To effectively manage this transition, outsourcing initiatives should be viewed as a development strategy and not simply as a means of offloading inefficient processes or excess staff. We have already discussed this aspect, but large shared service and outsourcing initiatives by major banks are generally not about shifting a problem. Outsourcing in a bank is not normally considered until back-office functions have been centralised, standardised and generally tidied up. If this is not done the benefits of the rationalisation will tend to accrue to the outsourcer rather than to the bank.

It is worth noting that some institutions are re-evaluating which of their functions are core to their business. Some have returned certain services (such as IT) that were considered non core into the value chain and, on occasion, brought functional service heads onto the main board. This is a sure indication that finding a correct answer to shared service and outsourcing issues is far from easy.

Long-term future in the finance sector

The demand for shared services in the finance sector is cyclical and depends largely on the prevailing trends towards centralisation or decentralisation of business functions. Certainly in the 2009 finance sector environment banks should be looking for all ways to save costs and increase efficiency. The diversity of applications for shared services within the finance sector, such as those illustrated below, suggests that shared services are here to stay.

Full automation – the e-bank

The next generation of shared services will increase its focus on e-business and fully automated banking. By automating shared services banks will be able to process transactions with minimal human intervention on a 24/7 basis. The improvements we have seen in service availability during the past 10 years will be extended and made possible by shared services.

Globalisation

Shared service centres will increase in geographical span of service provision. It will become harder to justify disparate sites working with different systems and standards. Banks find serving an international customer base extremely challenging where systems and processes are not necessarily transferable between countries. Their ability to achieve a standard quality of service can be threatened. While the use of shared services centres offshore has been relatively slow in key customer business development areas in banking, the take-up of this approach has been much faster in claims, collections, accounting, HR, etc.

Commercialisation

While the commercialisation of shared services within the finance sector can offer banks a number of opportunities to enhance their competitiveness and grow business, there continues to be some resistance to it due to a strong focus on security, banking core competencies and of course the regulatory/supervisory environment which has more impact on banking than in most other sectors.

Currently, across all sectors in Europe, only 12 per cent of shared services are sold to clients outside of the owning companies. The proportion is even lower in the finance sector. However, this will undoubtedly change as the development of a strategic approach to business management rapidly becomes a banking core competency.

FURTHER READING

'The Outsourcing Decision: A Strategic Framework' by Steven Globerman, Kaiser Professor of International Business, Western Washington University and Aidan Vining, CNABS Professor of Business and Government Relations, Simon Fraser University, Vancouver, B.C. (March 2004). This is a downloadable paper available on the internet: http://129.3.20.41/eps/it/papers/0404/0404007.pdf

Financial markets

TYPES OF FINANCIAL INTERMEDIARIES

A financial intermediary brings together borrowers and lenders providing aggregation, economies of scale, maturity date transformation and the pooling of risks. It is an institution that provides a borrower with the ability to borrow longer by aggregating smaller, shorter-term investments.

A financial intermediary typically facilitates the channelling of funds between lenders and borrowers. Lenders give funds to a financial intermediary such as a bank and the intermediary lends those funds to borrowers by way of a loan. The intermediary may lend the money to the financial markets (financial disintermediation). Financial intermediaries set prices, provide liquidity, provide a market place and help ensure delivery and performance.

The types of financial intermediary include:

- retail banks and clearing banks
- business banks
- private banks
- commercial banks
- corporate banks
- merchant banks
- investment banks
- finance houses
- building societies
- National Savings deposit department
- pension funds
- investment trusts
- credit unions
- financial advisers and brokers.

Financial intermediaries oil the wheels of commerce by providing the money needed to develop and carry on business. When funds dry up, business can go into recession. Intermediaries provide a useful way in which a lender can save money and at the same time make this money available to borrowers in the market. This pooling of funds reduces risks to the lenders since any individual loss is spread amongst the pool of lenders. Pooling also enables investors to enjoy the benefits of a larger portfolio. It is unlikely that any one lender will always be able to lend the exact amount that a borrower needs. By aggregation a financial intermediary enables the bringing together of groups of lenders with savers who wish to invest or borrow different amounts. One of the most important benefits provided by a financial intermediary is the provision of maturity transformation in that they bridge the gap between lenders who want liquidity and borrowers who want longer-term loans. Of course, herein lie the questions: how can an intermediary borrow short and lend long? What happens if there is a rush on a bank? How is this safely achieved?

We have so far in this text explained the risks of borrowing short for long-term needs. How, then, can a bank safely do it? We saw in 2008 and 2009 the problems that financial institutions can get into and how their problems can affect the global economy. Well, we have talked about aggregation and scale and these are two factors that help spread the risk. Two other important factors are:

- confidence
- regulation – prudential supervision.

BANK PRUDENTIAL SUPERVISION

Customer confidence in a bank is extremely important. We all witnessed the queues of Northern Rock depositors wanting to withdraw their cash and have seen what happens when confidence goes. Sound prudential supervision can help avoid this type of occurrence. The supervision of banks and financial institutions may be regarded as a function of a central bank. Sometimes it is given to another regulatory body. There are different arrangements in each country. In 1997 UK banking supervision was taken away from the central bank, the Bank of England, and placed with the Financial Services Authority, a statutory body. This was done in order to have a common regulatory framework. In mid-2009 the Conservative opposition party raised the idea that some FSA work should move back to the Bank of England. Some countries have adopted a system whereby the central bank is responsible for prudential supervision and the conduct of business regulation is given to a different body.

It is difficult to generalise but, as an outline, the type of reporting required by a typical financial services authority is given in the following table.

1. A general periodic liquidity questionnaire	This may be monthly or quarterly. Accordingly there is scope for 'window dressing' which defeats the purpose of this element of control.
2. A report on any mismatches	This type of report should be required daily and also include any off-balance sheet items.
a. A daily liquidity report – including acid tests	This is a daily acid test type of report.
b. A profile analysis of retail bank funding	This may be required daily or weekly and gives a profile of the range of retail funds.
c. A profile analysis of wholesale funding	This may be required daily or weekly and gives a profile of the range of wholesale funds.
d. Stress test	Monthly or quarterly.
3. Consolidated intra-day liquidity reports	Daily.
4. Consolidated group liquidity reports	Daily.
5. Risk asset capital limits	Weekly.

This list is by no means exhaustive but gives an idea of the type of measures that regulatory bodies impose upon banks around the world.

At this stage it is worthwhile viewing the regulatory and prudential requirements of other countries given on their web sites.

One of the most important measures is the 'mismatch report'. This shows to what extent a bank's assets and liabilities are not matched. What would happen if a large number of short-term depositors requested repayment? Would the bank have enough liquidity to meet their demands? Another measure is the amount of lending a bank has to any one customer.

Basel II

Basel II provides recommendations on banking laws and regulations. It was issued by the Basel Committee on Banking Supervision in June 2004. Basel II aims to create an international standard for banking regulators to use when drafting regulations about how much capital a bank should put aside to guard against financial and operational risks. The idea is that an international standard such as Basel II can help protect the international financial system from problems arising when major banks collapse. Basel II tries to accomplish this by establishing risk and capital management requirements to ensure that a bank holds appropriate capital reserves for the type of risk the bank is exposed to. It aims to ensure that capital allocation is risk sensitive, that operational and credit risks are separately identified and that economic and regulatory capital are more closely aligned so as to reduce the scope for regulatory arbitrage.

Central to Basel II are 'three pillars':

1. Minimum capital requirements.

2. Supervisory review.

3. Market discipline for greater stability.

The first pillar of minimum capital requirements identifies three principal elements of risk for a bank:

1. Credit risk.

2. Operational risk.

3. Market risk.

In future there will be closer links between the concepts of economic profit and regulatory capital.

Credit risk can be calculated by using one of three approaches:

1. Standardised approach.

2. Foundation IRB (internal ratings-based) approach.

3. Advanced IRB approach.

The standardised approach sets out the specific risk weights for certain types of credit risk. The second pillar specifies the regulatory response to the first pillar and a framework for dealing with all the other risks such as systemic risk, concentration risk, liquidity risk, legal risk, pension risk and reputation risk, to name a few. The third pillar increases the disclosure that a bank must make in order to better inform the markets.

THE MONEY MARKET

The money market is the market for short-term capital. The money market exists for the trading of short-term financial instruments and for short-term lending and borrowing. It is operated by banks, financial institutions and large organisations.

The money market comprises:

■ the primary market – also known as the official market where approved institutions deal in financial instruments with their central bank

- the Eurocurrency market – where banks lend and borrow foreign currencies
- the interbank market – where banks lend short-term funds to each other
- the CD market – where negotiable instruments known as certificates of deposit are traded
- the finance house market – where short-term loans are raised from money markets by finance houses
- the inter-company market – where there is direct lending and borrowing between the treasury departments of large organisations
- the local authority market – where local authorities borrow short-term funds by issuing short-term debt.

Some common money market instruments include:

- bankers' acceptances – drafts issued by banks that will be accepted for payment
- CDs – a deposit at a bank with a specific maturity date
- commercial paper – unsecured promissory notes with a fixed maturity date
- repurchase agreements – very short-term loans usually arranged by selling securities to an investor with an agreement to repurchase them at a fixed price on a fixed future date
- Eurodollar deposits – deposits made in US dollars at a bank or bank branch located outside the United States
- treasury bills – short-term debt obligations of a government. Normal maturity is between 3 and 12 months
- foreign exchange swaps – the exchange of currency in spot and the reversal of the exchange at a predetermined future date
- US federal agency short-term securities – short-term securities issued by US government-sponsored enterprises
- US municipal notes – short-term notes issued by US municipalities
- bills of exchange – bills used primarily in international trade being written orders by one person to his bank to pay the bearer a specific sum on a specific date some time in the future.

THE CAPITAL MARKET

This is the market for longer-term finance such as equities and corporate bonds. In the UK the London Stock Exchange (LSE) and the Alternative Investment Market (AIM) are the primary market for raising new and also a secondary markets for the trading of existing securities.

■ The LSE is for companies with a full stock market listing.

■ AIM is for smaller companies requiring less regulation.

Companies raise long- and medium-term capital by raising share capital (equity) or by raising loan capital (bonds, loan notes, debentures, loan stock and convertibles).

Stock exchanges

A stock exchange, securities exchange or bourse is an organisation (a corporation or mutual) that provides a trading floor and facilities for the trading of stocks and other securities by stock brokers and traders. They also provide facilities for the issuance and redemption of securities and other financial instruments. The principal types of securities traded on a stock exchange include shares, unit trusts and bonds.

A security can be traded on an exchange only if it is listed there and this requires meeting the stock exchange rules and regulations. Trading rooms are increasingly high-speed, low-cost electronic facilities with a central record-keeping back office. Only members of a stock exchange can actually trade on an exchange.

Initial offerings of stocks and bonds are carried out on the primary market, with subsequent trading being undertaken on the secondary market.

Some of the major stock exchanges in the world are:

Americas	NASDAQ
Americas	Toronto Stock Exchange
Americas	NYSE
Asia Pacific	Australian Stock Exchange
Asia Pacific	Hong Kong Stock Exchange
Asia Pacific	Shanghai Stock Exchange
Asia Pacific	Tokyo Stock Exchange
Europe	Frankfurt Stock Exchange
Europe	London Stock Exchange
Europe	Madrid Stock Exchange

The above are the larger exchanges. There are, of course, many other smaller exchanges in other countries which would be used for dealing in instruments of those countries.

The Alternative Investment Market in the UK

This is the divisional market of the London Stock Exchange enabling smaller companies to float shares under a more flexible and less regulated system than applies to the main market. Some of the stringent regulations applicable to large companies are not relevant or appropriate for small companies and this market provides a place for these small companies. AIM was created in 1995 and has helped thousands of small companies raise many billions of pounds. Because of the advantages offered by AIM there are generally more companies each year moving from the main market to AIM than there are moving from AIM to the main market. AIM is becoming an international exchange.

As primary markets, stock exchanges enable companies to raise new finance through the issuance of new shares or loan notes. To raise funds in the UK from a public capital market a company must be a plc (a public company). As a secondary market the stock exchange enables existing investors to sell their investments. The stock exchange enables owners of a company to float shares on the market and realise some cash and it also enables takeovers by the issuing of shares to fund the takeover. The market also gives access to institutional investors such as insurance companies and pension funds which, in the UK, have the largest amounts of funds to invest.

International money and capital markets

BACKGROUND

The international money and capital markets exist as places where large companies may raise large amounts of finance. The Eurocurrency markets are international money markets. The Eurobond markets are international capital markets.

THE EUROCURRENCY MARKET

The Eurocurrency market is a money market for borrowing and lending currencies that are held in the form of deposits in banks that are located outside the countries where the currencies are issued as legal tender. For example, when a UK organisation borrows in a foreign currency from a UK bank, the facility will be named a Eurocurrency loan. When a UK company borrows US dollars from its UK bank, the loan will be named a Eurodollar loan.

Eurodollars are deposits that are denominated in US dollars at a bank outside the United States. They are not under the supervision of the Federal Reserve and as a consequence are subject to less regulation than similar deposits within the United States. Eurodollar is a misleading term because there is nothing consistently European about a Eurodollar. A US dollar-denominated deposit in Australia would be deemed a Eurodollar deposit.

The Eurocurrency markets, therefore, simply involve depositing funds with a bank which is not in the country of the currency of denomination and then re-lending these funds, usually for a short time. Many Eurocurrency transactions take place between banks domiciled in different countries and are documented as negotiable certificates of deposit (NCDs).

INTERNATIONAL CAPITAL MARKETS

A large company may decide to borrow directly from private investors rather than banks and may do this by issuing bonds, notes or paper through the international capital markets. The bank acts as a middle man by finding investors. The markets include Eurobonds, Euronotes and Eurocommercial paper. There is also a market for Euro-equity.

EUROBONDS

A Eurobond is a long-term fixed-interest loan raised in the Euromarkets usually by large blue-chip, multi-national organisations. They are bonds issued in a European capital market, normally in a currency that is different from the country of issue. Eurobonds are sold internationally and are effectively long-term loans (typically of between 10 and 15 years) raised by international organisations. Eurobonds may be convertible and carry the right to convert into equity shares. Eurobonds are generally issued in bearer form and are, therefore, normally a form of negotiable debt transferable on a Eurobond market.

Eurobonds are used by large organisations that are first-class credits to:

- raise long-term (5–20 years) loan finance for capital-expenditure programmes
- enable borrowing that is not subject to exchange-control restrictions
- raise money at a time when market conditions are favourable
- raise money quickly

Of course, a borrower making a Eurobond issue will have to consider the foreign exchange exposure of a currency loan over a long period. If the borrowing is used to purchase an asset in another currency then there is a mis-match that could result in exchange losses or gains which will need to be managed.

The investor who subscribes to the bond issue will want to ensure that:

- the borrower will pay back and that the borrower is of a sufficiently high quality in terms of credit rating
- the return on the investment is adequate and is tax free
- the bonds or notes are of a high enough quality to make them readily marketable and that there is a ready market available
- the bonds are issued to bearer since investors generally want marketability and anonymity.

There may be an international syndicate that handles the issue on behalf of large organisations and issues are normally placed whereby the consortium finds banks and other institutions which will underwrite the issue. The subsequent sale and purchase by investors takes place in the secondary markets.

The order of events in a Eurobond are are as follows:

1. The issuer (the borrower) appoints a managing bank to handle the bond issue. This will normally be a merchant or investment bank.
2. The managing bank is also known as the lead manager. It might also invite other banks or financial institutions to underwrite the issue.

3. The managing bank will invite a number of other banks to co-manage the issue.

4. The managing banks will expect fees. This may be 0.5% of the total issue amount. In addition it will require payment of expenses.

5. When the issue is underwritten the managing bank will place it with a number of selling banks, some of which may be the underwriters. A commission is paid to selling banks.

6. A prospectus is issued and the selling banks try to place their allotments with clients.

A single bank might take on an entire issue as a 'bought deal'.

Eurobond interest rates

Interest rates on a bond issue are either variable or fixed. A variable rate issue is known as a floating rate note (FRN). These may incorporate a minimum guaranteed rate to the holders so that however low the market rates go, the holders will receive a minimum. They effectively convert to a fixed rate at a certain market level and are sometimes called 'drop lock floating rate notes'. Floating rate notes are essentially debt securities bonds in any currency entitling the holder to interest. FRN coupons are reset from time to time so as to match the London/Euribor interbank offered rate. The rate agreed is the benchmark rate plus an additional spread. It is reset every 3–6 months.

EURONOTES

Euronotes are short-term debt instruments whereas Eurobonds are longer-term instruments (bonds). A Euronote may be called a NIF (note issuance facility) or a SNIF (syndicated note issuance facility). A Euronote facility is available only to top-class 'rated' companies.

Euronote facilities are usually for periods of between 5 and 10 years and during this period the borrower is able to issue a series of notes with maturities of 3 or 6 months. Therefore, a 5 years facility may be between 10 and 20 note issues, each with different interest rates reflecting the current market conditions.

The Euronote facility may be established through a tender panel which comprises a syndicate of banks. When a tender panel of banks takes up an issue of Euronotes it will place them with other investors.

EUROCOMMERCIAL PAPER (ECP)

Eurocommercial paper (ECP) are short-term negotiable debt instruments but offer greater flexibility and lower issue costs than Euronotes.

When a company wishes to raise funds through the issue of commercial paper it will arrange for the issue to be undertaken by a number of dealers. This may include a leading UK ECP dealing bank, a US bank and/or a Swiss bank. Interest rates will be based on market rates. The borrower is able to choose the precise maturity date/period. This is much more flexible than the standard 3- or 6-month Euronote periods. This flexibility enables a borrower to follow the market and choose a time and rate that are suitable.

USING THE EUROCURRENCY MARKET TO HEDGE AGAINST FOREIGN EXCHANGE RISK

Example

If a company has a commitment to pay a large sum in a foreign currency in a few months' time it can use the Eurocurrency market to hedge against the exchange exposure. There are, of course, other options available, such as the forward exchange market, and a company treasurer will need to compare all options and choose the lowest-cost option that also offers the necessary flexibility.

Assume that a UK company must pay US$10,000,000 in 90 days' time to a US supplier. The following interest and exchange rate rates are known:

	US$ Deposit rate	US$ borrowing rate	UK£ deposit rate	UK£ borrowing rate
30 days	2% p.a.	3% p.a.	3% p.a.	4% p.a.
90 days	2% p.a.	3.5% p.a.	3.35% p.a.	4.45% p.a.

	US$/£ sterling exchange rate US$ = £1
Spot	1.4500
30-day forward	1.4524
90-day forward	1.4530

Using the forward market the cost in 90 days will be:

US$10,000,000 @ 1.4530 = £6,882,313

By putting off payment for 90 days the company is saving interest expense for 90 days at 4.45% p.a. or investment opportunity for 90 days at 3.35%. Since the company is a borrower, the cost saving will be £6,882,313 @ 4.45%/4 = £76,566. Therefore, the net cost of using the forward market is **£6,805,747** (£6,882,313 − £76,566).

Using the Eurocurrency market would require paying out $10,000,000. This means lending in the foreign currency to the Eurocurrency market. The US$ deposit rate for 90 days is 2% p.a., which equates to 0.5% for the 90-day period. The present value of US$10,000,000 in 90 days using 0.5% is:

$$\frac{US\$10,000,000}{1.0050} = US\$9,950,249$$

Using the spot rate of 1.45 gives sterling of $\dfrac{US\$9,950,249}{1.45} = £6,862,241$.

On this occasion, using the forward exchange market has produced a lower basic cost. At this point these costs would both be increased to reflect fees and expenses and normally the lower cost would be chosen, provided that the cost saving was worthwhile. Otherwise, the most convenient method would be selected. Assuming the company had access to funds, it might choose to purchase the currency on day one at the spot rate. It would then have the cost of the funds during the 90-day period to take into account and can compare this total cost to the other two options.

To make proper comparisons requires obtaining simultaneous quotations from more than one institution. To quickly compute these and respond to the dealer will require fast computations. The company will need dealing lines in place and it is normal for the corporate treasurer to have worksheets ready and to co-ordinate and manage a small team to obtain best quotations.

INTERNATIONAL CAPITAL MARKET ASSOCIATION (ICMA)

For updates on international capital markets, details of courses and membership, the ICMA web site is www.icmagroup.org.

The following extract regarding ICMA has been taken from its web site:

ICMA is a unique self regulatory organisation and an influential voice for the global capital market. It represents a broad range of capital market interests including global investment banks and smaller regional banks, as well as asset managers, exchanges, central banks, law firms and other professional advisers amongst its 400 member firms. ICMA's market conventions and standards have been the pillars of the international debt market for over 40 years, providing the self regulatory framework of rules governing market practice which have facilitated the orderly functioning and impressive growth of the market. ICMA actively promotes the efficiency and cost effectiveness of the capital markets by bringing together market participants including regulatory authorities and governments.

Strategic financial management

DEFINITION

Strategic financial management (SFM) is the identification of financial strategies available and capable of maximising an organisation's net value through both the creation of value and the financial support of an organisation's business strategy. SFM creates both value and organisational agility through the allocation of scarce capital resources among competing business opportunities. It is an aid to the implementation and monitoring of business strategy and helps achieve business objectives. Strategic financial management integrates financial management into business strategy and operations.

We have already discussed a number of financial management tools and processes. In Chapter 1 we talked about the relationship of financial management with corporate strategy. This chapter summarises the relationship between strategic management and financial management and discusses the strategic financial management interfaces.

CREATING VALUE THROUGH FINANCE WHILE STILL SUPPORTING OVERALL BUSINESS STRATEGY

Pay dividends or re-invest? Future opportunities require financial agility

Chief executives and chief finance officers often face the question of whether to pay surplus cash to their shareholders or invest it back in the business. They question how their company should be geared and whether new projects should be financed by debt or by equity.

We have discussed in Chapters 11 and 13 the problems of achieving the right debt versus equity capital structure that is needed to finance both operations and strategic investments. It is a problem that company executives grapple with constantly. We have also discussed the tax benefits of debt (interest expenses are tax deductible but dividends are not). There is the argument that using debt increases returns on shareholders' funds and low-interest-rate environments like 2009 in the UK and US make debt seem even more attractive.

High gearing, however, may not be consistent with a company's overall business strategy. Too much debt might put constraints on future strategic opportunities. The tax benefits of high gearing may be more than offset by a lack of flexibility and loss of business opportunity. Whilst high gearing might create value through finance, this needs to be balanced with having sound financial policies that support business strategy. Equity offers a greater flexibility to take advantage of new investment opportunities. Of course, if a company has few investment opportunities then the position would be different.

Having the optimum capital structure requires finding a balance between financial flexibility and financial discipline. A company's underlying capital structure may at times enable the creation of value. When a company's shares are under or overvalued the directors might change the company's capital structure to create value by buying back undervalued shares. However, strategic financial management is not just about creating value through clever finance but is first and foremost about finance strategy supporting the overall business strategy. A company with opportunity needs financial agility and strategic financial management can enable this.

THE STRATEGIC FINANCIAL MANAGEMENT PROCESS

Objectives and governance

The strategic financial management process starts with an understanding of objectives and corporate governance. This includes a definition of the principal aims, objectives, key tasks and sustainability goals and how these form a basis upon which detailed business plans and budgets are prepared. We have discussed budgeting and planning and the encouragement of performance through goal alignment and congruence in Chapters 5 and 9. The objectives will include the fulfilment of stakeholder needs. Stakeholders include shareholders, lenders, employees, customers, governments, suppliers, directors and others. The needs of stakeholders may conflict and this is where strategic financial management processes need to ensure the concepts of goal congruence are achieved through professional directorships (both executive and non-executive) and through sound corporate governance.

The system of corporate governance by which an organisation is directed and controlled includes risk management, the system of internal controls, an 'ethical watchdog' and methods of accountability to all stakeholders.

Although one aim of strategic financial management is to create value and financial efficiency, its principal objective must always be to support the goals, ethos and ethical values of the organisation. Strategic financial policy setting, therefore, starts with an understanding of organisational objectives and corporate governance. It is not something that is prepared in isolation.

Strategy and business plans

The strategic planning process follows corporate objectives setting. Divisional and functional directors, starting at a zero base, develop their plans and strategies to achieve their contribution towards the achievement of corporate goals. From this process will arise the development and identification of opportunities and capital investment decisions which support corporate goals, goal congruence and alignment being part of the planning process. This is how strategic planning is linked with investment decisions. Financial plans and first-stage budgets are prepared to meet the agreed divisional and departmental objectives. At this stage draft income and expenditure budgets are available from which financial projections and analysis are undertaken using ratio and other forms of financial analysis already discussed.

An analysis of business strategies available will be undertaken and this may use any of a number of techniques including SWOT analysis, the Seven S model, the value chain, sector analysis, integration and expansion strategies, competitive strategies, portfolio strategy, synergy, incrementalism, the Ansoff Matrix, Porter's Five Forces model, The Prisoner's Dilemma, the BCG portfolio chart, the ADL Strategic Business Unit model and many others. Details of these and other strategy concepts are easily found now on the web or in *Mastering Strategy* (Financial Times, Prentice Hall, 2000). The executive team will discuss and agree strategy and it is the role of the financial strategist to form sound financial strategies that support the chosen business strategy whilst at the same time creating value from financial policies. For example, if a company has adopted an expansion strategy requiring new investment then the financial strategy that will support this may include a moderate level of gearing that enables agility and ease of funding acquisitions rather than a more highly geared (possibly lower-cost) capital structure that will not necessarily enable funds to be available at an opportune moment. The financial implications of allowing for a successful exit strategy are also a necessary part of a strategic financial plan.

If part of the business strategy includes a takeover or merger then the techniques we have discussed for valuing individual shares and for valuing businesses will be used to develop the strategic financial plan.

During the planning process entry and exit barriers and sources of competitive advantage will be identified. These have associated financial implications which, whilst not necessarily forming a part of the immediate cash or profit plans, are relevant to long-term financial planning and policies.

Risk evaluation

The financial plan needs to evaluate all risks and identify hedging options. To do this requires an understanding of the following concepts and the application of a number of techniques, including the cost of capital, the cost of equity (the capital asset pricing model and the dividend growth model), the cost of debt, the weighted average cost of capital, the impact of capital structures on the cost of capital, the identification of interest rate and foreign exchange risk, yield curves and hedging techniques (using forwards, futures, options, swaps, FRAs and other products). These aspects have been described in Chapters 15 and 16. The strategic financial plan will evaluate all risks and provide appropriate financial strategies for hedging.

Investment decisions

The planning process will 'trigger' an investment review and the capital budgeting process. In Chapter 17 we discussed the six-step model for capital investment decisions identified in 1967 by Paul King and how these are aligned with business goals and how sponsors are developed. The steps are: triggering, screening, definition, evaluation, transmission and decision.

During the evaluation stage the following financial methods and techniques are employed: relevant cash flow, payback method, return on capital employed, accounting rate of return, discounted cash flow, net present value, internal rate of return, capital rationing simulations, portfolio theory and CAPM, tax planning and financial engineering.

A financial assessment is made of expansion strategies, organic growth, mergers and acquisitions, takeovers, offensive and defensive strategies, corporate reorganisation, corporate restructuring, going private and share repurchases.

Ongoing treasury management and financial forecasting

Strategic financial management is also concerned with ongoing treasury management and financial planning for short-, medium- and long-term needs. Clearly on a daily basis the treasurer or financial manager will want to ensure that the best possible rates are obtained for investments and borrowings and this will be done within the policies set out above whereby the financial plan supports the corporate goals and risk profile. For example, it would be wholly inappropriate for a treasurer to invest funds with a BBB-rated bank if this rating represented a risk profile that was higher than agreed in the corporate strategic financial plan. The strategic financial plan should set guidelines for investment risk and liquidity.

The treasury management function will include responsibility for optimal liquidity management, borrowing, investment of cash surpluses, interest rate risk management, foreign exchange risk management, optimal pooling of funds, money transmission and banking.

Financial environment and sensitivity analysis

A company does not operate in a vacuum and is a part of the global economic environment. Both local and international factors affect the availability of funds, as we saw in an alarming way in 2008 and 2009. The strategic financial plan must be prepared within the broader context of the local and global financial environment, showing the threats and opportunities that this creates to corporate plans. A knowledge of this financial environment will enable better forecasting, scenario and sensitivity analysis to be undertaken. Knowledge is required of trends in global competition, the role of multinationals in the world economy, free trade, protectionism, trade agreements, common markets, the role of the World Bank and the International Monetary Fund (IMF), economic relations between developed and developing countries including problems of debt and development, introduction of a single currency, exchange rate determination, influences on exchange rates, models of exchange rate determination and different forms of exchange rate system.

Global financial management

Any organisation that has cross border transactions will encounter added risk and uncertainty that needs careful financial analysis and planning. Issues such as double taxation, transfer pricing, foreign exchange exposure, international dividend policy, overseas cost of capital, overseas investment appraisal, international capital markets, international cash management, international trade and payments and global treasury management need to be considered if they impact upon the business plan.

If a company is importing or exporting overseas it will need to understand its exchange exposure and how to hedge against currency risk. A company that has overseas assets or subsidiaries will need to understand the implications for its dividend policy of global taxation, the possibility of double taxation and the rules in relation to transfer pricing. An understanding of the basic OECD rules in relation to transfer pricing is given in Chapter 3.

Corporate mergers and acquisitions

The strategic financial plan will include the identification of possible M&A threats and opportunities. Chapter 18 covered defensive tactics, acquisition consideration, the market value of shares during takeover, the effect of takeovers and mergers on EPS and dividend cover, reverse takeovers, demergers, the City Code, documents in a takeover and cross border M&A. The valuation of business and securities was discussed in Chapter 14. The directors of a company receiving a bid must always act in the best interests of their company, their shareholders, creditors and employees. If they feel that the offer is not in the best interests of the company then they may decide to contest the offer. However, it is illegal to block, obstruct and not treat shareholders equally. Chapter 18 explains the responsibilities of directors and how they should act in an ethical and legal manner.

The cost of capital and capital structure

The cost of capital can be calculated in a number of ways, including WACC, CAPM, dividend growth and MM. These methods, together with an explanation of capital structures are covered in Chapters 11, 12 and 13. The capital requirements of an organisation will be determined during the planning process and it is the role of the strategic financial plan to identify the most appropriate structure to support the overall business plan while at the same time being financially efficient.

THE STRATEGIC FINANCIAL MANAGEMENT INTERFACE WITH CORPORATE STRATEGY

At the core of corporate strategic management is strategic analysis, defining strategic options and then implementing the chosen strategy. These three core elements can be further broken down into core strategic activities. Strategic financial management processes interface with these core items as shown in Figure 22.1.

There is no particular sequence and the figure is just a simplification of the process. For example, at the core of corporate strategic management is defining strategic options and choices. This requires setting out the reasons for making choices, identifying options and evaluating the options to help make choices. The financial management interface at this evaluation stage will include the use of tools such as payback analysis, IRR, NPV, ARR, DCF, interest rate risk analysis, exchange rate risk analysis, taxation, etc. Figure 22.1 gives examples of some of the financial management tools available for use at each stage of the strategic business plan.

From this interface we might conclude that corporate strategy is more ambiguous and perhaps more qualitative in approach whereas financial management has a more precise and measurable approach. The interface between corporate strategy and strategic financial management is better understood if we define strategic management as a mechanism for assessing strategic choices and performance using the techniques of strategic analysis and financial analysis. This is done to help executive teams recognise the financial constraints and opportunities surrounding their strategic vision. It is a more engaging process than conventional financial management.

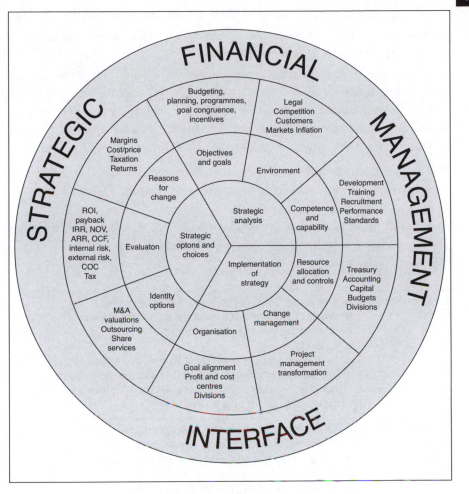

- Strategic analysis ask questions such as: is the mission achievable, what are the strategic goals and objectives, what strategies do we adopt to achieve our goals, what activities should we undertake and how do we control these activities?

- Financial analysis will ask questions such as: how does the mission relate to shareholder value, are the objectives and goals achievable within the financial constraints, how can financial resource development enhance objectives and goals, what financial value do the proposed strategies have, what is the value of the proposed activities and finally what profit and financial value is there to be gained from completion of the activities?

In Figure 22.1 we also mention strategic choices and strategy implementation. Financial evaluation and analysis interfaces with these two corporate strategy elements in the following manner:

- Strategic choices include finding the most suitable, realistic and acceptable routes that bring competitive benefits and increase shareholder value.

- Strategy implementation involves defining the organisation and resources and managing change and transformation.

- The strategic financial management interface with strategic choices and implementation is concerned with the financial analysis and evaluation such as cost–benefit analysis, risk and return analysis, scenario sensitivity analysis, constraint and opportunity identification, value-added analysis, resource costs and the value of change.

We can see from the above paragraphs that strategic financial management integrates our strategic thinking with financial analysis, planning and controls.

An example of a strategic financial management interface with corporate strategy within a technology company (DataBank Systems BNZ, ANZ, Westpac/NBNZ).

Value creation	■ Identify the principal activities that create value. ■ Identify the internal and external drivers for change. ■ Identify the critical success factors (CSFs). ■ Evaluate. ■ Understand the financial value by evaluating the financial implications of change, including regulation (normally negative), socio-economic (negative and positive), technology (should be positive but could be a threat).
Analysis and control	■ Link strategy, planning, budgeting and programming. ■ Define the strategic business units (SBUs) ■ Integrate the planning and budgeting processes. ■ Measure performance of SBUs. ■ Are resources built up from a zero base? ■ Is there a system of internal charging? ■ Use cost and management accounting techniques to measure performance and decide on courses of action. ■ Market and competitive analysis, including price determination. ■ Analysis of financial performance and predictions for the future. ■ Financial analysis and ratio analysis to identify areas for performance improvement. ■ Identify the activities that change shareholder value. ■ What is actually driving cost? ■ Prepare a 'dashboard' to guide the organisation to enhance value creation and achieve guide goals. ■ How can the business be streamlined or is there a more efficient business architecture that will reduce costs?

Investment decisions	Use Paul King's (1967 Queens' College Cambridge) six-stage model for investment decisions: ■ Triggering – recognise trigger events and links to corporate strategy and plan. ■ Screening – decision whether to pursue or not. Strategy discussion. ■ Definition – explain, identify alternatives, assumptions and sponsors. ■ Evaluation – financial analysis of consequences, cost–benefit analysis, payback, IRR, NPV, DCF and other appraisal methods. ■ Transmission – communicate throughout the organisation and obtain wider organisational commitment. ■ Decision – evaluate choices, determine value, formal business case. Decide on an appropriate cost of capital to be used in evaluation. How does the investment opportunity link or relate to other investment opportunities or current investments? How does the investment opportunity create value? Define the critical interdependencies. Prepare a sensitivity analysis.
Mergers and acquisitions	Identify merger and acquisition opportunities that fit with organisational strategic objectives. Determine how the acquisition or merger will create value and define how this will be measured. What are the risks and uncertainties of the acquisition and how will they be managed? What options are available? How will the investment be funded, what is the cost of funds and what are the other associated costs, both actual and opportunistic? How will the target's cost structure look after acquisition?

Example of strategic financial management interface with strategy within an IT company

This IT manufacturing and software supplier had prepared a conventional SWOT analysis. SWOT is the acronym for strengths, weaknesses, opportunities and threats and is used by many organisations to define the relationships between key environmental influences and an organisation's strategic capability. It is used in developing new strategies and in the case of our IT company defined the financial management interfaces and opportunities relating to the business strategies. Below is an example of some of the more significant factors identified in the analysis.

Strengths	Weaknesses
Technological leadership Brand Staff knowledge Product leadership	Marketing performance Channels to market High gearing High level of fixed costs Staff levels Lack of agility
Opportunities	**Threats**
Takeover of niche suppliers New product developments	New entrants raiding niche product market Interest rate increases Legislation increasing cost base

The company had a strong brand, experienced staff and product development leadership in key areas. However, it did not have good marketing ability and channel strategy. Agile new entrants and niche players often stole the lead. The company had a high cost base with a high proportion of fixed costs and staff numbers were up, with a low staff turnover. Added to this the company had borrowed externally in recent years and was now vulnerable to increasing interest rates. The first objective of high-level strategy was to increase agility and remove some of the threats. Appropriate financial strategies to support this include:

Financial strategy	How this helps business strategy
Hedge against further interest rate increases	Reduces exposure to increasing interest rates
Explore strategies to reduce gearing	Reduces exposure to increasing interest rates
Explore areas of overstaffing and seek opportunities to use contract staff	Improves financial agility and ability to take advantage of new opportunities for the takeover of niche suppliers and new product development
Explore M&A opportunities and have potential funding in place	Will reduce the semi-fixed cost base and increase agility. Contract staff may not necessarily be more expensive than employees. This will not be a 'quick fix'
Look for opportunities to replace fixed costs with variable costs. Sell buildings and lease back. Use more external suppliers on contract basis	Ability to purchase niche suppliers. Ability to take on new markets and also rationalise staff numbers. Potential for better market penetration
	Reduces fixed costs and improves agility and market responsiveness

These financial strategies will support the chosen business strategies. The financial manager will, of course, always explore efficiencies in the provision of finance. However, he will do this within the broader strategic financial strategy that supports business strategy. The IT company in question did in fact sell premises and lease them back and increase its market agility and responsiveness while reducing its fixed costs.

Example of strategic financial management interface with customer strategy in a UK clearing bank

The corporate banking division of a UK clearing bank wanted to raise the level of customer relationship with certain prime customers to one of being a valued business partner. At the present time the relationship between the bank and these customers is simply the reactive provision of basic services. The bank feels that by increasing the level of customer relationship it will add more value to the customer, thereby increasing customer retention and the potential for more bank-fee income.

To improve customer relationships requires two things:

1. An investment in technology to improve connectivity and links into the customer's treasury department.
2. A change of ethos in bank–customer relationship management.

Item 1 requires an investment of funds. Item 2 does not necessarily require significant additional funds. This is demonstrated in Figure 22.2.

To connect better with the customer and become a trusted business partner the bank will need to invest in technology that will enable it to link directly with the customer's treasury function. However, if it does this without simultaneously improving the quality of bank-staff relationship management capability (a change of ethos) it will simply have spent money on improved technology without increasing the level of service. The result will be a position at the bottom far right of the box, that is, money spent with no additional income.

If the bank simply improves the quality of staff and moves up on the 'ethos' axis it will merely frustrate the customer since the connectivity to complete the transactions and benefit from the improved bank-staff relationship will not be there.

This is a simplified example showing that investment strategy should interface with broader organisational changes in order to realise the benefits of the investment.

Figure 22.2

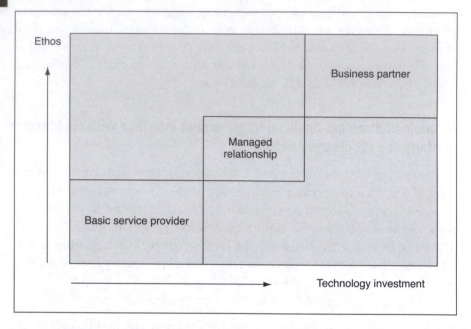

FINANCIAL MANAGEMENT IN A RECESSION

I do not think there are many people who can accurately predict when a recession will hit. There are plenty of people who do predict that a recession will happen but then there are also plenty of people who predict that the weather will get worse when it is currently sunny.

Recessions and downturns happen. Sometimes they develop into full-blown depressions. In the UK, for example, we have recently experienced the following recessions:

1973–1975	Most sectors lost about 30% of their value.
1980–1982	Most sectors lost less than 15% of their value. Energy suffered more.
1990–1991	Most sectors lost less than 15% of their value. Finance suffered more.
2001	Most sectors lost more than 20% value. IT and telecoms lost more.
2008–	Finance sector lost up to 90%.

If we look at the fall in share price during 2008 we can see clusters of industry sectors with similar reductions in their share price. For example:

Sector	Company	2008 share price movements
Oil and gas	Royal Dutch Shell	−14%
Oil and gas	BP	−14%
Retail	Sainsbury	−23%
Retail	Tesco	−25%
Finance	Barclays	−69%
Finance	LTSB	−73%
Finance	HBOS	−90%

Now, some of these share price movements simply reflect the overall market sentiment during a recession and more than offset movements due to a company's good financial performance. For example, Shell posted exceedingly strong results in January 2009 and so did Sainsbury. When we consider the finance sector movements we might assume that these reflect their troubled performance.

What can we deduce from this high-level observation that will be of use to the financial manager? Several things in fact:

1. Recessions happen – regularly.

2. In the UK we have had five in 35 years.

3. They have occurred at intervals of between 7 and 11 years.

4. It has, in the past, taken about 2 years to get out of recession.

5. Market sentiment will push down your share value and offset or partially offset increases in value due to good performance.

6. Not surprisingly, businesses within sectors are affected in similar ways.

7. Just because a sector is hit badly in one recession does not mean it will be similarly hit again in the next recession.

These observations, obvious as they are, seem to be ignored often by companies in their strategic financial management and strategic business plans. An acknowledgement of their existence and a contingency plan (or perhaps an exit strategy) to accommodate the inevitable can be useful if there is a belief and desire for survival. However, there is another view that thinks that the inevitable seasons of economic and business activity are a healthy way of pruning and encouraging new growth. This view suggests going with the flow and starting afresh with new ideas.

Whatever your view on this, whether it is better to defend or go with the flow and start again, there is no doubt that you will have more options available if you take defensive and other actions to protect your wealth. Since this text on financial management includes creating value and wealth protection, we will follow the proposition that it is better to attempt to make a business more robust to the inevitability of recessions.

Consumer/discretionary spending tends to lead the way into and out of recession. The 2008/2009 recession seems so far to be following this pattern. The three big differences in this recession from the past four are:

- the global nature of the recession
- a shift in economic influence and world power bases
- e-business that will accelerate recovery and new business.

These similarities and observations may give companies some idea of what to expect, how to protect their businesses and how to position themselves for the future. However, there is a trade-off in that some of the measures required to protect liquidity and availability of funds during a recession may increase the current cost of capital. This is the point where a financial manager is required to think strategically rather than tactically and accept, for example, a less immediately efficient financial structure in order to preserve some future flexibility.

The first thing to establish is how a recession might affect your organisation. As we have seen from the past it is difficult to predict how each sector will be affected. What we can do, however, is make certain assumptions on the possible downturn in key areas of business and plot various scenarios together with a sensitivity analysis to see how important each variable factor is to the desired end result. For example, run the business plan:

- assuming a 30% drop in sales
- assuming a reduction of 5% in interest rates
- assuming an increase of 5% in interest rates
- assuming a credit crunch.

Run these through, one at a time, to determine the effect that each change has on cash and on profits. Remember, cash is all important in a recession, especially if there is a credit crunch.

Having run these basic scenarios, establish whether the organisation has enough cash to survive for the predicted 2 years of recession and credit crunch. If it has not enough cash to survive then determine what can be done now to protect liquidity and flexibility. Also, examine areas of fixed cost that perhaps could become variable. Consider the following:

- dividends versus cash retention
- lower financial gearing
- lower level of fixed costs
- more robust income even if it produces a lower margin.

What we are talking about here is a lower level of gearing in all areas, not just finance. For example, a service company might take on a greater proportion of maintenance work (at a lower margin) than creative work (usually at a higher margin) because it might decide that the maintenance work will continue during a recession. These actions might create a diminution in current value and it is up to the executive team to decide whether this is acceptable to shareholders.

Once actually into a recession, the following actions are usually considered:

- reduce costs
- reduce capital expenditure
- increase efficiency
- increase productivity
- increase market share
- new products and areas
- seek bargain acquisitions
- exit poor markets
- shore up risk management
- buy bargain resources.

Remember that the companies that fare well and stand up to recessions better are those that have provided a better level of customer service and product offering and are generally more diversified in the sense that they provide some services/products that are more recession robust, for example essential maintenance services in addition to new builds.

CONCLUSION

Strategic financial management is a method that uses the techniques described in this book to integrate and link strategy to value and to finance. The techniques help evaluate and are applied to value management, analysis and controls, investment decisions and M&A.

Financial management has an interface with every stage of strategic management and by using the techniques discussed you should now be able to:

- evaluate the financial consequences of a company's strategic decisions
- choose appropriate sources of finance to support business strategy and understand risks and costs
- understand the business environment and the impact of global affairs on an organisation

- assess investment opportunities, decisions and strategies
- understand risk and engage appropriate risk-management techniques
- optimise the use of financial resources
- understand cash and treasury management
- have knowledge of creating value
- analyse and control business performance.

It is easy to get wrapped up in academic debate on many of the topics covered in this book, particularly strategic financial management, when in fact a professional and pragmatic approach is what is really needed to arrive at sensible, workable solutions to real business problems. I hope that I have struck the right balance in this chapter and that this SFM analysis will have real practical use for professionals and students. To help summarise the SFM approach the following schedule may be useful:

Value	
	1. Identify and understand the main activities in the organisation that create and generate value.
	2. Identify activities that actually destroy value.
	3. Determine how these activities work with the overall business system and processes.
	4. Determine the factors that can change or influence these activities that have an effect on value and perform a sensitivity analysis.
	5. Determine the key elements that affect value and cost and see how these can be managed better.
	6. Determine financial management strategies that support the value-creation strategy.
Accounting costs and budgets	1. Define appropriate profit, cost centres and strategic business units that support value creation.
	2. Consider internal charging for all internally provided services.
	3. Ensure that customers of services have the ability to accept the lowest-cost provider (internal or external) of a service.
	4. Ensure a form of zero-based budgeting exists and that internal support providers cover their costs with income generated from customers.
	5. Ensure that budgets are aligned with corporate goals and objectives.
	6. Measure the relative performance of strategic business units.
	7. Have clarity on the strategic goals and mission of the organisation and ensure that this is communicated throughout the organisation and in the annual report.
	8. Measure performance.
	9. Prepare and act on budget variance analysis.
	10. Make use of a management control 'dashboard'.
	11. Identify and measure areas that add value and those that reduce value.

	12. Make use of financial and management ratio analysis. 13. Ensure that resources are allocated in a way that will increase value and competitiveness. 14. Ensure that any surplus funds create maximum value and do not destroy value. 15. Compare organisational costs with those of competitors. 16. Determine how the business could be more efficient, how costs can be reduced and consider outsourcing and shared services.
Investment decisions	1. How does an investment opportunity relate to the organisational goals and objectives and how does it relate to other investments in the organisation? 2. Ensure a capital investment appraisal process is in place and that no elements of it are by-passed. 3. Use King's capital investment process defined in Chapter 17: triggering, screening, definition, evaluation, transmission, decision. 4. Determine what will happen to organisational profits and cash if an investment is not made. 5. Does the investment create value? 6. How does it relate to other projects? 7. What are the risks? Prepare a sensitivity analysis. 8. Determine an appropriate cost of capital and calculate the NPV.
Mergers and acquisitions	1. How does the proposed acquisition or merger relate to the organisational strategic objectives? 2. How will the acquisition create value, for example, is it creating synergy, a new area or does it provide general defence? 3. Are there alternatives? 4. Determine the risks that come with the acquisition or merger and prepare a sensitivity analysis. 5. Determine the full investment required to both acquire and integrate. 6. Ensure that the funding strategy supports the strategic opportunity and is robust through various future economic and business scenarios.

Earlier in this chapter we talked about corporate governance and an 'ethical watchdog'. In the final chapter we will discuss the basics of ethics and professionalism as they relate to financial management and particularly to bankers. This is intended to provide useful practical advice on how to recognise and deal with an ethical problem rather than to engage in an academic debate on morality and ethics.

23

Professionalism and ethics – what happens if it all goes wrong?

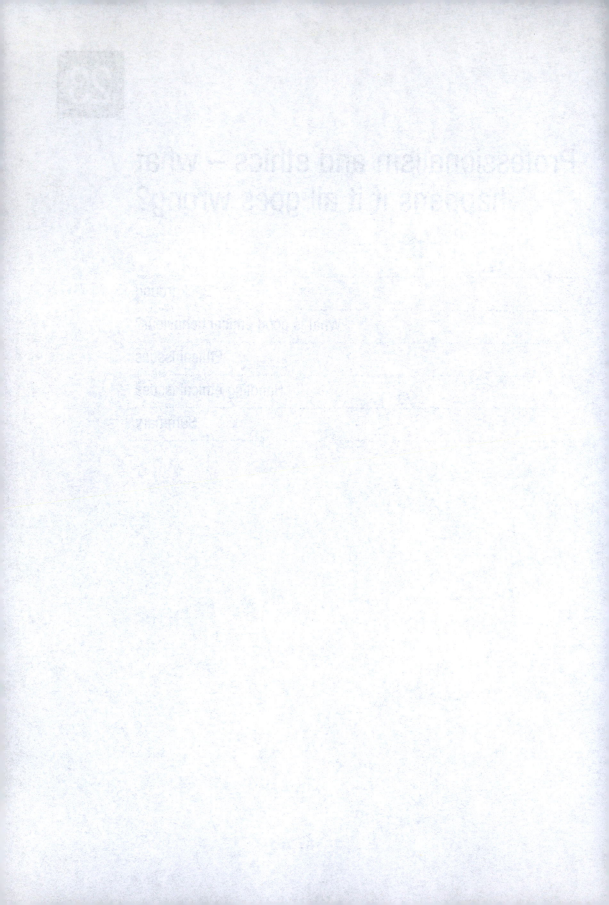

BACKGROUND

In the previous chapter we talked about corporate governance and the ethical watchdog. In this chapter we will explain how professionalism and ethics form a vital element of sound financial management.

We have seen in 2008 and 2009 the results of unprofessional and unethical behaviour and how this has affected financial markets and global economies. Our major financial institutions are paying fines of hundreds of millions of shareholders' funds for violating US sanctions and other regulations and trusted 'professionals' are losing billions of investors' funds. Meanwhile, an investor might ask, 'How do I find a really ethical bank?'

From 1 August 2008 new students starting their Chartered Banker studies will need to show that they are aware of ethical issues and be able to demonstrate how they can handle these with professionalism and integrity. Professional accountancy institutions around the world have recently introduced ethics into their professional competence examinations. All professional institutions will have disciplinary procedures for members who breach ethical and professional standards.

This chapter may help you apply some simple rules to recognise an ethical problem and to deal with it. We will start from the premise that it is always easier to stay out of trouble than it is to get out of trouble. So, we will examine how to recognise and avoid a potential ethical problem. We will also examine how to review an ethical problem and decide on a course of action.

WHAT IS GOOD ETHICAL BEHAVIOUR?

We all have our own ideas about what is good ethical behaviour, derived from our parents, schooling, religion, work associates, our own beliefs and many other influences. If I attempt to define what good ethical behaviour means to me, I am sure that you will be able to add to this with your own ideas and thoughts. In the profession of banking my own list includes:

- being truthful, honest and having integrity
- being fair
- being able to do what you say you are going to do
- being independent and impartial in advice
- having no prejudice
- having respect for others

- treating people as you would want them to treat you
- setting customer expectations and meeting them
- keeping a person's confidentiality.

You may express this differently and you may feel that I have omitted things. This is one problem with defining ethical behaviour, it can be very subjective and it is also easy to forget things. However, you might recognise that the above list attempts to:

- do good
- do to others as you would have them do to you
- be respectful
- show natural justice
- treat people the same.

As a finance professional, banker or accountant you should first of all be aware of your own institute's code of ethics and expectations of members. Then, having agreed on what you consider to be good ethical behaviour, you can attempt to recognise and deal with an ethical issue.

ETHICAL ISSUES

An ethical issue is when we are in breach or potentially in breach of any of our professional codes of ethics. This may arise when there is a threat to our ethical behaviour standards. Threats to ethical behaviour can arise from:

- self-interest
- familiarity
- conflicts of interest
- intimidation
- acting in two roles.

An example of the *self-interest* threat can arise when a professional puts his or her personal interests before those of a client, for example advising a client on a course of action that will increase your fee income rather than on the course of action that is best for the client. *Familiarity* can occur from spending too long on one account and perhaps losing some objectivity or accepting the status quo. It can also arise from being too close to the client on a personal basis. This can be avoided in a bank by client rotation, but might not be so easy in a smaller firm or consultancy. Conflicts of interest occur in almost any area of professional work, for example when you are advising two clients who have business relationships with each other or when you find that you have split loyalties. *Intimidation* can occur both internally and externally for any number of reasons. It is easy to recognise but not so easy to deal with, for example a tyrannical boss threatening a subordinate to take a particular course of action or else lose his job. A threat to ethical behaviour can occur when a person *acts in two roles*, for example both as accountant and auditor!

I am sure that you can think of many more threats to ethical behaviour. The important thing is to recognise a threat and avoid getting into trouble, remembering that it is easier to stay out of trouble than it is to get out of trouble. Many professionals who breach professional codes simply do not see the threat coming.

HANDLING ETHICAL ISSUES

When you recognise an ethical issue you will find it useful to have some guidelines on how to handle it. They tend not to go away and you will need to understand what options you have and which one to take. You will probably need to seek advice. Talking to your chums and your professional institute is most valuable. Having a structured method to do this will help. You will find that there are many models for handling ethical issues. They can be complicated. As a start and to keep things simple you could use the following simple method: FIAC (Facts, Issues, Alternatives, Choices). Or you can develop your own model. For the purpose of this short article I will use FIAC.

List the facts

List the essential elements of the case. What is being done? Who is asking what? Who will gain and who will lose? Identify all of the parties to the issue. You could describe these as stakeholders. For example, these could be yourself, your employer, your client, another connected business, the wider community, your profession, HMC, etc.

Identify ethical issues

Identify each ethical issue that is being affected by the fact of the case. For example, are you in danger of losing your independence, do you have a conflict of interest? List each ethical issue as you see it. This could be subject to review by an independent person/party to ensure that you have left nothing out.

Define and compare alternatives

You will need to define the alternative courses of action available to you. These will include doing nothing, going public, dropping the customer, reporting the case to the profession, reporting the case to the authorities, finding an alternative solution, getting the customer to do things differently.

When you have defined the alternatives you can list the advantages and disadvantages of each case. You will find that there are often conflicts, for example doing what is just and right for the public might result in a breach of customer confidentiality.

Choose

Having defined all of the alternatives it is 'make your mind up time'. This may not be at all easy and this is why it is best to seek advice from your fellow professionals and independent sources. Of course, you will aim to take the course of action that does the least amount of harm, but you may find that the decision is far from clear. Taking a systematic approach to solving an ethical dilemma and consulting your peers will ensure that your decision is seen as impartial and has the best chance of being the correct one.

SUMMARY

A finance professional carries additional moral responsibilities to those held by the general population because he/she is in an informed position and capable of making and acting on knowledge that the general public or clients cannot. Perhaps you cannot fairly be held accountable for failing to do something that you do not have the brief or ability to do, but if you do have the ability then you are fully accountable.

Professional knowledge brings with it authority and power. Clients will rightly place trust in a professional on the basis that the services provided will be of benefit to them. However, in the past few years much of this trust has gone. The managing director of one large firm recently said to me that the 'masters of the universe' who control our financial institutions had their ethical bone removed at birth.

Most professionals follow codes of practice that are enforced by their professional institution. These are designed not only to protect the public but also to maintain the integrity of the profession. Disciplinary codes and standards allow the profession to ensure practitioners meet standards. This is one reason why, when dealing with a financial institution, it offers some comfort to know if the individuals you are dealing with belong to a relevant professional institution. This, of course, is in addition to the 'comfort' brought by regulators and financial services authorities around the world. What we are talking about are individuals who seek to serve their clients in a professional and ethical manner and belong to a professional institution.

There are, of course, concerns about the validity of professional codes of ethics. Self-regulation might be seen as a self-serving, soft option. However, if a profession wishes to keep its standing it cannot allow this view to prevail. Professionals should always act in the best interest of their clients and to the best of their ability. Clients would be well advised to determine which professional code of ethics their advisers subscribe to.

Most professional institutions publish their own codes of ethical principles for their members and students to abide by. These can never be complete, but they do provide the basic tenets of ethical and professional behaviour and conduct. These codes can be summarised in the following principles.

Fundamental principles

Integrity	Be honest, fair, right and just.
	Act with integrity in professional and business relationships and in all transactions.
Objectivity and independence	Be impartial and intellectually honest.
	Show no prejudice or bias to any party.
	Have no conflict of interest.
	Be independent in all engagements.
	Do not put undue influence on others.
Competence	Ensure you are competent for the work you are doing. This includes being qualified through both qualification and experience and keeping up to date with latest practice.
	Have the ability to evaluate and supervise the work performed by staff.
Performance	Ensure professional obligations are completed in accordance with expectations that have been set and agreed with clients and customers. This includes ensuring both quality and time expectations are met.
	Carry out work with due care and diligence.
Behaviour	Act in a manner that is expected of a professional by a trusting client.
	Ensure client and employer confidentiality.
	Do not engage in activities that run counter to your profession.
	Do not mislead in terms of promotion and competence.
	Ensure that fees are fair and that there is a process for settling disputes.

In considering the performance of individuals involved in creating financial collapses and our current global recession it would be interesting to see how they compare with the above fundamentals. Indeed, how many of them belonged to a professional institution that required them to comply with a code of ethics?

Acknowledgement: In this chapter extracts have been taken from 'Professionalism and ethics' in the September 2008 edition of *Chartered Banker*.

Sustainability and financial management

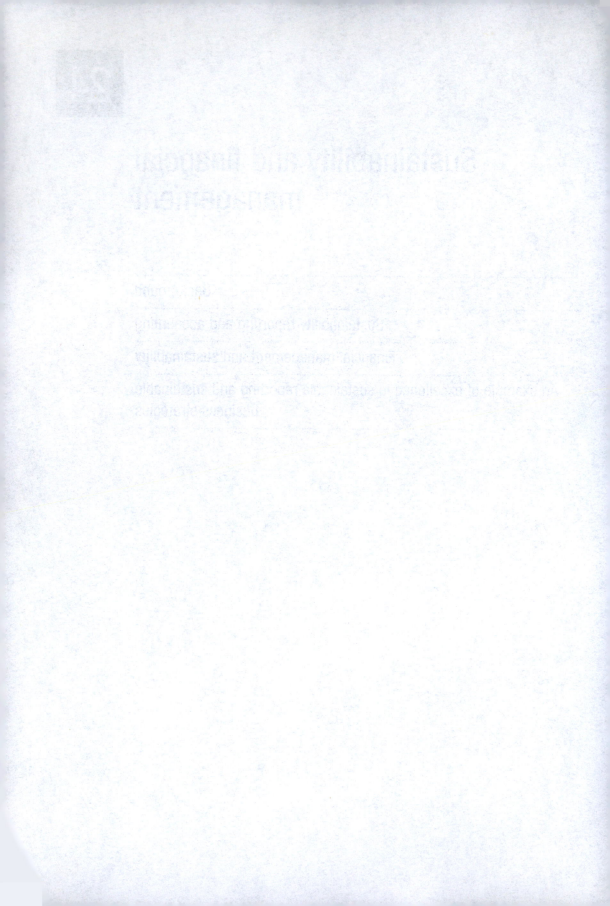

BACKGROUND

We have discussed why financial management is more than just ensuring transactional financial efficiency. It is also about ensuring that the correct types of funds are available to support business strategy and that they are obtained and used in an efficient manner. Good strategic financial management helps an organisation to achieve its goals efficiently and in a robust way that makes the best use of resources available and obtainable. Sustainable financial management goes further to ensure the achievement of goals and use of resources over a much longer term and with consideration to social and environmental consequences.

SUSTAINABILITY REPORTING AND ACCOUNTING

Just as financial accounting is a useful background to financial management so is sustainability accounting and reporting a useful backdrop to sustainable financial management. Sustainability accounting will provide information to support sustainable financial management and also to contribute to the governance processes that encourage sustainable outcomes in an organisation. Sustainability accounting also provides information regarding the sustainability of an organisation to internal and external stakeholders and investors.

Sustainability accounting includes a range of accounting approaches which aims to move an organisation towards decision making that is consistent with environmental and social sustainability as well as the more conventional economic evaluation approach. Fully integrated sustainable accounting is an approach that is yet to be completely developed. However, sustainability reporting to the public has been developed in most company reports and accounts for some years now and includes reporting on:

- carbon emissions
- environmental impact
- social responsibility reporting
- triple bottom-line reporting
- progress towards becoming a sustainable organisation.

Sustainable development reporting (SDR) and triple bottom line (TBL)

For some years now the cornerstone of SDR has been the triple bottom line (TBL) approach. TBL considers three aspects:

1. Environment.
2. Economic.
3. Social.

Some countries go one stage further by adding 'Cultural' to the list as a separate item, considering culture to be of major importance and not something to simply include under the 'Social' category.

For a clear example of TBL go to www.sanford.co.nz and view the report and accounts. The latest SDR shows clearly the TBL approach used in reporting to shareholders and stakeholders the progress that the company has made in sustainability.

An example of the possible contents of a TBL report is given in the following table. This is not set in stone and different organisations and countries have different approaches.

Environmental	Materials used
	Sustainable materials
	Emissions
	Renewable energy
	Output consumption
	Environmental impact
	Waste
	Penalties
Economic	Sales
	Profits
	Geographical analysis
	Market share
	Customer perceptions
	Total salaries and wages paid
	Economic value to local area
	Taxes paid
Social	Training
	Health
	Accidents and accident-prevention measures
	Equal employment
	Human rights
	Workforce home locations
	Contribution to employees
	Privacy
	Greater community

To prepare an SDR TBL report it is useful to consider the following aspects:

- resource costs
- scope of the report
- level of senior management commitment
- shareholder and stakeholder expectations
- environmental, economic and social issues in the industry
- environmental, economic and social issues in the community
- comparison of the environmental, economic and social issues with the company's own mission, values and objectives and decide whether these items need adjustment
- environmental, economic and social impact at each stage of production
- engagement with stakeholders
- key indicators, for example: Environmental = materials used, waste, renewable, etc.; Economic = sales, share price, taxes, etc.; Social = equal opportunities, pay, workers' locations, etc.

SDR and TBL reporting involves cost. This is the first stage of where it interfaces with financial management because in justifying the cost of SDR and TBL we can see the real benefits that it brings to an organisation and how these benefits flow into the organisation's mission and goals.

The following table shows the benefits of SDR and TBL and will form the basis for building up a sound business case.

Internal	External
Better motivated staff who can justify their work in terms of their environment	Enhanced brand and reputation
	A 'community licence' to operate
Aligned staff	More customer loyalty
Ability to attract good staff	Sustainable profits
Better understanding of risks and better risk management	Increase in sales and market share
	More media attention.
Increased sales	

FINANCIAL MANAGEMENT AND SUSTAINABILITY

By considering the above benefits of SDR and TBL we can begin to see that sustainable performance adds real business value and needs to be a part of an organisation's business strategy supported by a sound financial management strategy.

Sustainable strategies bring together long-term environmental needs with current requirements, finding ways to improve the current situation without damaging the future. This is all about setting both current and future needs and finding optimal solutions. There need not be a conflict between current and future needs; they may, in fact, be complementary and should be met in a way that ensures that environmental, economic and social dimensions are integrated into the business plan and strategy.

When identifying the sustainable strategies to be built into a business plan one should actively pursue those opportunities that support environmental, economic and social benefits. Avoid any narrow-view attitudes that might produce benefits in one area at the cost of damaging another. This means taking a broader view while simultaneously determining how contributions to broader outcomes can benefit the organisation. This is achieved only through a sustained process of engaging with communities and other stakeholders.

The financial management consequences of this include:

- having longer-term financial strategies in place to support sustainable developments
- identifying whether sustainable development will help obtain a lower-cost source of funds
- identification of the cost of not adopting sustainable strategies
- recognising that responsible financial management decisions evaluate the benefits of long-term sustainability and that all financial decisions should be based on full consideration of the environmental, economic and social consequences
- developing financing strategies for sustainability by building reserves and developing donor–beneficiary relationships.

The effect of sustainable strategies on the cost of finance

Lenders may consider environmental and social risks as an element of their decision criteria when deciding whether or not to provide finance. Clearly, under these circumstances, a company that has considered environmental and sustainability questions and has supported these with SDR is more likely to obtain the finance that it needs. SDR also indicates a level of forward thinking that is not provided in conventional historical financial reports. This type of thinking promotes new ideas and opportunity identification and helps assure lenders and investors. Increasingly investors in lending institutions are looking to see that their funds are invested in an environmentally efficient way and a lending institution that can demonstrate that it has a substantial portfolio of loans out to companies with sustainable strategies is likely to obtain a lower cost of funds. This would apply equally to direct equity investors.

Socially responsible investment is now an established and growing market, supported in the UK, for example, by FTSE4Good. Many investors will only invest in sustainable projects. Therefore, it is clear that having sustainable strategies in place will reduce the cost of funds and this is now a part of sound strategic financial management.

The integration of sustainability into plans, budgets and financial statements

When projects that meet sustainable objectives have been approved as part of the planning and budgeting process and integrated with other corporate objectives, a process of reporting progress against the projects needs to be developed. SDR and TBL reports need to be based on auditable facts and figures derived from the company's normal reporting system. This mechanism is known as sustainability reporting integration. While a method for full integration has yet to be developed and widely approved, it is essential that SDR reports are verifiable. In the UK companies are now required under the Companies Act to disclose and comment on environmental liabilities in their reports. The Act requires that:

> A director of a company must act in the way he considers, in good faith, would be most likely to promote the success of the company for the benefit of its members as a whole, and in doing so have (amongst other matters) regard to –
>
> a. the likely consequence of any decision in the long term
>
> b. the interests of the company's employees
>
> c. the need to foster the company's business relationships with suppliers, customers and others
>
> d. the effect of the company's operations on the community and the environment.

There is also now a reporting requirement for large companies to produce a business review that includes environmental matters. SMEs are encouraged to do the same.

Sustainability – opportunities and risks

Environmental and sustainability considerations bring opportunities to those who can develop and market new technologies successfully, for example low-emission vehicles and low-carbon services. They also bring risks such as the risk of flooding, new regulations, increasing costs of funds, damage to reputation and increased energy prices.

Reasons for the integration of sustainability into financial management

Sustainability should be integrated into business and financial management strategies in order to:

- take advantage of the opportunities it creates and to avoid the risks
- obtain a lower cost of external and equity funds
- ensure financial strategies support longer-term goals
- measure the risks of not achieving sustainability goals.

AN EXAMPLE OF EXCELLENCE IN SUSTAINABLE REPORTING AND SUSTAINABLE BUSINESS STRATEGIES

The following examples and extracts are taken from the annual report of Sanford Limited in New Zealand with its permission. Sanford Limited holds no responsibility for this reproduction.

One of the best examples of sustainability reporting and sustainable business strategy is shown each year in the Sanford report (www.sanford.co.nz). This is a substantial New Zealand deep sea fishing company that has taken sustainability to the core of every business activity, positioning its current activities with long-term sustainable operations. This means ensuring that fish stocks are managed and not depleted. As a Maori once said to me, 'take a bit for today but leave something for tomorrow'.

The extracts below from the Sanford annual report explain how the quota system and sustainable harvesting work and how Sanford uses sustainable policies throughout its business, matching current value creation with future long-term sustainability.

Background

New Zealand has one of the most advanced systems in the world for ensuring the sustainable utilisation and management of wild fisheries. The system (called the Quota Management System or QMS) is based on proportional harvest property rights allocated in perpetuity (called quota or ITQ) that may be purchased or sold subject to certain qualifications in respect of enterprise ownership and aggregate quota owned. An annual harvest right is generated from quota ownership based on the percentage of the Total Allowable Commercial Catch (TACC or sometimes called TAC).

This amount of quota – in tonnes (Annual Catch Entitlement or ACE) – is the amount that can be caught. Strict regimes are in place to ensure compliance with catch landing and reporting requirements to ensure that quota rights and responsibilities are protected.

Scientific assessments are carried out on fish stocks annually or when required and the TACC and all quota is adjusted proportionally up and down depending on the state of the resource.

Sanford commits totally to comply with the rules and regulations in respect to Fisheries and other relevant New Zealand Law. Sanford actively participates in the collection and analysis of data to ensure realistic and cost effective research programs are developed to underpin the sustainable utilization and management of New Zealand's marine resources.

Taking sustainability to the core of the business

The potential impact of climate change has become one of the most important concerns of the 21st century. Combine the agricultural effects from shifting weather patterns, the availability of clean water and the demand of an ever-increasing world population on food supplies, and the need for sustainable food sources becomes very significant. Fishing and aquaculture have the distinct advantage of being from renewable sources, if managed responsibly. As a well-established seafood company, Sanford Limited has long supported "Sustainable Seafood". We subscribe to the New Zealand Quota Management System (QMS), which ensures the long-term health of New Zealand's wild fish stocks, and actively invest in sustainable aquaculture projects. At Sanford we also recognise the need for a business to be sustainable in all its activities. As part of the Environmental Management System (EMS) review, we recognised the need for a Sustainability Policy. This policy is designed to complement the existing environmental policy, which underpins the EMS. It is also to ensure we assess our business decisions for environmental, social and economic sustainability to ensure continuous improvement and growth of the Company, and enduring stakeholder benefit. The Emissions Trading Scheme Bill has a potentially huge impact on the economic sustainability of the New Zealand fishing sector. The allocation of units, equal to 50% of the impact of fuel costs for a three-year period, will help lessen the blow somewhat. However, in an industry that is heavily reliant on fuel for energy, these costs, combined with rising fuel prices, mean fuel-saving initiatives are even more important. Operating in a socially responsible manner and supporting those communities in which we operate remains key to the sustainability of Sanford. The ongoing viability of some of these communities is essential for us to continue to access the hard-working and diligent pool of labour that we presently have in our fishing fleets, marine farms and processing factories. Sanford continues to respond to stakeholders by reporting our progress as comprehensively as possible. This year, defining the report content, including the materiality of topics, was completed. A list of draft topics was circulated to the executive team. Their feedback was then discussed at their meeting in early September and the inclusion and priority of each topic was agreed. We have aimed to report topics of relevance and interest, as well as the outcomes of our activities during the 2008 financial year.

* * *

Achieving sustainable development is perhaps one of the most difficult and one of the most pressing goals we face. It requires on the part of all of us commitment, action, partnerships and, sometimes, sacrifices of our traditional life patterns and personal interests.

Some sustainable activities

Sanford Snapshots

In our staff rooms and communities

- We contributed to 126 employee KiwiSaver funds

- We took part in Environment Canterbury's annual oil spill training exercise

- We worked with the local community to avert potential oil leakage from the San Cuvier in our business

- We replaced the environmental policy with a sustainability policy in this report

- We achieved a C+ grade against the Global Reporting Initiative guidelines

- We invested in light fuel oil use in our deepwater fleet

- We expanded our product range and quota with the purchase of the Jones Group assets

- We avoided two potentially major floods at the Kaeo plant through mitigation activity in our environment

- We attained six out of the seven environmental targets set for 2008

- We continued our ISO 14001 and Marine Stewardship Council certification

- We cleaned up a beach in South Georgia

- We took part in an industry workshop on sustainability reporting

Sustainability Policy

This policy, and supporting quality, environmental, social and economic systems, aims to promote sustainable fishery practices, and related development initiatives, which will be productive indefinitely. Sanford is committed to operating in a sustainable manner in all aspects of the business. New Zealand's Quota Management System (QMS) is one of the most advanced systems in the world for ensuring the sustainable utilisation and management of wild fisheries. As part of this system, Sanford believes in promoting New Zealand's commercial fishing industry and in protecting the ocean ecosystem. The New Zealand Aquaculture Strategy, developed by the New Zealand Aquaculture Council and endorsed by the New Zealand Government, is the principal document for ensuring the sustainable management of aquaculture interests. As part of this industry, Sanford believes in promoting New Zealand's aquaculture industry and in protecting the associated ecosystems. Sanford's sustainability policy encompasses activities that are wholly owned and operated by the Company. In those operations in which Sanford has partial influence, through percentage stake or management collaboration, we aim to operate according to this policy.

Sanford aims to deliver sustainability through:

1. Promotion of all aspects of sustainability in our governance, by:

■ considering all aspects of sustainability in our business planning and operations, including achieving a reasonable balance between conflicting demands;

■ endorsing and complying with relevant legislation, regulations, codes of practice and other voluntary requirements to which we subscribe, and maintaining good working relationships with administrating agencies;

■ engaging with key stakeholders about our strategic intent and performance;

■ improving our performance by establishing appropriate objectives and targets, completing regular audit and review of our policies, activities and practices, and acting on complaints;

■ reporting on key, readily measurable aspects of our performance and strategic intent.

2. Respect for the environment through our activities and influence, by:

■ supporting sustainable use of marine resources;

■ minimising any adverse impacts of our activities on the environment (including biotechnologies, resource efficiency and waste production);

■ reducing the likelihood of accidental discharges of pollutants and having contingency plans in place to deal with these should they occur;

■ working proactively with our suppliers to increase supplier participation and commitment to sustainable development principles.

3. Respect for our stakeholders through our activities and influence, by:

■ providing a safe and healthy working environment that supports individual development, team-working, positive work/life balance, and job
satisfaction;

■ ensuring that staff are part of ongoing dialogue about our sustainability;

■ strengthening relationships and providing confidence to regulators,
banks, insurers and financial markets;

■ maintaining and enhancing relations with the communities in which we
operate;

■ being honest and transparent in our communications, both internally
and with external stakeholders.

4. Generation of economic benefit for New Zealand, our Shareholders and
   Sanford, by:

■ creating meaningful employment, and making an appropriate rate of
return on equity;

■ supporting the sustainable development of New Zealand fisheries;

■ maintaining financial viability and maximising profitability for our
Shareholders;

■ delivering to stakeholders through economically sustainable business
ventures.

International responsibilities

Sanford Limited also has responsibilities to international stakeholders,
and nowhere is this more apparent than in our activities in the southern
oceans around Antarctica, and in the waters of the Western and Central
Pacific Ocean.

Convention for the Conservation of Antarctic Marine Living Resources

Sanford Limited undertakes exploratory fishing for Antarctic Toothfish in
the southern oceans around Antarctica, under a licence granted by the
New Zealand Government and consistent with the Conservation
Measures approved by the Convention for the Conservation of Antarctic
Marine Living Resources (CCAMLR). CCAMLR came into force in 1982, as
part of the Antarctic Treaty System. We take our responsibilities for
research and seabird mitigation very seriously, as required by CCAMLR.
Indeed, we are proud of our record in seabird mitigation – not once in the
six years we have been undertaking exploratory fishing under a CCAMLR

licence has Sanford caught a single seabird, a record that we fully intend to maintain. Website www.ccamlr.org

Coalition of Legal Toothfish Operators

Illegal, unregulated and unreported fishing for Toothfish in the waters around Antarctica (while never recorded in the Ross Sea) is recognised by Sanford and other responsible fishing companies as a significant problem. Sanford Limited complies with all reporting requirements of CCAMLR, the New Zealand Government and other international bodies, and is able to provide full documentation for its total catch of toothfish. In addition, Sanford Limited is a founding member of the Coalition of Legal Toothfish Operators, an organisation established to help authorities reduce the incidence of illegal, unregulated or unreported fishing of Toothfish. Website www.colto.org

Western & Central Pacific Fisheries Commission

New Zealand is a signatory to the Convention on the Conservation and Management of Highly Migratory Fish Stocks in the Western and Central Pacific Ocean which, after 4 years of negotiations was opened for signature on 5 September 2000 and came into force on 19 June 2004. The objective of the Convention is to ensure, through effective management, the long-term conservation and sustainable use of highly migratory species within the Convention Area.

Environmental awareness

Sanford is responding to existing and emerging environmental issues by seeking to improve performance standards in all its operations and through active participation in industry environmental initiatives and forums.

Environmental performance improvement is being achieved by

■ the implementation of Environmental Management Systems (EMS) incorporating compliance with ISO 14001 standards. All shore based and on board processing facilities are certified to ISO 14001 standard.

■ continually investigating the implementation of methods to improve the Company's eco-efficiency in terms of farmed and harvested seafood, energy, water, packaging and waste management.

■ protecting and enhancing the natural environment through active management programs to prevent events such as oil spills from occurring, and formal contingency planning in the event they do. We also undertake active maintenance of marine areas nearby to where we operate.

Health benefits

There is increased consumer recognition of the correlation between seafood and healthy living. Globally, governments are increasingly focused on nutrition and health. Many countries are battling lifestyle diseases, and this trend is rising. Scientific evidence shows that the consumption of seafood has positive health benefits for all age groups, and significantly higher benefits for certain medical conditions. Recent research papers advocating fish as part of a healthy diet are available at www.seafood.net.au.

For an example of excellence in sustainable reporting visit the Sanford website at http://live.isitesoftware.co.nz/sanford/documents/sdr/sustainable_Development_Report_-_published_17_December_2008.pdf

Appendices

Discounted cash flow tables showing discount factors to three decimal places

Years	1	2	3	4	5	6	7	8	9	10	11	12	13	14	15
1	990	980	971	962	952	943	935	926	917	909	901	893	885	877	870
2	980	961	943	925	907	890	873	857	842	826	812	797	783	769	756
3	971	942	915	889	864	840	816	794	772	751	731	712	693	675	658
4	961	924	888	855	823	792	763	735	708	683	659	636	613	592	572
5	951	906	863	822	784	747	713	681	650	621	593	567	543	519	497
6	942	888	837	790	746	705	667	630	596	564	535	507	480	456	432
7	933	871	813	760	711	665	623	583	547	513	482	452	425	400	376
8	923	853	789	731	677	627	582	540	502	467	434	404	376	351	327
9	914	837	766	703	645	592	544	500	460	424	391	361	333	308	284
10	905	820	744	676	614	558	508	463	422	386	352	322	295	270	247
11	896	804	722	650	585	527	475	429	388	350	317	287	261	237	215
12	887	788	701	625	557	497	444	397	356	319	286	257	231	208	187
13	879	773	681	601	530	469	415	368	326	290	258	229	204	182	163
14	870	758	661	577	505	442	388	340	299	263	232	205	181	160	141
15	861	743	642	555	481	417	362	315	275	239	209	183	160	140	123
16	853	728	623	534	458	394	339	292	252	218	188	163	141	123	107
17	844	714	605	513	436	371	317	270	231	198	170	146	125	108	93
18	836	700	587	494	416	350	296	250	212	180	153	130	111	95	81
19	828	686	570	475	396	331	277	232	194	164	138	116	98	83	70
20	820	673	554	456	377	312	258	215	178	149	124	104	87	73	61
21	811	660	538	439	359	294	242	199	164	135	112	93	77	64	53
22	803	647	522	422	342	278	226	184	150	123	101	83	68	56	46
23	795	634	507	406	326	262	211	170	138	112	91	74	60	49	40
24	788	622	492	390	310	247	197	158	126	102	82	66	53	43	35
25	780	610	478	375	295	233	184	146	116	92	74	59	47	38	30

Discount factor are given to 3 decimal places with the decimal point omitted.

Formulae: $\dfrac{1}{(1+i)^n}$ where i = rate of discount and n = number of years

Use the above formulae if you need to extend the table's rows or columns

Example of use: The value of £1 in ten years' time when the discount factor is 5% is 60p (£0.614)

Compound interest

n \ i	3%	4%	5%	6%	7%	8%	9%	10%
1	1.03	1.04	1.05	1.06	1.07	1.08	1.09	1.1
2	1.0609	1.0816	1.1025	1.1236	1,1449	1.1664	1.1881	1.21
3	1.0927	1.1249	1.1576	1.91	1.225	1.2597	1.295	1.331
4	1.1255	1.1699	1.2155	1.2625	1.3108	1.3605	1.4116	1.4641
5	1.1593	1.2167	1.2763	1.3382	1.4026	1.4693	1.5386	1.6105
6	1.1941	1.2653	1.3401	1.4185	1.5007	1.5869	1.6771	1.7716
7	1.2299	1.3159	1.4071	1.5036	1.6058	1.7138	1.828	1.9487
8	1.2668	1.3686	1.4775	1.5939	1.7182	1.8509	1.9926	2.1436
9	1.3048	1.4233	1.5513	1.6895	1.8385	1.999	2.1719	2.358
10	1.3439	1.4802	1.6289	1.7909	1.9672	2.1589	2.3674	2.5937
11	1.3842	1.5395	1.7103	1.8983	2.1049	2.3316	2.5804	2.8531
12	1.4258	1.601	1.7959	2.0122	2.2522	2.5182	2.8127	3.1384
13	1.4685	1.6651	1.8857	2.1329	2.4099	2.7196	3.0658	3.4523
14	1.5126	1.7317	1.9799	2.2609	2.5785	2.9372	3.3417	3.7975
15	1.558	1.8009	2.0789	2.3966	2.759	3.1722	3.6425	4.1773
16	1.6047	1.873	2.1829	2.5404	2.9522	3.4259	3.9703	4.595
17	1.6529	1.9479	2.292	2.6928	3.1588	3.7	4.3276	5.0545
18	1.7024	2.0258	2.4066	2.8543	3.3799	3.996	4.7171	5.5599
19	1.7535	2.1069	2.527	3.0256	3.6165	4.3157	5.1417	6.1159
20.	1.8061	2.1911	2.6533	3.2071	3.8697	4.661	5.6044	6.7275

Useful financial formulae

Where:

P = Principal sum

i = Interest rate

n = Number of years

m = Number of months

Then:

Basic compounding	$P(1 + i)^n$
Frequent compounding	$P(1 + \dfrac{i}{m})^{mn}$
Present value	$\dfrac{1}{(1 + i)^n}$
Annuity	$P \left(\dfrac{(1 + i)^n - 1)}{i} \right)$
Present value of annuity	$P\left(\dfrac{1 - \dfrac{1}{(1 + i)^n}}{i} \right)$
Effective rate	$(1 + \dfrac{i}{m})^m - 1$
Repayments	$\dfrac{Pi\,(1 + i)^n}{(1 + i)^n - 1}$

Mastering Financial Management chapters relevant to professional examination syllabi

ACCA FINANCIAL MANAGEMENT (F9)

ACCA Detailed Syllabus (2008)	Mastering Financial Management chapter
A Financial Management Function	
1. Nature and purpose of financial management	1,22
2. Financial objectives and relationship with corporate strategy	1,8,22
3. Stakeholders and impact on corporate objectives	1,22
4. Financial and other objectives in not for profit organisations	1,22
B Financial Management Environment	
1. The economic environment for business	1,22
2. The nature and role of financial markets and institutions	1,20,22
C Working Capital Management	
1. The nature, elements and importance of working capital	10,11,12,13
2. Management of inventories, accounts receivable, accounts payable and cash	10
3. Determining working capital needs and funding strategies	10,11,12,13,20,21,22
D Investment appraisal	
1. The nature of investment decisions and the appraisal process	17
2. Non-discounted cash flow techniques	17
3. Discounted cash flow techniques	17
4. Allowing for inflation and taxation in DCF	4,17
5. Adjusting for risk and uncertainty in investment appraisal	Whole text

ACCA Detailed Syllabus (2008)	Mastering Financial Management chapter
E Business Finance	
1. Sources of, and raising short term finance	11,20
2. Sources of, and raising long term finance	11,12,13,15,20,21
3. Internal sources of finance and dividend policy	15
4. Gearing and capital structure considerations	11,12,13,20,21
5. Finance for small and medium sized entities	11,15
F Cost of capital	
1. Sources of finance and their relative costs	11,12,13,20,21
2. Estimating the cost of equity	11,12,13,20,21
3. Estimating the cost of debt and other capital instruments	11,12,13,20,21
4. Estimating the overall cost of capital	11,12,13,20,21
5. Capital structure theories and practical considerations	11,12,13,20,21
6. Impact of cost of capital on investments	11,12,13,20,21
G Business valuations	
1. Nature and purpose of the valuation of business and financial assets	14
2. Models for the valuation of shares	14
3. The valuation of debt and other financial assets	14
4. Efficient market hypothesis and practical considerations in the valuation of shares	14, 18 Whole text
H Risk management	
1. The nature and types of risk and approaches to risk management	15,16
2. Causes of exchange rate differences and interest rate fluctuations	14,16
3. Hedging techniques for foreign currency risk	15,16
4. Hedging techniques for interest rate risk	15,16

CHARTERED INSTITUTE OF BANKERS IN SCOTLAND FINANCIAL MANAGEMENT

Chartered Institute of Bankers in Scotland syllabus	Mastering Financial Management chapter
1. Introduction to finance	12
2. Business and corporate form	2
Sole traders	2
Partnerships	2
Limited companies	2
3. Capital and financing	
Owners funds	13
Loan capital	13
Equity of debt	13
4. Assets	
Working capital	2, 12
Fixed assets	2
Cash and investments	2, 12
5. Cash flow	
Profit and cash – their relationship	2
Cash flow forecasts	7
Debtor/creditor management	12
Cash flow statement	7
6. Financial accounts	
The trading and profit and loss account	2
Balance sheet	2
Published financial accounts	2
Directors' report	2
Auditors' report	2
7. Regulation and accounting standards	2
8. Planning and control	
Planning and strategy	Whole text
Strategic planning process	Whole text
Financial planning and control	Whole text
Performance measurement in the control system	Whole text

Chartered Institute of Bankers in Scotland syllabus	Mastering Financial Management chapter
Control strategies	8
9. The role of the accounting function	
The accounting function and external interface	2
Accounting and the organisation	2
Strategic management accounting	5
Accounting systems	2
Audit	2
Fraud prevention	2
10. Costing	
Problems of costing	5
Types of costing	5
11. Budgets and budgetary control	
Budgeting and strategic planning	7
Budgetary control	7
12. Performance management	
The performance hierarchy	2
Social responsibility objectives	23, 24
Performance measurement – benefits and drawbacks	9
Standards and targets	9
Reward systems	9
Growth and survival	Whole text
Profitability measures	2, 10
Liquidity and gearing	11, 12, 13
Non-financial performance indicators	24
Problems with measurement	Whole text
The balanced scorecard	
13. Ratio analysis	
Analysis of the business	2
Types of ratio	2
Preparing the report	2
Inter-firm comparison	2
Gearing and capital structure	11, 12, 13

Chartered Institute of Bankers in Scotland Syllabus	Mastering Financial Management Chapter
Overtrading	11, 12, 13
14. Sources of finance and capital structure	
Sources of finance for the small business	11
The capital structure decision	13
Cost of capital	12
Capital asset pricing model	12
Capital budgeting	5
Capital rationing	17
15. Management of working capital	
Working capital ratios	2, 10
Measuring the length of the working capital cycle	10
Managing stock	10
Creditors	10
Debtors	10
Cash and investments	10
16. Managerial decision making	
Information requirements	Whole text
Classification of costs	6
The decision making cycle	Whole text
Break-even analysis in decision making	6
Relevant costs and scarce resources	17
Limiting factors	Whole text
Product mix decisions	8
Customer profitability analysis	8
17. Risk and uncertainty	
Sources of risk and uncertainty	Whole text
Dealing with risk and uncertainty	Whole text
18. Investment appraisal	17
19. Valuation of companies and securities	18

INSTITUTE OF CHARTERED ACCOUNTANTS OF ENGLAND AND WALES

Detailed syllabus (2008)	Mastering Financial Management chapter
1 Financing options	
a. explain the general objectives of financial management and describe the financial strategy process for a business	1, 22
b. describe the impact of financial markets and other external factors on a business's financial strategy, using appropriate examples to illustrate the impacts	1, 3, 4, 20, 21, 22
c. explain the characteristics, terms and conditions and role of alternative short, medium and long term sources of finance available to different businesses	11, 20, 21, 22, 24
d. describe the implications of terms included in loan agreements in a given scenario (e.g. representations and warranties; covenants; guarantees)	
e. explain the processes by which businesses raise equity, capital and other long term finance	11, 13, 20, 21
f. explain the roles played by different stakeholders, advisors and financial institutions in the financial strategy selected by a business	11, 13, 22
g. identify the possible conflicts of objectives between different stakeholders in a business	11, 13, 22
h. compare the features of different means of making returns to owners and lenders, explain their effects on the business and its stakeholders, and recommend appropriate options in a given scenario	11, 12, 13, 22
i. identify and calculate a business's future requirements for capital, taking into account current and planned activities	10, 11, 12, 13, 14, 18, 22
j. assess the suitability of different financing options for a given business	10, 11, 12, 13, 18, 22
k. calculate and interpret the costs of different financing methods (before and after tax) and the weighted average cost of capital	12, 13
l. calculate and interpret the cost of capital of a business in a straightforward scenario	12, 13
m. explain, in non-technical terms and using appropriate examples, the effect of capital gearing/leverage on investors' perception of risk and reward	10, 11, 12, 13
n. describe options for reconstruction (e.g. group reconstruction, spin-off, purchase of own shares, use of distributable profits)	18

Detailed syllabus (2008)	Mastering Financial Management chapter
2 Managing financial risk	
a. identify and describe the key financial risks facing a business in a given scenario	15, 16
b. explain how financial instruments (e.g. derivatives, hedging instruments) can be utilised to manage financial risks and describe the characteristics of those instruments	15, 16
c. perform non-complex calculations relating to financial derivatives and other financial products and discuss the results	15, 16
d. explain different methods of managing interest rate exposure appropriate to a given situation and perform non-complex calculations to determine the cost of the hedge	16
e. explain different methods of managing currency risks appropriate to a given situation and perform non-complex calculations to determine the cost of the hedge	15
f. explain methods of managing other key financial risks and perform non-complex calculations to determine the cost of particular methods	15, 16
g. identify appropriate methods of financing exports, including: – bills of exchange – letters of credit – export credit insurance	11
3 Investment and financing decisions	
a. select and justify investment appraisal techniques which are appropriate to the objectives and circumstances of a given business	17
b. explain the investment decision making process	17
c. select and justify an appropriate discount or interest rate for use in selected investment appraisal techniques from information supplied	12
d. choose appropriate values to be used in selected appraisal techniques from information supplied, taking account of inflation and tax	12, 17
e. identify environmental factors that may affect financing for investment in a different country	17
f. apply appraisal techniques and demonstrate how the interpretation of results from the techniques can be influenced by an assessment of risk	4, 12, 17

Detailed syllabus (2008)	Mastering Financial Management chapter
g. recognise how the results of the appraisal of projects or groups of projects are affected by the accuracy of the data on which they are based and factors which could not be included in the computational analysis	4, 12, 17
h. calculate the optimal investment plan when capital is restricted	17
i. recommend and justify a course of action which is based upon the results of investment appraisal and consideration of relevant non-financial factors and which takes account of the limitations of the techniques being used	17
j. identify and calculate the financing options, costs and benefits of activities in a given situation, referring to levels of uncertainty and making reasonable assumptions which are consistent with the situation	17
k. compare the financing costs and benefits (including those that are not separately quantifiable) of various courses of action, using appropriate appraisal techniques	17
l. recommend relevant methods of funding for a given situation, stating their sources and justifying the selection	17
m. draft a straightforward investment and financing plan for a given business scenario	1 to 23

CHARTERED INSTITUTE OF PUBLIC FINANCE AND ACCOUNTANCY

Chartered Institute of Public Finance and Accountancy syllabus – financial management learning outcomes	Mastering Financial Management chapter
A) Determine appropriate approaches and techniques to solve problems and meet decision-makers' and other recipients' needs.	
A1) Evaluate the organisational, professional and regulatory environments in which the professional accountant is expected to operate.	
A2) Determine the information required by specified decision makers.	Whole text
A3) Formulate problems which are to be solved and determine an appropriate approach to solving them, recognising relevant constraints and assumptions.	Whole text
A4) Determine the decisions which are required to resolve the problem, taking into account appropriate decision-making criteria for the organisational and environmental circumstances.	Whole text
A5) Determine ethical judgements and decisions required based on an understanding and application of ethics knowledge and ethical sensitivity.	23
A6) Determine appropriate planning, analytical and decision-making techniques, demonstrating awareness of their limitations.	5,6,7,8, 9,10,11,12,
A7) Present first draft or final documents to communicate proposed approaches and techniques which meet the requirements of specific recipients / decision-makers.	Whole text
B) Apply appropriate professional and technical skills, knowledge and techniques to facilitate organisational problem solving and decision-making.	
B1) Analyse and interpret complex policy, operational, financial and budgetary documents.	5
B2) Apply appropriate planning, analytical and decision-making techniques correctly, demonstrating awareness of their limitations.	5,6,7,8,9
B3) Evaluate the findings of preliminary analysis, and determine and apply further appropriate analytical and decision-making techniques as necessary.	Whole text

Chartered Institute of Public Finance and Accountancy syllabus – financial management learning outcomes	Mastering Financial Management chapter
C) Evaluate the results of technical analyses for an organisation and formulate appropriate conclusions and recommendations.	
C1) Evaluate the results of technical analyses and formulate conclusions and recommendations appropriate to an organisation's political, cultural and economic/environmental context.	24 Whole text
C2) Evaluate the meaning and implications of conclusions and recommendations for an organisation's management/financial management strategies and policies, in the context of appropriate professional standards and ethics.	Whole text
D) Present information, analyses, conclusions and recommendations effectively.	
D1) Present information, analysis, conclusions and recommendations using methods and formats appropriate to the needs of recipients / decision makers.	Whole text
D2) Determine the type of information and level of detail appropriate to specific recipients / decision-makers	Whole text
D3) Present clear and concise written reports, minutes, briefing notes etc. to communicate information, analysis, conclusions and recommendations to decision-makers	
E) Manage activities and resources to meet defined requirements within time constraints.	
E1) Determine all requirements, their relative priorities and the appropriate proportion of available time required.	
E2) Simultaneously manage a number of activities to achieve all the set objectives within the time available	

Further reading

Mastering Derivatives Markets: A guide to the products, applications and risks by Francesca Taylor. Published by FT Prentice Hall.

Mastering Financial Calculations: A guide to the mathematics of financial market instruments by Bob Steiner. Published by FT Prentice Hall.

'The Outsourcing Decision: A Strategic Framework' by Steven Globerman, Kaiser Professor of International Business, Western Washington University and Aidan Vining, CNABS Professor of Business and Government Relations, Simon Fraser University, Vancouver, B.C. This is a downloadable paper available on the internet: http://129.3.20.41/eps/it/papers/0404/0404007.pdf

Exploring Strategic Financial Management: Integrating corporate strategy with financial management by Tony Grundy with Gerry Johnson and Kevan Scholes. Published by FT Prentice Hall.

Exploring Corporate Strategy by Gerry Johnson and Kevan Scholes. Published by Prentice Hall.

Tax Strategy for Companies by Malcolm Gammie. Published by Longman.

Handbook of UK Corporate Finance edited by Janette Rutherford and David Carter. Published by Butterworths.

Currency and Interest Rate Swaps by Schuyler K. Henderson and John A.M. Price. Published by Butterworths.

Key Management Ideas by Stuart Crainer. Published by Financial Times Pitman Publishing.

Balance Sheets and the Lending Banker by J.H. Clements and L.S. Dyer. Published by Europa Publications.

'Professionalism and Ethics' by Clive Marsh. *Journal of the Chartered Institute of Bankers in Scotland*, September 2008.

'Invoice Finance' by Clive Marsh, *Journal of the National Institute of Accountants of Australia*, January 2008.

'Banks and Shared Services' by Clive Marsh, *Journal of Banking and Financial Services*, the Australasian Institute of Banking and Finance, November 2004.

Management Accounting for the Lending Banker by M.A. Pitcher. Published by the Chartered Institute of Bankers.

Managerial Accounting by Moore, Jaedicke and Anderson. Published by South-Western Publishing Co. in the USA.

The author recommends the above as relevant further reading. Not all these works are currently in publication but they are generally available through websites or directly from the professional institute mentioned.

Index